# VERNON LEE

# Vernon Lee

*Aesthetics, History, and the
Victorian Female Intellectual*

 Christa Zorn

Ohio University Press
ATHENS

Ohio University Press, Athens, Ohio 45701

© 2003 by Christa Zorn

Printed in the United States of America

Ohio University Press books are printed on acid-free paper ∞

12 11 10 09 08 07 06 05 04 03  5 4 3 2 1

*Jacket and Frontispiece:* Photograph of Vernon Lee in 1914 courtesy of Colby College
Special Collections, Waterville, Maine.

Library of Congress Cataloging-in-Publication Data
Zorn, Christa, 1954–
     Vernon Lee : aesthetics, history, and the Victorian female intellectual / Christa Zorn.
        p.  cm.
     Includes bibliographical references and index.
     ISBN 0-8214-1497-6 (alk. paper)
      1. Lee, Vernon, 1856–1935—Criticism and interpretation. 2. Feminism and
literature—Great Britain—History—19th century. 3. Literature and history—Great
Britain—History—19th century. 4. Women and literature—Great Britain—History—
19th century. 5. Women—Great Britain—Intellectual life. 6. Modernism (Literature)—
Great Britain. 7. Women intellectuals—Great Britain. 8. Aestheticism (Literature)
I. Title.

PR5115.P2Z98 2003
824'.8—dc21

2003040570

*To E. F. Zopp*

# Contents

# Acknowledgments

Since this book began as a dissertation at the University of Florida, it has gone through numerous drafts. Along the way, several people have read and discussed with me the manuscript at different stages of completion. I would like to thank all those whose generous advice, support, and suggestions have made this a better book. I am especially indebted to Alistair Duckworth, Elizabeth Langland, David Mann, and Susan Mann. My thanks also go to Patricia O'Neill for helping me think through the project from a new perspective.

I am greatly indebted to Indiana University Southeast for awarding me two Summer Faculty Fellowships, Grants in Aid, and an Overseas Travel Grant, all of which helped me conduct the research for this book, here and in Great Britain.

I owe special thanks to Patience-Anne W. Lenk at the Miller Library for her help with the Vernon Lee papers in the Colby College Special Collections, Waterville, Maine; to Patricia Burdick and Margaret Libby for assisting me with the Vernon Lee photos from the Colby College Special Collections at the Miller Library; to the Principal and Fellows of Somerville College Oxford; to Pauline Adams at the Somerville College Library for her assistance with the Vernon Lee Papers; and to Martin Rosen for bibliographical help and to the interlibrary loan staff at the Indiana University Southeast Library.

I would also like to thank David Sanders of Ohio University Press for his patience with my manuscript and Nancy Basmajian for her astute and clarifying copyediting. I am also grateful for the two outside readers, who have given me the best critical advice I could hope for.

The last section of chapter 6 appeared in a different form in the *Victorian*

*Newsletter* 91 (Spring 1997) as "Aesthetic Intertextuality as Cultural Critique: Vernon Lee Rewrites Walter Pater's 'La Gioconda.'" I am grateful to Ward Hellstrom for the permission to reprint.

The following libraries have kindly granted permission to quote from manuscripts in their possession: Miller Library, Colby College Special Collections, Waterville, Maine; Somerville College, Oxford; University College London Library. The photograph on the cover has been reprinted with kind permission from the Colby College Special Collections, Waterville, Maine.

My warmest thanks to Carola Costa-Angeli, owner of the Vernon Lee villa "Il Palmerino" in Fiesole, for inviting me to the villa and for sharing her knowledge of Lee with me in 1993. Thanks to her efforts, in 1995 "Violet Paget (Vernon Lee)" was inscribed on a commemorative plaque on her grave in the Cimitero degli Allori in Florence.

Finally, it is impossible to measure the support of Fred Zopp, or adequately to express my gratitude for his intellectual and emotional sustenance; for accompanying me on my research trips; for editing my writing; and, most of all, for his belief in my work. I dedicate this book to him, as he lives on in it.

# Introduction

The four decades spanning the turn of the twentieth century (1880–1920) encompass a wide array of writers and intellectual circles. The period has challenged advocates of periodization with its heterogeneous movements known by such names as naturalism, symbolism, Parnassianism, Pre-Raphaelitism, aestheticism, or decadence. Critics often speak of the fin de siècle as an interregnum, which "requires notice but suggests brevity" (R. Williams, 162), or as an age of transition between romanticism and modernism, designations which, according to Sally Ledger and Scott McCracken, have lent this period "backwater status in literary and cultural criticism" (1).

What all these labels have in common is their mapping of history in men's terms based on a small set of canonized male writers so that women's texts, as Elaine Showalter puts it, "must be forcibly assimilated to an irrelevant grid" (*New Feminist Criticism,* 203). Organized by the modernist notion of the masterwork, British literary history for a long time operated on the misconception that there were no significant women writers—especially of prose texts other than the novel—in the decades between George Eliot and Virginia Woolf. However, literary scholarship in the last thirty years has found in this "gap" an unusually large number of women working independently as novelists, critics, journalists, and travel writers. These New Women, as Talia Schaffer and Kathy Alexis Psomiades demonstrate in *Women and British Aestheticism,* "Malet, Ward, Lee, Meynell, Margaret L. Woods, Ethel Lillian Voynich, Ouida, Mary and Jane Findlater, Syrett, Tomson, Egerton, and Olive Schreiner, constitute an impressive group of ambitious women writers who enjoyed strong sales and critical acclaim" (16). Many of them were zealously engaged in experimenting with new literary forms, typically considered a trademark of the modernist avant garde. George Egerton's impressionist stories, Olive Schreiner's allegories, Charlotte Mew's eerie visions, and Vernon Lee's ironic-fantastic tales are exemplary stylistic innovations even before the formative years of modernism (1910–25).

Several recent studies of the late nineteenth century converge on the claim that the "gap" between Victorianism and modernism is largely the product of modernist self-fashioning, which placed all the merits of innovation in the high (male) modernist league while readily dismissing New Women writers as a "special interest" group. But female intellectuals of the late-Victorian and early modernist periods who voiced their aesthetic, social, and political concerns to the public attracted as much critical attention as the writers who have now become canonized.[1] The reassessment of conventional period lines and categorizations during the last three decades has produced an impressive body of scholarship on late-Victorian women writers and, simultaneously, interesting new readings of "eminent" Victorians from Ruskin to Carlyle.[2] A large-scale revision of tightly defined standards is producing a new awareness of the material role the fin de siècle played in modern intellectual and literary movements and of the wide-ranging involvement of women writers in all of them.[3] Ann Heilmann, for instance, has credited the scholarship of the last few decades with highlighting the New Women's involvement in larger cultural developments rather than internally categorizing their writing under a narrow label. Ann Ardis's and Lyn Pykett's important studies both redefine the unhappy relationship between New Women and modernism by removing from it the hierarchical distinction between "high" and "low" art and revealing how the construction of the New Woman's special interest split her from the developments of high modernist (male) discourses. By analyzing New Women's texts beyond literary judgment, these critics have enabled us to re-evaluate neglected writers in their historical and political context apart from established aesthetic paradigms. Although Ardis's and Pykett's evasion of aesthetic assessments has its problems, I would not go quite as far as Schaffer in stating that their studies "[leave] the impression that they could find nothing positive to say about their [New Women's] texts," an impression that "may be more damaging, in the long run, than the canonical impulse they are trying to avoid" (12). After all, if critics had not looked beyond established aesthetic standards, the current debates about the role of modernism in shaping our literary judgment would not have been as challenging and prolific. The tendency to analyze literary works as "texts" or historical documents is not just a feminist specialty but is common to all cultural criticism. However, Schaffer's criticism is right on target when she cautions us not to speak of "feminist" or "New Women" texts without proper historical contextualization or sufficient differentiation. Her critical analysis of these terms clears the way for the long-overdue discussion of the relationship between New Women and female aesthetes: "Unfortunately, New Women criticism has neglected the female aesthetes as completely as aesthetic criticism has," with the result that the female aesthetes have been "falling between two stools" (7). Schaffer's and others' recent scholarship that highlights the enormous complexity of late-Victorian gender politics has already produced a more diversified picture of these intellectual groups.

As more and more women writers have become visible in the "gap" between George Eliot and Virginia Woolf, a much more differentiated picture of the fin de siècle emerges, leading to questions about the ways in which Victorian, modern, and even postmodern critics claimed and "dis-claimed" boundaries. The increasingly complex and specific readings of New Women literature are testimony that we are now at a point where any singular concept of the New Woman in the late nineteenth century does not render sufficient historical accuracy. Eventually, more varied modes of criticism, combining social, political, psychological, and cultural approaches, have provided more insight into the diversity, transformative force, inventiveness, and even contradictions among New Women writers.

Vernon Lee, for instance, distanced herself from suffragist rhetoric, feminist activism, and, later, from aestheticism; and yet, in more than one way, her assertive (and sometimes arrogant) unorthodox scholarship opened alternative venues that have since become effective in feminist and other innovative forms of criticism. Lee's long neglect, even at a time when feminist scholars were discovering forgotten women writers in great numbers, could be a reminder to us that, instead of making her fit topical agendas, we should pay more attention to the way her texts inspired contemporary attempts to come to terms with new developments for which the available interpretive models had no answers.

Scholarship devoted to the late nineteenth and early twentieth centuries has for some time recognized the presence of women who called into question the normative horizon of established "masterworks" and the way criticism has formed itself around and against certain prime texts.[4] Women's contributions to the development of modern prose styles, in particular, have not been evaluated sufficiently. Even though Andrea Broomfield and Sally Mitchell's anthology *Prose by Victorian Women* has made available a good number of obscured texts, few studies as yet have focused on women's cultural and historical scholarship, or what the Germans call "Kulturwissenschaft." Although New Women studies have shed light on a significant female writing tradition outside the Victorian novel, they have almost exclusively assumed women's home base to have been in fiction, and preferably with a feminist cause. But as cultural critics, philosophers, and scholars, women of the period are still underrepresented in modern scholarship.

We know now that the division of intellectual labor between the sexes was not true even for the nineteenth century. Virginia Woolf in *A Room of One's Own* (1929) could reflect on a number of women who had made a name for themselves in traditionally "masculine" fields: "There are Jane Harrison's books on Greek archeology; Vernon Lee's books on aesthetics; Gertrude Bell's books on Persia" (83). The irony is that Woolf's modernist focus and her disavowal of her indebtedness to nineteenth-century writers have an undermining effect on her tribute to earlier women's essay writing. Woolf permits only a few token women into her otherwise all-male genealogy to give more force to her own "takeover of this genre" (Bowlby, xxvii).[5]

Woolf's and other modernists' distancing from immediate predecessors has helped shape our present image of the fin de siècle. Through their emphasis on form and their denial of old Victorian morality, modernists aligned themselves with the aesthetic movement, thus creating our traditional image of the late nineteenth century's indulgence in style.[6] More recent scholars of the fin de siècle—such as Sally Ledger, Scott McCracken, Linda Dowling, Yopie Prins, Talia Schaffer, and Kathy Alexis Psomiades—have opened the years from 1880 to 1920 to a new critique with their emphasis on "cultural politics." These scholars have focused on the multiplicity of cultural forms and have asked new questions, such as, In what ways did female writers establish their relationship to literature and history and how did they affect the intellectual debates? As Rita Felski puts it in *The Gender of Modernity,* "By refusing to ontologize particular spheres of culture . . . [and b]y affirming women's historical presence within spheres often seen as the province of men, . . . feminist critics challenge all attempts to confine women to a circumscribed and devalued sphere of activity" (205). To avoid easy generalizations, critics reevaluate the period by looking at individual figures, recovering some lesser-known works, and thereby complicating our understanding of others. As Schaffer aptly observes, "If we can put Ouida, Malet, Wilde, and James on the same list, perhaps everyone on that list will benefit" (17).

In employing more diversified critical terms, scholars have been able to examine more subtly the differences among fin-de-siècle writers (male and female) in a broad spectrum of discourses associated with aestheticism, socialism, and feminism. Most writers of the time made a living from contributions to periodical literature that did not follow our modern generic distinctions between historical, philosophical, and political essays and literary criticism. To quote Schaffer again, "it is vital to remember that during this period these writers enjoyed multiple, flexible, social and professional networks" (16), effects of their wide-ranging experiences which cannot be easily subsumed under one rubric. Late-Victorian women writers wrote prolifically and received much critical acclaim, but their texts were not usually collected for academic recirculation in later years. Exclusion most likely operated in some of the same (academic) institutions that are now involved in its reversal. When modernism, with its trademarks of "pure style," academic rigor, and impersonal detachment, became the dominant literary trend, women writers of the previous era were snubbed for their moral tone, their singular concerns, or their lack of disinterestedness.[7] Because they lacked academic training and professional specialization—deficiencies that were not considered impediments for the Victorian man of letters—they were deemed amateurish or hopelessly old-fashioned. Thus, the late-Victorian period offers a particularly interesting context for evaluating the writing and the social authority of what we may call the public intellectual, a term that bridges and goes beyond the Victorian sage and the modernist aesthetic critic. The evolution of the latter reflects the growing professionalization of intellectual life, which replaced the Victorian generalists by academic specialists who no longer imagined their audience to be the community at large.

Vernon Lee, today one of the most underread and underrated critics from the period between 1880 and 1920, provides an apt model for the study of the public intellectual in that era. Her prominence as a female aesthete with a strong ethical agenda has been obscured by modernist writers as they distanced themselves from the Victorians' moral and political "impediments." Modernist critics were irritated by Lee's verbosity and ignored her intellectual boldness and experimentation. René Wellek, for instance, speaks for many of them in dismissing Lee's writing as "long-winded, earnest moralizing about dead public issues" (166). At the same time, Wellek accentuates Lee's similarity to Walter Pater, whose influence on modernist aesthetics has become widely acknowledged. Pater himself had praised Lee's expression as "sustained and firm,"[8] but Virginia Woolf found that she lacked "the exquisite taste and penetrating clearness of sight which make some essays concentrated epitomes of precious things" (*Essays of Virginia Woolf,* 158).

Twentieth-century literary history often held a constricted view of Lee as an aesthete who wrote in the fashion of Walter Pater and Henry James, but—reiterating Woolf's verdict—was impeded by her Victorian garrulity. Since Lee has been remembered mainly through her links with aestheticism, few critics are aware that she also contributed significantly to cultural, psychological, and social criticism, and to historical scholarship. Modeling her career on the Victorian "man of letters," Lee published her first historical study at twenty-four and became a prolific contributor to contemporary criticism of art and history. She was one of the most popular travel writers at the turn of the century and also achieved wide recognition for her novels and short stories. She kept extensive diaries and journals that attest to the seriousness with which she took her intellectual work and to her constant attention to contemporary issues, not infrequently giving financial support to those in need.

Lee's identity as a writer cannot be described easily. Peter Gunn, her biographer, admits that he "can only define her by saying that she is an essayist who is at once an aesthete, a psychologist and an historian" (219). "The difficulty of writing about her is that she is such a various author," says Desmond MacCarthy in "Out of the Limelight" (1941). But he is optimistic about her future place in literary history: "she will be read by posterity" because of her "intellectual curiosity and imaginative sensibility" (quoted in Gunn, 220). Two years before Lee's death in 1935, when she was in despair over her deafness, MacCarthy wrote to console her, "and remember, dear Vernon, that those who are with you always want much more to hear what *you* have to say than to express their own opinion" (16 May 1933, Somerville). In the end, it was not MacCarthy's optimism but Percy Lubbock's resigned attitude—"It was impossible to control or to civilize Vernon Lee" (quoted in Gunn, 182)—that characterized Lee's reception in modern literary history, which never found a suitable spot for her work. Lee irritated her critics by presenting in the same text unreconciled viewpoints and by deliberately crossing genre boundaries, which she found stifling: "The Essayist is an amphibious creature, neither fish, flesh, nor fowl," she wrote in 1883, "something of the nature of the centaur" (*Ottilie*, 7–8). Following her creed, she produced countless unorthodox prose texts—"dialogues," "fancies," "idylls," and "studies"—which, in her lifetime, reached third and fourth editions but were overlooked by later generations.

The uneven judgments of Lee's work make us ponder her role in the ideological middle ground between Victorianism and modernity and ask how a more conscious inclusion of her works can redefine our current ideas about the formation of literary movements and traditions. It is noteworthy that the terms in which Dinah Birch describes Ruskin (in *Ruskin and the Dawn of the Modern*) equally characterize Vernon Lee:

> His refusal to limit himself to any single field of thought lies at the heart of his project as a mature critic. But it also became an important reason for the decline of his reputation in the twentieth century. Specialization and profes-sionalization had come to dominate scholarship. Ruskin was suspicious of both. (1–2)

Studies of the late nineteenth century have often emphasized the outsider sta-tus of innovative writers because of their gender or their class. But what do we make of the fact that a conspicuous number of New Women writers, such as Olive Schreiner, George Egerton, and Vernon Lee, spent large periods of their lives outside Britain? In other words, how does nationality come into play? Vernon Lee grew up a Victorian, but did not visit Britain until her early twen-ties. The family's meandering between France, Germany, and Italy and her proficiency in four languages gave her a cosmopolitan European rather than a British identity. Trained by a free-spirited mother for a writing career as other women were for motherhood and domesticity, Vernon Lee introduced herself to the British audience in 1878 with an intellectual history of eighteenth-century Italy that received rave reviews, especially impressive for an author so young; as Harriet Waters Preston, the *Atlantic Monthly* critic, remarked in 1885, *Studies of the Eighteenth Century in Italy* was "an amazing production for a woman, and especially a young woman." The book brought Lee immediate recognition for her scholarship and erudition, qualities that came to be validated at a time when intellectual disciplines established new professional standards.

Her follow-up Renaissance studies, *Euphorion* (1884) and *Renaissance Fancies and Studies* (1892), include a great amount of her own primary historical research and her extensive studies of secondary sources. Lee's historical texts are continuously intertwined with the narrative of her personal encounters with history. Her impressionistic style won her the admiration of Pater and James, but it was not "scientific" enough to impress pedantic German scholars.[9] From our postmodern perspective, Lee's mingling of public and personal history, popular and "high" culture reminds us of a cultural studies approach, while her sense of realism lends her texts a documentary character associated with twentieth-century journalist-writers, such as Vera Brittain or Rebecca West.

Vernon Lee published more than forty books on aesthetic, historical, philosophical, and social issues. She was a regular contributor to some of the foremost critical journals: from the liberal *Contemporary Review* and the popular *Blackwell's Magazine* to the more elitist *Fortnightly Review, Atheneum,* and the *Nation.* In the *Wellesley Index to Victorian Periodicals* (5 vols., 1966–90), Lee is one of only eleven women with more than fifty entries—a distinction all the more remarkable for the fact that there are thirteen male contributors with more than fifty entries under the letter "A" alone. Remarkable also in that her literary authority derived solely from her writing outside the academy, which in her time empowered the scholarly expert as it marginalized the dilettante and the generalist.[10]

Lee's intellectual position favored an aesthetic credo indebted to natural philosophy and social realism. She employed her unique aesthetic approach freely, especially when she wanted to set herself apart from her peers, namely Ruskin or Pater. Although emotionally closer to Ruskin's ethical demands, she disparaged him like an older self she felt she had left behind. She played Ruskin against Pater in *Belcaro* (1881), rebutting the former as the old Victorian monument he had already become by that time. But she soon became suspicious of exquisite pleasures for their own sake, and developed her own aesthetic that emphasized a socially responsible appreciation of art and beauty. While still applying Pater's impressionism to illuminate new vistas in the historical landscape, she also criticized his omission of the "cruellest realism" (*Euphorion,* 1: 133). In the second half of the 1880s, especially in *Juvenilia* (1887), she became increasingly self-conscious about her art criticism, lamenting the uneven distribution of aesthetic pleasures among the different classes in European society. The ongoing theme in her writing then becomes the relationship between individual and society, artist and audience viewed from various social and intellectual standpoints and expressed in different textual forms, "somewhere in the borderland between fact and fiction" (*Baldwin* [1886], 14).

Unlike other equally prolific women writers, Lee owed her reputation not so much to her novels but to her prose and journalism. She saw herself as an essay writer and was bemused when in the early 1880s *Fraser's Magazine* asked her to write a serial novel. "Think if I were a novelist!" she wrote to her mother. "But even had I time, I would shrink from writing what would certainly be vastly inferior to my other work" (letter to Mrs. Paget, 1881, Colby). Little did she know at the time how prophetic her words would become: three years later, Henry James wrote to a friend about her novel, *Miss Brown,* "It is very bad, *strangely* inferior to her other writing . . . a rather deplorable mistake" (quoted in Edel, 677). In the novel, Lee mixed fact and fiction (or should we say, art and life?) in such an unambiguous way that she offended the aesthetic sets around Oscar Wilde and the Rossettis. Like Lee herself, the heroine of her three-decker novel explores women's aesthetic and social roles beyond the contemporary stereotypes of femininity while struggling with the "right" and "wrong" uses of art. A satirical attack on the aesthetic movement, the novel reflects Lee's conflicting views of art and society in the 1880s. She uses the rather limited viewpoint of an Italian servant girl to show what aestheticism might look like from among the lower classes. At the same time, she explores the moral responsibilities of the artist toward the public in an era of growing mass audiences.

*Miss Brown* marks Lee's transition from a Paterian aesthete to a socially and morally engaged writer. Still, she kept returning to the question of aesthetics by expanding into the empirical dimension of the field and measuring the psychological effects on the "consumers." Lee introduced to her British audience the concept of empathy, developed by the German school of psychological aesthetics from Lipps to Vischer to Groos. She applied her psychological studies to literary texts in *The Handling of Words,* a collection of essays written over several decades but published together in 1923.[11] Her minute exploration of the reading process—down to the counting of certain words—has been considered exemplary for "practical criticism" (David Lodge) or an early model of reader-response criticism. Stuart Sillars, in his review of the 1992 edition of the book, finds that she not only anticipates "the kind of thing later popularized by I. A. Richards," but also "reader response and even Barthes's narratology" (117).

Acutely aware of the psychological powers involved in the reading process, Vernon Lee aimed consistently to develop in her reader what she called "a habit of thinking, an attitude . . . of wider influence than [any] rules of conduct" (*Gospels of Anarchy,* 39). While referring to every major philosopher from Plato to William James and every literary work from the *Iliad* to *Hedda Gabler,* Lee cultivated an independent, reasonable voice, ready to test any intellectual position against her own experience. In her first Renaissance study, *Euphorion* (1884), she had questioned the merely theoretical knowledge of scholars from the perspective of one who had actually lived among the ruins: "I have seen the concrete things, and what I might call the concrete realities of thought and feeling left behind by the Renaissance" (1:16). Still, she is eager to prove her familiarity with current academic research, as, for example, in the appendix to *Euphorion,* which cites an impressive range of scholarly works in four languages.[12] Such attestations, while typical of the amateur trying to impress the professionals, also reveal her indebtedness to earlier writers and writing traditions. In *Euphorion* she harks back to Roscoe, Gibbons, Michelet, and Symonds; in *The Handling of Words,* she gives credit to mentors including Carlyle, Michelet, Ruskin, and Pater, showing that the creation of any art requires an "appreciative engagement with one's predecessors" (Stetz, 47). Nevertheless, Lee emphasizes the originality of her own method. She offers her individual impressions, "developed by means of study" (*Euphorion,* 1:16) and concrete experience, as perspectivial correction of theoretical scholarship, cautioning her readers—as Ruskin had done—about the limitations of abstraction and "pure" science. She doubted that universality or objectivity in history had any claim to reason, asking scholars to be aware of "this inevitable one-sidedness" (2:225) of their own viewpoint.

To her, the study of the past, or any subject, should not be like the dissection of a lifeless object, "a thing so utterly dead as to be fit only for the scalpel and the microscope" (1:12), but rather a "historic habit" that mediates between past and present, historian and subject matter. Historians should explore not only "facts" but "thoughts and feelings," as well as "sensations and temperaments," and thus include intuitive and impressionist methods in their investigation (*Renaissance Fancies,* 237–40). Interested in psychological rather than factual history, she constructs a historical voice that is individual and not institutional. At times, the sense of her idiosyncrasy is so strong ("giving way to personal and perhaps sometimes irrelevant impressions," *Euphorion,* 1:14) that we may overlook her indebtedness to academic scholarship. Her "personal impression," as we shall see, is a historical method based on extensive research, but conducted from a new angle: from a different social and geographical perspective as well as from outside the academic mainstream.

This did not mean that she spoke from a marginal or defensive corner. On the contrary, the irreverence of her critical voice gave her the semblance of an intellectual authority that often enough irritated her colleagues. Untrammeled by any authority, Lee ignored doctrine and dogma, always ready to propound the validity of her own viewpoint in cleverly constructed arguments. Her contemporaries, bemused or irritated by her irreverence, typically banned her voice by satire and caricature, which depreciated her critical intelligence. Max Beerbohm, for instance, "improved" the title page to his own copy of Lee's essay collection *Gospels of Anarchy* (1908) with the following caption:

> Oh dear! Poor dear dreadful little lady! Always having a crow to pick, ever
> so coyly, with Nietzsche, or a wee lance to break with Mr. Carlyle, or a sweet
> but sharp little warning to whisper in the ear of Mr. H. G. Wells, or Strind-
> berg or Darwin or D'Annunzio! What a dreadful little bore and busybody!
> How artfully at this moment she must be button-holing Einstein! And Sig-
> nor Croce—and Mr. James Joyce! (Gunn, 3)

Beerbohm's gloss is a gibe at her intellectual belligerence. What strikes us even more than his incomparable wit is the phalanx of luminaries he deploys to put the "poor, dear, dreadful little lady" in her place. He reveals a certain discomfort with prominent intellectual women, similar to that of Henry James, who labeled Lee as "brilliant" but "uncanny," or J. A. Symonds, who called her "cocksure." Such strictures on behavior, we can assume, were applied in their severity especially to women writers, even when their intellectual abilities were generally admired. "Cleverness" for the Victorian woman was something like a backhanded compliment (V. Colby, 175). Used in the "proper" combination of productive skill with beauty and charm, cleverness could be an asset. But the word also suggested something less desirable in women, especially when paired with overconfidence.[13]

Contemporary reviews of Lee's work imply that the greatest challenge came not from her gender but from the formal transgressions in her "cross-disciplinary" style. As suggested by Sally Ledger and Roger Luckhurst in the introduction to their anthology *Fin de Siècle: A Reader in Cultural History, c. 1880–1900* (2000), cross-disciplinary and idiosyncratic writers, such as Andrew Lang and W. T. Stead—not to forget even Ruskin's unorthodox side—appeared to be on the increase in this period and symptomatic of its "bizarre collocations of interest" (xxii). Studying the cross-disciplinary and even contradictory texts of contemporary writers like Stead or Lee can be helpful in opening up forgotten and unusual connections between discursive constellations in the late nineteenth century. Terry Eagleton gives the late Victorians more credit for their intellectual flexibility than he gives us for our "well-policed frontiers of the mind": "Fin-de-siècle intellectuals blend belief systems with staggering nonchalance, blithely confident of some invisible omega point at which Baudelaire and Kropotkin consort harmoniously together and Emerson lies down with Engels" (12).

To find out exactly how the Victorians transgressed intellectual boundaries, we can only profit from looking at writers who worked across disciplines, especially women writers, whose general amateur status may have been conducive to greater disciplinary and thematic flexibility. Victorian women not only rewrote or reacted to their "fathers'" texts, but were more directly engaged in constructive exchanges with male writers than has been assumed. Frances Power Cobbe (1822–1904), for instance, carried on a spirited correspondence with famous intellectuals of her time, including Charles Darwin, who incorporated her suggestions in the development of his theories. Olive Schreiner (1855–1920) exchanged views on sex, gender, and politics with Karl Pearson, Havelock Ellis, and Edward Carpenter. And Vernon Lee's regular discussions with Walter Pater on their ongoing historical studies have been well documented. She also conducted an involved correspondence with the German aesthetic psychologist Karl Groos (1861–1946) that reveals the interest they had in each other's experiments and theories.[14]

Vernon Lee's close friendships with other women also displayed a professional dimension, but had no effect on her becoming a feminist. Her involvement with the Woman Question did not surface in her writing until the 1890s and even then it was with a certain skepticism. Although she wrote one important essay on the Woman Question—"The Economic Parasitism of Women" (1902)—she never saw herself as a "woman" writer, nor was she an outspoken feminist. Unlike other New Women writers, Lee does not make gender an issue in her texts. This ought not come as a surprise. To give her voice intellectual authority, Lee resorted to a kind of reasoning found in the province of men. Like other women who wrote theoretical texts, such as Harriet Martineau, Lee avoided drawing attention to her gender, well aware that women were not judged by the same standards as men. "I am sure," she wrote to a friend in 1878, "that no one reads a woman's writing on art, history or aesthetics with anything but unmitigated contempt" (quoted in Gunn, 66). Obviously, Lee overcompensated for this prejudice by an assertiveness sometimes bordering on brusque impudence, which probably earned her the unflattering epithets by J. A. Symonds or Bertrand Russell.

How then does Vernon Lee's work allow us to test our assumptions about the role of the intellectual woman at the turn of the century? How does she alter the history of aestheticism? The intellectual authority she gained from her literary and critical writings suggests that our notions of the public intellectual—Victorian sage or modern critic—are much too narrow. Modeled on a small elite of educated men, these terms, if applied unmodified, simply reproduce the same parameters of literary history. In the wake of modernist self-fashioning, contemporary readers have readily accepted the idea of the modern specialist replacing the Victorian generalist, who, somewhat idealized by T. W. Heyck, was in close contact with the community (228). This community as we now know was imagined to be similar to the writer: university-educated, cultured, aloof—and male. Today, critics ask how the story of the intellectual in the years between 1880 and 1920 changes when viewed from the woman writer's perspective. Concretely, what does the omission of Vernon Lee's work tell us about our concept of that literary period and our authorization of certain intellectual discourses? Since the core of Lee's writing falls within the formative years of modernism, her case can provide some insight into the relationships between cultural and intellectual authority, knowledge, gender, and institutional power.

At the end of the nineteenth century, according to Heyck, an "intellectual class" was forming and the earlier Victorian generalist was superseded and disparaged by both the aesthetic critic and the academic specialist. Intellectual authority was institutionalized through a series of academic standards and procedures, such as disinterested research uncluttered by social or moral attachments. In their rejection of Victorian ways and their turning away from society at large (Heyck, 225–26), the otherwise dissimilar pair of the modern university scholar and the aesthetic critic converged. The university-trained, professional critics distanced themselves from Victorian "men of letters" whose amateur status—a sign of gentlemanly pride in previous time—appeared hopelessly outdated as the century drew to a close. Vernon Lee's novel *Louis Norbert* (1914) reflects this development, but also suggests her ideal of an intellectual method: an aristocratic dilettante woman is joined by a pedantic young (male) scholar in investigating a seventeenth-century mystery. The young professor soon has to admit that his scholarly training is too far removed from social reality to solve the case, and it is only by combining forces—amateur intuition and academic rigor—that the project can succeed.

If we accept the account of the decline of the "man of letters" as a consequence of the rise of the professional intellectual, it seems obvious by which standards Lee became marginalized, as Wellek's comment reveals: "The essays are not nourished by any critical erudition; she is rather an imaginative personal writer who must not be judged for her contribution to scholarship" (165). Even Ian Small's critical study, *Conditions for Criticism: Authority, Knowledge and Literature in the Late Nineteenth Century* (1991), operates from an abstract intellectual position (like Wellek's) in which gender is considered immaterial.[15] Small argues that neither Pater nor Wilde came to be considered serious academic writers when literary criticism became institutionlized during their time. Ironically their exclusion helped shape the standards of a contemporary academy which marginalizes some of its most innovative contributors. Although Small gives some room to Lee in his discussion of literary authority, his argument is based on the traditional assumptions about intellectuals who, in Deirdre David's words, were "virtually always of the male sex and masculine gender" (1). Small explains intellectual structures abstracted from empirical dimensions, such as those represented by gender studies. Yet it cannot be denied that in academic criticism, gender has always been a social and an institutional factor which determined who could speak on what matters.[16] If we measure Lee's aesthetic theories only abstractly, we cannot fully recognize the scope and intention of her work—especially its experiential side. Because social authority and intellectual authority are not identical, critical practice needs a historical perspective in which intellectual, institutional, and social conditions are taken into account. Otherwise, if treated as a timeless operational device, professional criticism simply reproduces the accepted terms of its practice. Therefore, this study focuses on the question of how Vernon Lee revises the familiar story of aestheticism from a woman writer's point of view within a certain historical context. Or: what does she offer the postmodern reader in reassessing intellectual history and the role of the critic at the fin de siècle?

When nineteenth-century beliefs in the spiritual and moral function of art began to lose ground to modern formalism, Lee claimed intellectual responsibility toward the audience, a stance that distinguished her from the leading figures in the aesthetic movement who favored detachment and isolation. Arguing for aesthetic "empathy" that elevates individuals *and* creates community, she believed in the purifying effect of art on the individual and, therefore, pleaded for an art that benefits each person. Early in her career, Lee had advocated aesthetic disinterestedness, but later she became fearful that artistic detachment would ultimately separate intellectuals from human matters and alienate artists and critics from the community at large. Lee was not alone in deploring the distance between intellectuals and society and their unwillingness to act as cultural leaders. In a *Blackwood*'s article of February 1872, Robert S. Lytton expressed similar regrets for the barrier "between the erudite oligarchy who think and write" and the "plebeian public who only read and talk" (202 and 216). Lytton's snobbishness aside, the rift between intellectual artistic elites on the one hand and mass audiences on the other was perceived as real by many critics of the time. The rarified aesthete came to symbolize this gap, especially in the travesties and satires from Gilbert and Sullivan's *Patience* to George Du Maurier's *Punch* cartoons. But there were also constructive solutions for a new aesthetics in the public sphere. Christian and socialist discourses—especially when aesthetically joined, as in William Morris's arts and crafts movement—challenged aestheticism's cult of the individual. Similarly, many New Women writers made a claim for social awareness and responsibility. Like the "social-problem novelists" of the time, writers like Charlotte Perkins Gilman or Vernon Lee attributed the alienation of the self to the social and economic conditions while "suggesting that collective action pointed a way out of self-fragmentation" (Heilmann, 167).

Vernon Lee's "aesthetic empathy" proposed a form of fin-de-siècle communitarianism. Unlike Pater and Wilde, she did not fashion her aesthetics as a cult of the artistic individual but consistently redirected her view toward the audience. She cautioned other writers against an unrestrained indulgence in individual temperament because she was convinced that the writer's influence extended far beyond the moment, depositing, like a kind of residue, a lasting effect in the reader's psyche.

In "Gospels of Anarchy" (the reference to Arnold in the title is intended) Lee takes to task the tacit determinism of the age, the Nietzschean yea-sayers and fatalists who aestheticized the inevitable and left individual agency in limbo. "For science teaches us that all the life we human beings call progress, is not a mere affirmation so to speak of mere passive being, but . . . the perpetual assertion of fitness against unfitness, a constant making of inequality" (35). Against passive acceptance, she invokes a principle of (active) "selection and rejection" by a cultivated, reasonable human consciousness.[17] Lee mimics Darwinist language but modifies its determinist tilt by inserting a human agent who retains the principle of selection as an active choice. It is this choice paired with intellectual discipline and responsibility which for her defines the modern critic whose influence began to grow as audiences increasingly relied on mediated versions of reality. She believed in cultural production guided by a striving for the best without being elitist, and she demanded the highest aesthetic and ethical discipline from any writer—literary critic, artist, or otherwise. Like Arnold, Lee valued moral and cultural leadership but, unlike him, she did not locate it in academic authority. Her exclusion from a university career predicated an alternative path for the public intellectual which encompassed nonacademic discourses as long as they were morally and aesthetically sound.

Vernon Lee presents a historical site and a set of texts for the exploration of an alternative public voice in literature and criticism. She was prominent enough to attract an audience whose members included noted intellectuals such as Walter Pater, Henry James, and Virginia Woolf. Straddling both the Victorian and the early modernist periods, Lee exemplifies the changing role of the public intellectual while simultaneously establishing continuity between the nineteenth-century "man of letters" and the modernist aesthetic critic. Her relegation to obscurity has been prompted by a prejudice against intellectual women and a modernist anti-Victorianism which proclaimed "disinterestedness" and split sentiment from style. But the very forces which may be responsible for Lee's obscurity have now come under scrutiny. The present reassessment of modernism from broader cultural perspectives has led to renewed interest in writers like Lee, who wrote intelligently and energetically on a variety of topics for an audience they imagined to be large and diverse. Indeed, the creative mingling of intellectual and popular discourses as a form of writing can be associated most significantly with the figure of Vernon Lee.

Although my study raises the question to what extent Lee's marginalization is the product of pervasive gender bias in literary history, I am not interested in "discovering" her as another obscured woman writer. Nor do I find that Lee can be subsumed wholly among the "forgotten female aesthetes" if her role is conceived as "the junction between two other controversial public movements, the aesthetes and the New Women" (Schaffer, 18). However, Schaffer offers a viable redefinition of the female aesthetes that allows for the inclusion of a complex, multitalented writer like Lee. Schaffer's emphasis on the aesthetes' wide range of experience and their "multiple, flexible, social, and professional networks" (16) affords a fitting context for Vernon Lee. Lee's cross-disciplinary aesthetics—to use Schaffer's words—"accommodated a vast range of political positions" and "permitted the construction of a female subject as contradictory as the author's own politics" (16).

I would venture even further and suggest that Lee can be read as a category of her own. Her still undecided literary status serves as a point of departure, from which I investigate the various ways in which she addressed intellectual issues across the disciplines and outside academically defined styles. "Like the age to which it responded, Lee's was a complex genius" (Navarette, 145) and like her age, Lee oscillated in her argument between liberal tolerance and strong doctrinal misgivings, expressed in the mixed idiom of rationalist progressivism and aesthetic conservatism. It is her very unevenness, her Whitmanesque advertising—"and if I contradict myself, I contradict myself" (epigraph to *Baldwin*)—that identifies her so strikingly with the spirit of the age aptly described by Karl Pearson in *A Grammar of Science* (1892) as

> an era of great self-assertion and of excessive altruism; we see the highest intellectual power accompanied by the strangest recrudescence of superstition; there is a strong socialist drift and yet not a few remarkable individualist teachers; the extremes of religious faith and of unequivocal freethought. (3–4)

The frantic cross-fertilization between forms of knowledge that can often be found in "the same individual mind, unconscious of its own want of logical consistency, will often exhibit our age in microcosm" (Pearson, 4); it can be located in the idiosyncracies of its public intellectuals, from W. T. Stead to Andrew Lang, and surely including Vernon Lee.

Lee's disinclination to commit to any particular discipline has proven to be especially challenging for literary history's genre-oriented view. Thus, the reader may be surprised to see the chapters of this study answering to these same categories. This is intentional. For once, a critique of literary history is not achieved by denying the existence of formal differentiation but rather by reassessing the meanings assigned to these forms by individual writers. Lee was at home in almost all genres (except poetry), testing their expressive possi-bilities for her writerly intent. If she felt constrained by one form, she tossed it aside, risking to be misunderstood. Her struggle with traditional genre catego-ries reflects her struggle for an independent and yet recognizable voice.

Chapter 1 of this book introduces Lee as a European rather than wholly British writer and critic, with a unique upbringing between cultures in an in-tellectually ambitious home. While scholars have nodded to her cosmopolitan background as a biographical curiosity, hardly anyone has treated her European-ness as an integral part of her work. It can be argued that her cultural range gave her the diverse critical perspectives that we would associate with the emerg-ing figure of the public intellectual. Her European perspective is significantly tinted with her short but intense identification with British aestheticism, namely through the influence of Ruskin and Pater. Lee felt authenticated as an intellectual through her European experience, but she gained professional rec-ognition through her scholarship and erudition in aesthetic and historical top-ics that preoccupied her British contemporaries.

A brief summary of Lee's reception in the twentieth century and a discussion of the growing number of critical studies in recent years leads to a review of dif-ferent critical approaches suitable for reassessing her works in her most prolific phase of writing, from 1880 to about 1915. Lee imagined herself as part of a fel-lowship of (male) writers but, at the same time, she was known for her emotional or erotic ties with women. Thus, I investigate how her multiple identifications may have contributed to the ironic or ambiguous voices in her texts.

Critics have habitually lined up a string of famous influences to enhance Lee's own standing in literary history. While many studies have foregrounded her resistance to literary authorities, few have shown that she herself has been a source of influence for a variety of writers including Bernard Berenson, Oscar Wilde, Richard Le Gallienne, I. A. Richards, and even Virginia Woolf. The at-tention that Lee has received in the last few years has begun to change her role in literary history: from the marginal space of an "obscure" woman writer during most of the twentieth century, she has been moved into the more prominent po-sition that George Bernard Shaw had marked for her: "Vernon Lee is the Eng-lish of the English, and yet held her intellectual own all through. I take off my hat to the old guard of Victorian cosmopolitan intellectualism" (Gunn, 203).

Lee's first book, *Studies of the Eighteenth Century in Italy,* established her as an expert in Italian history and culture, which she considered her intellectual home from which she challenged especially pedantic German Historicism. She tried to shake off the universal (male) voice of historical scholarship by approaching history through biography, impression, and experience. Chapter 2 investigates how Lee sought to transcend her individuality by posing as a mediator of sorts between different cultures, genres, identities, and ages. Her blending of fact and fiction was most creative and provocative in the area of history writing, a traditionally "masculine" genre.

There is no doubt that history was a site of controversy throughout the nineteenth century, and as Rohan Maitzen has shown in *Gender, Genre, and Victorian Historical Writing,* women historians could "take advantage of instabilities in existing models of history" (xiii). However, if Lee "feminized" historiography, it was less by drawing on new models that "replaced the public sphere with the private" (xiv) than by broadening the base for historical subjects which included not only women but other neglected social groups. Like many contemporaries, Lee found the Renaissance attractive for its diverse cultural messages indicating transition and innovation, but she questioned the strong genteel focus of Renaissance scholarship. Strikingly modern, her studies direct us to a more diversified concept of historical relevance, anticipating the criticism expressed by George Parfitt a full century later: "We are now saying that 'the Renaissance' indicates a minority or élite tendency within a period. . . . There is little in 'the Renaissance' for peasants of either sex, and probably not much for artisans either" (84).

Since Lee was not viewed too favorably by the following generation of modernists, Woolf's exacting criticism affords an opportunity to discuss in chapter 3 Lee's relationship to feminism. I show that Lee's distance from contemporary feminist discourses does not necessarily make her an antifeminist. Although Lee did not participate actively in the turn-of-the-century debates on the "New Woman," her independent life as a female intellectual and her close collaboration with other women make her a model New Woman. In an extremely ironic article of 1902 (her introduction to the Italian translation of Charlotte Perkins Gilman's *Women and Economics*) Lee appears to endorse a feminist standpoint. She declares her advocacy of the Woman Question, not as a political activist, but rather from the position of a cultural critic. In this chapter I show how she uses the traditional form of the essay creatively to suggest alternative ways of knowing. Although chapters 2 and 3 appear to overlap in topic matter, there is a clear distinction: chapter 2 emphasizes discipline (historiography); chapter 3 focuses on genre (essay).

Lee reveals her most innovative textual operations in the development of her philosophical dialogues. For instance, in "On Friendship" (*Althea*) she finds a way of writing into her text an alternative, woman-centered subjectivity. In Chapter 4 I explore how she evokes a lesbian dimension by both activating and redefining classic forms of masculine homoeroticism. Lee replaces Plato's exclusive male round by men and women modeled on her acquaintances, with Althea stylized as a "boy" who resembles Lee's partner, Kit Anstruther-Thomson. This chapter also traces the evolvement of Lee's own critical voice from the mid-eighties to the mid-nineties: from questioning the exclusivity of the male subject and its "cunning abstractions," to an assertive alternative (female) voice. Lee's ambivalent identifications with Baldwin as her literary self in the 1880s reaches a new dimension in the next decade, when he is absorbed into Althea's abstract lesbian position.

Chapter 5 presents Vernon Lee as a novelist in *Miss Brown* (1884), which attracted enough public attention to have been called a bestseller. Lee's novel, criticized for its tactlessness and moral tone, exposes the less desirable sides of aestheticism, especially its constraint of women in their sexual roles. The question is: Can Lee remove the sexual and misogynist assumptions of aestheticism to make it commendable for women seeking an identity different from languid virgins or men-eating femmes fatales? Her portrayal of the aesthetic movement in the form of the "bildungsroman" creates a bizarre tension which mocks the irreducible contradiction between liberal female *Bildung* and male-defined social contract. Things get even more complicated when class difference is thrown into the mix as Lee's growing social awareness would demand. By using an Italian servant girl as her protagonist, Lee challenges the function of astheticism in a social context. When she stages an encounter between aesthetic and socialist movements, neither comes out a winner, mainly because of the limited roles they offer women.

Like the exotic-looking Miss Brown, the female characters in Lee's supernatural tales reflect the decadents' ideal of female beauty. But whereas Anne Brown reveals the naive and troubled morality of a realistic character, the women in Lee's fantastic stories remain enigmatic and unreal. Chapter 6 covers three of Vernon Lee's better-known fantastic tales—"Dionea," "Prince Alberic and the Snake Lady," and "Amour Dure"—whose narrative structures combine the traditional ghost story with aesthetic symbolism. Vernon Lee's search for alternative forms of female subjectivity is embedded in the uncanny dimensions of these stories which recreate the contemporary social and psychological climates in which "otherness" is evoked in images of strange beauty. The uncanny appears as gendered productions of fear and desire which operate as powerful agents in fin-de-siècle cultural and social life. I have chosen these stories because, to my mind, they summarize the approach of this study, which addresses at once questions of genre and gender, textuality and sexuality, history and myth—questions that were at the center of Lee's vast and varied work.

# 1 Life and Letters
## *Vernon Lee's Role in Literary History*

BIOGRAPHICAL NOTES

*I absolutely prohibit any biography of me.*
*My life is my own and I leave that to nobody.*

—VERNON LEE

Vernon Lee's instructions to Irene Cooper Willis, her executrix, were meant to keep her private life closed to the public. Lee allowed, however, that her papers—letters, journals, and unpublished manuscripts—could be used privately.[1] The modern reader may wish that Vernon Lee had heeded her friend, Edith Wharton, who admonished her, in a letter of 4 December 1932: "Take my advice and sit down at once and do your memoirs! They will be a hundred times better worth it than mine" (Somerville). For a controversial writer like Vernon Lee, the absence of personal memoirs has led to bold speculations or distortions. Lee's biographer, Peter Gunn, who was the first (1964) to include the materials from Colby College (thanks to Cooper Willis's liberal interpretation of Lee's ruling), regards Lee's private papers as an essential corrective for a study of her life:

> It would indeed be possible to write of Vernon Lee's life and intellectual de-
> velopment from her own books, which furnish us with many biographical
> details; also from the lives, memoirs and letters of her contemporaries; or

from hearsay. But such procedure might have the effect of placing on the facts gathered from these sources constructions which, although not actually false, were partial and therefore misleading, if they were not corrected by what we know from her letters and journals. (ix)

Since the following study is not intended to be a biography, the excursion into Lee's life will be brief and, in Gunn's words, will focus on "Vernon Lee's life and intellectual development from her own books." Of primary interest are the literary sublimations of her aesthetic relationships with life and art from early on.[2]

Vernon Lee's education, like that of many upper-middle-class girls, was conducted mostly at home and in several European countries. When growing up, she spoke better French than English, which made her hesitate "between becoming a French or an English writer" (*Handling of Words,* 293); her first publications were in French and in Italian, and from her twenties on, she considered Italy her home. Returning to Italy from England in September 1886, she wrote to her mother, "For all my interest in England, this is *my* country" (8 September 1886, Colby). Lee had visited England briefly at the age of six but did not return until 1881, when her "slightly foreign precision of vocabulary and intonation" and her social manners struck her English audience as odd.[3] Yet, Lee's publication history is tied up with England, where the growing interest in Italian history and culture offered a large market for her studies. In her early twenties, her visits to England had one main purpose: soliciting publishers for her manuscripts. Since England was her country of choice for publishing, critics have largely discussed her as a British author. But her extensive knowledge of French, Italian, and German literature, history, and science brought her the attention of a more international intellectual community than most of her British contemporaries enjoyed.[4]

Born near Boulogne-sur-mer, France, Violet Paget (of Welsh extraction on her mother's side and French or Polish on her father's)[5] spent her first twenty years moving from Germany, to Switzerland, to France and to Italy, accompanied by mentors, tutors, and friends from various national backgrounds. As a young girl, Lee was put in the care of Swiss and German governesses whose stories and legends developed in her a sense of Germany's romantic past. This sentimental side of her childhood remained an integral part of her aesthetic and political judgment. In "Christkindchen" (*Juvenilia,* 1887) she explores the magnetism of such early impressions upon the human mind, reminding us of Walter Pater's vaguely autobiographical tale "The Child in the House." A large part of Lee's education was conducted by her mother, Matilda Paget, to whom she pays homage in *The Handling of Words*. From her, Lee received rigorous training in math, grammar, and rhetoric and a general belief in the soundness of rational thought, which later impelled her crusade against turn-of-the-century antirationalism. Mrs. Paget put her daughter through a demanding intellectual training with little room for an "éducation sentimentale."[6]

In the winter of 1866–67, the Pagets became friends with the family of the painter John Singer Sargent when both were staying in Nice. John Sargent and Violet Paget also spent the winter of 1867–68 together in Rome, painting, exploring the churches and palaces, and listening to Mrs. Sargent's stories. According to Peter Gunn, Mrs. Sargent's enthusiasm for art and beauty complemented Lee's intellectual training.[7] Gunn names Mrs. Sargent as one of the three most influential women in Lee's upbringing (the third one being Marie Schülpach, her Swiss governess). In *The Sentimental Traveller,* Lee fondly remembers Mrs. Sargent, "this most wisely fantastic of Wandering Ladies," to whom she felt she owed the spiritual initiation into the Genius Loci: "Well, to return to myself, who owe her so much . . . I do not think my family ever realized Mrs. S—'s high vocation, for they did not know of the cultus of Genius Loci, or even of his existence. And it is certain that Mrs. S— never conceived the bare possibility of people as stay-at-home as we" (12).

The tutelage of Mrs. Sargent, her mother, and the array of Swiss and German governesses allowed Lee to develop a keen sense of knowledge even outside an academic context that could be enjoyed and taken for granted by her elder, Cambridge-educated half-brother, Eugene Lee-Hamilton. Vernon Lee was aware of the unequal opportunities for men and women but never really considered herself affected by them. Coming late to an interest in the Woman Question, she mentioned to Karl Pearson in 1888 that he had actually first drawn her attention "to that question, which the exceptional good fortune of my life had me to despise" (13 March 1888).[8] A decade later, she would credit Charlotte Perkins Gilman for having "converted" her to the Woman Question.

In general, Vernon Lee regarded gender issues within larger national-historical contexts. Her European orientation as an expatriate of sorts and her intellectual training modeled on the French woman of letters Mme de Staël helped shape her unique views. In her only feminist essay, "The Economic Parasitism of

Women" (1902), Lee typically puts nationality above gender, emphasizing "a family resemblance, after all, between the men and women of the same country." She argues that the rather masculine Englishwoman would match the "athletic, sporting, colonising Englishman," whereas "the ultrafeminine woman belonged, quite naturally, to the effeminate (French) man" (295–96). Notwithstanding the national stereotypes she enlists for polemical purposes, she also points to their social construction, deeming herself qualified to judge national variations, "living, as I do equally among Latins and Anglo-Saxons" (296).

Turn-of-the-century Europeans took pride in national difference and perceived national character as fomenting divisiveness. Lee's lack of (British) patriotism and her outspoken pacifism during World War I, as well as her slightly unrealistic defense of Germany, did not win her any points among her French and British friends. The political tensions of the time can be held at least partially accountable for Lee's intellectual isolation after World War I. One might speculate whether her attraction to aestheticism was a result of its universal symbolism, which spoke to aesthetic communities beyond national identity.[9]

Vernon Lee's family belonged to a set of cosmopolitan expatriates gathering in Paris, Florence, and Rome. Due to the unsettled finances of her mother's inheritance, which provided the family's income, the Pagets were forced to move their possessions back and forth between France, Germany, and Italy in the 1860s and '70s. In *The Sentimental Traveller* (1908) Vernon Lee recalls: "We shifted our quarters invariably every six months, and, by dint of shifting, crossed Europe's length and breadth in several directions. But this was *moving,* not *travelling*" (6). They avoided sightseeing and touristic places, even people, when they took their walks on public promenades "at unfrequented hours." Since they never went without books or without her mother's constant reading, explaining, or telling of stories, Lee endowed "every promenade in Europe, nay, every bench and bush thereof" with imaginary persons and places that sprang from her mind and blended with her surroundings. She developed a concept of "a Europe occupying other dimensions than that network of railways blobbed with hotels and customs houses across which I was periodically hurried from inventory to inventory" (14). The family's nomadic life-style did not provide a sense of home. So it is not surprising that her stories are filled with displaced characters, longing to return to a time or place. Lee forced her readers to look at places not as they were but colored with qualities "derived entirely from her imagination" so that "one cannot be sure if they ever had an existence of their own" (Ponsonby, 183–84).

Although the Pagets' financial situation was not always stable, they were never without governesses, footmen, or servants. Matilda Paget was entitled to her share of the lifelong interest from the family estate built from an extensive business in the West Indies. Her brother's poor administration kept the cash from reaching her at regular intervals. Toward her friends, Lee typically displays a facade of financial soundness, but in writing to her mother, she is much more straightforward, constantly fretting about insufficient means or inadequate publishing fees. On one occasion she declares that she "will not accept only £20 from Unwin" for her stories (25 July 1891, Colby); on another, she is proud to withhold an article from the *Fortnightly* because she was given only thirteen days' notice (3 August 1887, Colby). Lee's financial struggles did not put her on the brink of poverty, though. We can take her literally when she tells Eugene (31 August 1893, Colby) that she could "lack, at most, only luxuries" and, more importantly, that she did not depend on her writing for a living.

> On the other hand I consider that in a world where so many clever people (especially in England) have to write to suit the public from sheer lack of money, it would be shocking for me, who could lack, at most, only luxuries, to do such a thing. Of course it would be a bore if my writing ceased to bring in anything at all; but I think it better to restrict my expenditure than to increase my income.

Lee's assertion of her independence curiously echoes Eugene's letter to his mother (7 January 1870, Colby) after his failure to publish a historical article on Pope Sextus V: "In a few years, I doubt not I shall be in the position to make a worthy contribution to historic literature and to publish it at my own expense. Independence is a most desirable thing."

Lee's declaration also points to a complicated brother-sister relationship. After all, *she* achieved recognition for the "great" books *he* had meant to publish but allegedly was prevented from writing by his mysterious physical paralysis. Since Violet's father, Henry, was not given much say in the family, her half-brother Eugene—twelve years her senior—provided some of the paternal directives for his sister's education. During his student years in Oxford and diplomatic training in London in the mid-sixties, Eugene sent to their mother a stream of priggish instructions for "Baby's" education. Unanimous in their advocacy for a rigorous and systematic training of Violet's intellectual talents, brother and mother—often speaking in a parental "we"—crammed her day with extensive lessons in French, German, Italian, and the "rational" subjects of history, philosophy, and geometry. Vernon Lee's early letters to Eugene (whom she addressed with the German "Bruder") are full of reverence and attempts to impress him with her intelligence and learning. Her own success as a writer came early and soon surpassed Eugene's own efforts. When he failed to place his first article in 1870, she had already published a story, "Les Aventures d'une pièce de monnaie," in the Swiss journal *La Famille*. In 1873 a sudden strange paralysis, which made it impossible for him to work, led to an early release from the diplomatic service and sent him back to his mother's overly indulgent protection. His physical frailty turned him—not yet thirty—for twenty years into an invalid around whom the whole household was organized. Although it may be doubted that Eugene Lee-Hamilton used his illness to escape comparison with his half-sister, as Burdett Gardner has argued, the paralysis kept him from leading a "normal" and productive life. In her teens, Vernon Lee was in charge of attending to his needs, such as governing the flow of his visitors or reading to him every afternoon.

Eugene's physical weakness put him in a somewhat feminine position, but his educational bonus and his older-brother role endowed him with masculine authority over his younger sister. Her gradual separation from Eugene, indicative of her general emancipation from authorities, runs as a subtle theme through the first two decades of her writing, but most candidly in her novella *Ottilie* (1883). In the thinly veiled autobiographical plot, she investigates a brother-sister relationship during the German "Sturm und Drang" period. Her introductory comments are not far from the truth: "People at W— maintained that in all these [literary] productions the sister had done at least half the work; and indeed the general opinion seems to have been that she was the master mind of the two" (18).[10] From her correspondence with Kit Anstruther-Thomson we know that Lee considered herself the stronger personality. Once she learned that Eugene's paralysis was in all likelihood caused by autosuggestion, she became less and less patient with his disease[11] and began asking for more attention to her own physical problems: "I do not say I am not capricious; I *am* capricious about my food," she wrote to her mother, "because my digestion is bad" (18 November 1890, Colby).

In 1873 the Pagets settled permanently in Italy, first in Rome and then in Florence. At her salons, Mrs. Paget hosted an illustrious set of international artists and intellectuals. An article by Mary Robinson (poet and close friend of Vernon Lee in the early 1880s) in *Country Life* gives us a glimpse of these guests: "—there was Mr. Benn, the philosopher, Ouida, Barzellotti, Paul Bourget, Princess Gortchakoff" (28 December 1907, 935–37). Celebrities from Henry James to Edith Wharton regularly flocked to the "Casa Paget," where they could expect intelligent and inspiring conversation.

Intellectual and social decorum placed Vernon Lee within the educated upper-middle classes of nineteenth-century Europe. Her upbringing by an ambitious, free-thinking mother, however, differed considerably from that of other women in her social class. She was educated not for domestic or marital life, but rather for an intellectual career (V. Colby, 248). At age thirty-six Lee had to beg her mother to provide for Lee to learn how to cook, so that she could prepare meals suited for her ill health, an undertaking she considered "a very good investment of my time" (VL to MP, 18 November 1890, Colby). Lee identified herself from early in life with what was considered a masculine career, impressing literary colleagues with her erudition and independent thought and challenging them with her sharpness and lack of tact. In nineteenth-century terms, Lee was leading a man's life in a woman's body, which she aptly describes as a mixed gender identity in her preface to *Baldwin:* "The accident of education . . . has placed this not very feminine man to some measure at a woman's standpoint" (5). Familiar with but not entrenched in traditional gender roles, she repeatedly explored the cultural conditions of their construction in her writing.

Lee often describes her identity as the product of personal influences, coincidence, and a sense of the various places in her family's perpetual movements. The determinants in Lee's life intersected at such unusual angles that they were bound to complicate her perception and performance. As Gardner puts it, "all simple formulas for understanding her must be abandoned forthwith" (87). Lee's reluctance to align herself with one nation, one culture, or one gender provoked all those who desired clearly defined boundaries. She was writing simultaneously for and against Victorian middle-class ideology, which promoted the values she was taught to embrace but felt driven to defy. This conflict became evident in Lee's relationship with Mary Robinson, the daughter of a London banking family, hosts of one of the famous salons at the time. The Robinsons' salon afforded Lee opportunities for artistic, literary, and political contacts—essential for a burgeoning young writer—but she also felt stifled by its intellectually stagnant and snobbish atmosphere. Eager to wrest

Mary from the "lazy stagnation" of Victorian middle-class life, Lee risked a
rupture with the family to enlist Mary as her champion in the struggle against
the petty domesticities of her hosts. After "escaping" with Mary to a cottage in
Sussex, she wrote to her mother (22 July 1882, Colby):

> Poor little Mary. . . . Her own intérieur, I think, is getting more and more in-
> sufficient for her. She is growing and it is shrinking. I mean that it is becom-
> ing more and more dead alive and commonplace. All that little literary
> society which seems, in pre-Raphaelite days, to have met at 84 Gower Street,
> seems dispersed or melted away, and 84 is getting more and more common-
> place and languid. To me it had grown excessively tedious. That perfect
> peace, which Mrs. R. boasts of so, is not the result of real sympathy, but of
> mere lazy stagnation.

Although the break with the Robinsons had highly personal reasons, the rhetoric she used to describe the conflict reveals her quick judgment of the intellectual set she had been so eager to meet only a year before. As much as she
admired the intelligence of artists like Oscar Wilde (who was a regular guest
at the Robinsons'), she was a caustic critic of the snobbery and complacency
found in these circles.

Vernon Lee was an outsider in Victorian English society, but she also shared
its high moral standards and beliefs in progress and improvement. She frowned
upon "immoral" artists and all forms of (male) egocentrism or self-indulgence,
which did not protect her from sharing some of the same foibles she was criticiz-
ing. After the calamity of *Miss Brown,* she wrote in her diary on 31 December
1884:

> [P]erhaps the British public is right; perhaps I have no right to argue on the
> matter, because I may be colour blind about the data. Here I am accused of
> having, in simplicity of heart, written, with a view to moralise the world, an
> immoral book. (Gunn, 105–6)

Like Pater, Lee was drawn to Italian art and history, which she studied through
his aesthetic impressionism to validate her own eclectic method against the systematic approaches that her half-brother Eugene found so admirable in John
Addington Symonds and among German historians. From the mid-1880s on,

her aesthetic philosophy became inflected with a sympathy for deprived social groups. Pained "with the force of great class evils" (*Juvenilia,* 12), she felt urged to address the great social questions brought to her attention, for instance, by her activist friend Isabella Ford and the Fabian Society. Lee's growing consciousness of social inequality aroused her interest in the Woman's Rights movement, but her dislike of the militancy among British suffragettes kept her from getting more involved in political feminism.

Until about World War I, Lee focused on aesthetic psychology, adapting the concept of empathy ("Einfühlung") from the German schools of Fechner, Vischer, and Lipps for literary analysis in *The Handling of Words* (1923). During the war years, she became a fervent pacifist, thus gaining the regard of George Bernard Shaw and Olive Schreiner, but estranging other British friends, such as H. G. Wells, especially when she campaigned for a more benign view of Germany. In the 1920s, she had already lost a great number of her readers. Her philosophical treatises did not find the same reception as her writings before the war. Even though her aesthetic-psychological study *The Handling of Words* was well received and is still quoted today, her most influential time as a public intellectual was over. Her death in 1935 startled the international community—almost incredulous that she was still alive.

## INTELLECTUAL DEVELOPMENT AND CRITICAL RECEPTION

*Of course I have played my cards as badly as I could have done with regard to securing a public; but I have written, for the last ten years with the determination never to write a thing which did not happen to interest me at the moment, and with the desire to prevent myself getting into intellectual ruts. At thirty seven I have no public, but on the other hand, I am singularly far from being played out and crystallized, as I see most writers become even before that age. (VL to Eugene Lee-Hamilton, 31 August 1893, Colby)*

Vernon Lee's self-reflection in a letter to her half-brother came at a time when she had published already a dozen rather successful books and was just preparing *Althea: A Second Book of Dialogues* for publication. Her books were being reviewed in leading journals of the time, including the *Athenaeum,* the *Spectator,* the *Academy,* and the *Nation.* With hindsight, Lee's complaint about her perceived marginality appears more prophetic than factual. Distancing herself from a larger reading public was as much a gesture of frustration as an act of intellectual independence. Apart from being an expression of personal sentiment, Lee's words reflect the dilemma of the public intellectual caught between the emergence of mass consumerism on the one hand and withdrawal into academic elitism on the other. Like most female aesthetes, Lee favored more inclusive forms of art but was wary of letting the marketplace dictate literary taste. She offered an alternative that melded aesthetic delight with individual intellectual responsibility. In a letter to Karl Pearson (3 March 1888), she called upon writers to use their "intellectual privileges—the privilege of comparative freedom from want, of leisure, of education, of subtlety of sentiment—[but] to employ them for the benefit of others" (Pearson Papers, UCL).

Lee's books on art and aesthetics were widely discussed in the late nineteenth century because of her independent and singularly unorthodox views. Yet she was never a "popular" writer. Two years before her death, Roger Fry, who felt indebted to her pioneering work in aesthetics, told her, "You've never had the reputation you deserve, but no doubt it'll come."[12] Inspired by John Ruskin, Walter Pater, and Henry James, Lee herself came to influence other critics: from Bernard Berenson to Roger Fry and even Virginia Woolf. In her reviews, Woolf was a pungent critic of Lee's prose style, but was impressed by her enthusiasm and erudition. Being fully conversant with the latest theories on art and science, Lee participated zealously in the debates on aesthetics, morality, evolution, and belief. When Virginia Woolf reviewed *Laurus Nobilis* (a collection of essays on art and ethics) for *TLS* in August 1909, she called Lee a "first-rate disciple," who "has read Plato and Ruskin and Pater with enthusiasm because she cares passionately for the subjects they deal with." Just how much Woolf engaged Lee's concepts of beauty to arrive at her modernist feminist aesthetics has been demonstrated recently by Dennis Denisoff in a striking intertextual reading. Denisoff shows how contexts and images from Lee's fiction are obviously reworked in Woolf's *Orlando*.[13] This connection is somewhat surprising, given the effort Woolf made to distance herself from Victorian writers like Lee. Most modernist writers severed their ties to the previous age to practice their new aesthetics of cool intellectual detachment. "Art is icy," Henry James had once admonished Lee, when he found the moral tone of *Miss Brown* lacking in aesthetic distance. Concerned with the aesthetics of form, James—like other modernist critics—overlooked Lee's talent for satire and irony, which rose to full prime in "Lady Tal," her satiric portrayal of a Jame-

sian novelist. With "Lady Tal" Lee fell out of favor not because she had failed
to write like James, but because she had written all too James-like.

Lee's exchanges with Henry James give us an inkling of the literary standards emerging between the Victorian and modernist ages, often expressed in
gendered terms. James saw himself as a paternal mentor for Lee and similarly
tried to "direct" a host of other female writers, such as Constance Fenimore
Woolson or Mrs. Humphry Ward. While his letters to Lee deliver his critique
civilly and courteously, the correspondence with his friend Perry is more straightforward, revealing his uneasiness about women writers. James and other contemporaries labeled Lee's assertiveness as unwomanly and herself as ugly, a
particularly crafted ruse considering her passion for beauty and aesthetics. Obviously, the intellectual woman's voice had little erotic appeal and was censored on
account of her sex, an effect Lee had tried to avoid all her life. Although James
admired Lee's cleverness, he did not always receive it benevolently because, we
may suppose, she did not present it with feminine charm. In his letters, he calls
Lee "the most intellectual person in Florence" but at the same time finds her "ex-
ceedingly ugly" (3:166–69). Bertrand Russell, too, finds her "incredibly ugly," although, as he implies, she obviously did not repel female admirers: "[She was]
always able to win the devotion of young girls who were both intelligent and
beautiful. This I suppose, was due to the brilliancy of her intellect" (quoted in
Gardner, 59–60).

When the female intellectual emerged as an identifiable cultural figure,
men's strictures turned overly defensive, suggesting an entrenched male intellectual establishment. Examples range from the notorious *Saturday Review* opposition to feminism to such desperate defenses against intelligent and aggressive
women as in P. G. Hamerton's works (David, 17). The uneasiness of Victorian
writers toward "clever" women is clearly felt in J. A. Symonds's correspondence
with Vernon Lee. In reference to her scathing review of Professor Villari's *Nic-
colo Macchiavelli* in the *Athenaeum* (7 July 1883), he tells her that "he [Villari] was
irritated by certain airs of superior knowledge intelligence & wisdom in a young
lady who certainly could not know so much of the subject as he did" (March
1884). Symonds's explanation of Villari's feelings only thinly veil his own irrita-
tion towards Lee, which transpires in a letter to her a month later:

> I feel that you imagine yourself to be so clever that every thing you think is
> either right or else valuable. . . . You get the charm of printing a clever woman's

aperçus, recording in the press her passing thoughts, stereotyping her table
talk, by your method. But you miss, according to my notion, the supreme
grace of dignity & sweetness & nobility. (4 April 1884)

Critical reactions to Vernon Lee have always been colored by a certain anxiety
over prominent female intellectuals. The gender bias lasted well into our own
century. Even her apt biographer, Peter Gunn, maintains that she offended her
contemporaries with unfeminine brusqueness and lack of humility. Thus, modern reevaluations of Vernon have to take into consideration the complicated roles
of women writers and the strictures on them in the nineteenth and early twentieth centuries. This pertains especially to those who, like Lee, subsumed the position of public intellectual and so invaded what was clearly a male domain.

The varying reactions to Lee afford insight into the instability of contemporary literary standards. Often enough, her books are simultaneously praised
and criticized—for precisely the same reasons. A few exemplary reviews from
her most productive years exhibit these inconsistent judgments. Lee's first aesthetic treatise, *Belcaro: Being Essays on Sundry Aesthetical Questions* (1881), finds
an enthusiastic Cosmo Monkhouse who—at this point still unsure of her
sex—thinks it rare to find "so much thought in so easy a style" (*Academy,* 18
February 1882, 112). The American critic, Harriet Waters Preston, although
generally supportive of Lee's writing, deplores the book as a "rather scatter-
brained declamation," which she hopes is only a youthful "fling" (*Atlantic
Monthly,* February 1885, 219–27). Lee's first study of the Italian Renaissance,
*Euphorion* (1884), receives praise from the *Athanaeum* for its "well-defined
ideas . . . clear impressions, and vigorous and persuasive sorts of writing" (5
July 1884, 7–8), but is rebuked by the *Saturday Review* because of the author's
confusion of "impressions with ideas" (6 September 1884, 317–18). A similar
rift in opinions runs through the commentaries on *The Spirit of Rome* (1905), a
collection of essays on the "Genius Loci." Whereas the *Times Literary Supplement* reproves the unpolished character of her "200 pages of scattered adjec-
tives and convulsed interjections" (13 October 1905, 339), the *Academy,* using
almost the same words, finds that "the essence and spirit of Rome breathes in
these disconnected and scattered leaves from an old diary. Each word is exactly
the right and vivid one" (14 October 1905, 1073–74). What some critics label as
sheer incompetence, others welcome as innovation, depending on the journal's
overall political view. Sometimes the critics simply find fault with Lee's style:

repetition, nonchalant word choice, convoluted sentences, or her peculiar use of semicolons.[14]

As a historian and aesthete, Lee was often measured against more established writers, such as J. A. Symonds or Walter Pater. The *Saturday Review* considers Lee's *Euphorion* clearly inferior to Symonds's Renaissance studies, especially since she did not read his work on the subject—an intolerable mistake for a neophyte and a woman (6 September 1884, 317–18). The most relentless critic is W. J. Stillman of the *Nation*, who calls her downright ignorant in matters of art and "absolutely devoid of aesthetic sense," a judgment which is highly unfair and simply false (22 January 1885, 76–77). Critics who compare Lee with Pater generally find her a "worthy disciple" but cannot warm up to her style since it "has not the polish which endeared Pater to his readers" (*Times*, 13 December 1895, 13). Pater himself, in a letter to Lee, praises *Euphorion* for its "very remarkable power of style—full of poetic charm . . . , justly expression, sustained and firm," but then adds, "as women's style so seldom is" (4 June 1884, Colby)—a rather back-handed compliment that reveals the gender bias in nineteenth-century literary criticism.

The other quibbles critics have with Lee concern her lack of objectivity. Sydney Waterlow, the reviewer of *The Beautiful: An Introduction to Psychological Aesthetics* (1914) in the *International Journal of Ethics,* is symptomatic in calling the book fatally flawed in its neglect of "one important characteristic of aesthetic judgments, their objectivity" (460). It seems that the readers of her essays expected a more straightforward form of writing, at a time when the conversations about the arts moved from the salon into the academy, where they were increasingly subjected to professional academic standards. Impressionist and evocative styles, usually associated with poetics, were separated from more analytical and scholarly discourses. Lee's textual hybrids did not satisfy those who split expository from imaginative writing; critics such as E. Purcell, writing in the *Academy,* accused her of "losing her grasp on reality by stretching out into associations and accidental remembrances" (19 July 1884, 37–38).

Lee's writings on art and history are not intended to be objective. Throwing aside Hegelian determinism and abstract theory, Lee tried to enter cultural and social systems through individual contemplation. In her historical fiction, for instance, the perspective is personal rather than institutional,[15] which implies, as Hilary Fraser puts it, that Lee brings back "the emotions in our responses to and representations of the past" (227). How much Lee attempts to overrule historical chronology can be shown by her total disregard of Karl Hillebrand's advice on *Ottilie*. The German historiographer corrected several dates to make the narrative historically plausible, but none of the later editions of the book show any signs of alteration.[16] Less pedantic critics call her unorthodox approach fresh and original, and therefore, the reviewer of *Spirit of Rome* ascribes to her a "distinguished place in that school of French and English writers called the 'literary Impressionists.'"[17]

Lee's fictional work, in general, was treated more generously. Except for *Miss Brown* (1883), which caused personal offence, and *The Ballet of Nations* (1915), which was in radical opposition to the political climate during World War I, her fiction received favorable reviews. Should we presume that she was less likely in her fiction to trespass into male territory, or was fiction simply more flexible in absorbing uncommon styles and subjects? In any case, the ideological separation between fact and fiction became imperative even in this genre. Lee's story "Amour Dure" (working title: "Medea da Carpi") was first rejected by *Blackwood* because she "put the historical facts into a fictitious frame," whereupon Vernon Lee commented, "Isn't that a joke?" (VL to MP, 25 July 1885, Colby).

All told, Lee's reviewers are divided over modes of representation in the late nineteenth century—such as Andrew Lang's realism-romance debate—a division which points to the contemporary apprehension about literary standards in a rapidly transforming culture and its aspirations for modernity. Virginia Woolf would later accuse Lee of relying too much on her own associations rather than keeping a steady eye on the object. It bothered her that Lee did not transform her impressions into "divine impersonality." In her review of *Laurus Nobilis* (1909), Woolf complained: "The very qualities of her style get in the way of any clear sight of the matter which she discusses; images and symbols, unless they spring from a profound understanding, illustrate not the object but the writer." Regardless of these concerns, even Woolf cannot deny Lee's sincerity and fervor for her subject: "we feel her enthusiasm; and that somewhat vague sensation is perhaps the most definite thing that we take away from her writing" (284).

In all their divergence, Vernon Lee's critics share a language that splices the idiom of difference and classification with gender. There is a clear demarcation between those who favor Lee as a new type of female writer, who "possesses a vigorous pen . . . unafraid to grapple with subjects women usually avoid" ("On Modern Thought," *New York Times,* 1 August 1886, 9) and those who rebuff her by using standard clichés about women writers. "There is also much careless thinking, not unusual in her sex in serious writing," finds James Jackson Jarves, the reviewer for the *New York Times* in 1879.[18] Three decades later, the idiom does not appear much different—only that femininity has slipped from character into style: "She writes with masculinity of thought and femininity of expression, and reasons about problems of duty and religion as if she were a philosopher" (*New York Times Saturday Review of Books* on *Gospels of Anarchy*, 1908). That "thought" was conventionally regarded as men's domain is revealed in a review which speaks of Lee as "the ablest living woman-thinker."[19] Superficially, such a phrase may appear to be a compliment, but the gender slant reinforces the familiar bias.

These comments show Lee to have been the unhappy recipient of conjectures about gender that had wide currency at the time. Subjects, styles, genres, and disciplines were categorized along the sex/gender divide. Positive traits are considered male attributes. Thus, Lee's style can be "vigorous," "strong," or "masterful." But she is said to have lacked the manly qualities of logic, unity, and synthesis. She is not systematic, objective, realistic, economic, or philosophical; in other words, she lacks the features of an academic (male) education. In the language of criticism, disadvantage becomes (female) deficiency: Lee's style is "wordy," "untidy," and "repetitious," with "too much detail" and "side-tracking," and, on the whole, "too tedious to read."

But Vernon Lee's books were indeed read so widely that Virginia Woolf cited her as the expert on aesthetics in *A Room of One's Own:* "There are Jane Harrison's books on Greek archaeology; Vernon Lee's books on aesthetics; Gertrude Bell's books on Persia" (83). Aware of the common prejudice that women were not fit to write about theoretical subjects, Lee was determined to ignore it wholeheartedly. In 1878 she wrote to Mrs. Jenkin, a novelist and friend of the Paget family:

> The *Academy* has been rather civil about my Fraser article. It has found out (Heaven knows how) that Vernon Lee is not a real name and put it in inverted commas. I don't care that Vernon Lee should be known to be myself or any other young woman, as I am sure no one *reads* a woman's writings on art, history or aesthetics with anything but mitigated contempt. (18 December 1878, quoted in Gunn)

Since anything from a woman's pen in a scholarly field would be treated with extra skepticism, it is remarkable that the reviews of *Studies of the Eighteenth*

*Century in Italy,* published when Lee was only twenty-two, were so positive throughout. Or were the critics so generous because the eighteenth century had been a neglected period on which nobody had yet done any important work?[20]

There have been sporadic periods of renewed interest in Vernon Lee. After her death in 1935, only a few of her books were republished, mainly her ghost stories. Her philosophical and historical essays, which constitute the bulk of her oeuvre, seldom attracted a publisher's interest in the twentieth century.[21] The most recent republications of her prose work include two library editions of her "New Critical" study, *The Handling of Words:* one in 1992 by Mellen Press, and the other in 1996 by Oxford University Press.[22] For a long time, Lee was best remembered for her fantastic tales, several of which have appeared in modern anthologies.[23] Her novella, "Lady Tal," became popular again when Elaine Showalter included it in the widely read *Daughters of Decadence* (1993). But most of Lee's nonfictional works, which she considered her major achievement, are out of print. The lack of access to Lee's works may also explain why even newer studies of the Renaissance, such as J. B. Bullen's *The Myth of the Renaissance in Nineteenth-Century Writing* (1994), completely ignore Lee's important contributions in this area of her expertise. However, the recent interest of feminist literary historians in women's nonfictional texts affords more ready access to some of Lee's theoretical studies. For instance, Andrea Broomfield and Sally Mitchell's anthology, *Prose by Victorian Women* (1996), has made accessible two important essays by Lee, "Gospels of Anarchy" and "Art and Man."

The history of Vernon Lee criticism follows a similarly uneven pattern. The first larger study of her works was published in 1932 by the Swiss scholar Max Bräm, who compares the Renaissance concepts of Vernon Lee, John Addington Symonds, and John Ruskin. Bräm's study—written under the influence of a longing for leadership and consolidation in the political crises of the early thirties—favors a unified image of the Renaissance, which, according to him, Lee fails to provide. Bräm therefore ranks her as inferior to Symonds and Ruskin.[24] Most other twentieth-century scholars of Renaissance studies ignore Lee's work. Hilary Fraser's *The Victorians and Renaissance Italy* (1992) for the first time supplements the standard experts from Ruskin to Pater with women's voices, including George Eliot, E. B. Browning, Christina Rossetti, and Vernon Lee. Being familiar with the recent reappraisal of Jacob Burckhardt as a cultural historian, Fraser can show that Lee, like Burckhardt, gave Renaissance studies in the nineteenth century a new accent by paying more attention to the broad spectrum of people involved in the "making" of the Renaissance. Much like Burckhardt's *Kultur der Renaissance in Italien* (1860), Lee's study of Italian literature, art, and music paved the way for what now has come to be called "cultural studies." Fraser recognizes Lee alongside Pater, Symonds, and Ruskin as a historian in her own right, "an acute critic of her contemporaries' attitude towards and treatment of the past and as a more subtle historiographical practitioner than she might at first appear" (228).

The 1950s were another period of renewed interest in Vernon Lee. In 1952, after a twenty-year silence, the *Colby Library Quarterly* announced that "thanks to Miss Irene Cooper Willis, of the Inner Temple, London, the Colby Library has received the private papers and correspondence of Vernon Lee (Violet Paget)" (Libbey, 117). The first to make use of these papers was Burdett Gardner, for his dissertation, "Violet Paget" (1954), which was not published until 1987 under the title *Vernon Lee: Lesbian Imagination Victorian Style*. Gardner's book is packed with quotations. He managed to interview more than twenty people who had known Vernon Lee, and ploughed through much of her vast correspondence and forty-three books. Unfortunately, his investigation singles her out negatively as a lesbian. The leading question—"what effect did her neurosis have upon her entire literary product?"—reflects the homophobia of the 1950s and seriously mars his whole approach.[25] Gardner remarginalizes Lee by subsuming her formidable literary qualities, her wit, and her imagination under the problematic notion of "lesbian neurosis."[26] He insists that Lee's deprivation of maternal love led to her (de-)formation as a lesbian. Although Gardner's book does shed some light on the family's psychological difficulties, his reading of Lee's texts as immediate expressions of her "great psychic handicap"(38) is unacceptable today.

Studies of Vernon Lee from the 1960s and '70s ignore or play down her preference for women. Peter Gunn's thorough biography of Vernon Lee (1964) pays much attention to her literary talent but, in opposition to Gardner's sensationalism, prudishly neglects her sexual inclination. Gunn foregrounds the worship of Vernon Lee as a child prodigy, which to him furnishes the main cause for her arrogance and egocentrism. However, he fails to relate her conduct to the historical climate of the nineteenth century, which was not very encouraging for intellectual women. Vineta Colby's chapter in *The Singular Anomaly* (1970), "The Puritan Aesthete: Vernon Lee," discusses Lee in the context of four other "minor" female novelists: Olive Schreiner, Mrs. Humphry Ward, Eliza Linton, and John Oliver Hobbes. Colby draws on biographical material, and investigates briefly Lee's friendships with women, such as Mary Robinson, Ethel Smyth, and Kit Anstruther-Thomson. Although Colby is more skeptical of comments by Lee's contemporaries than is either Gardner or Gunn, she still adjudges Lee as secondary to the great masters, notably Henry James, and "of ebullient talent rather than of creative genius" (258–69).[27]

In 1983 there appeared two comprehensive bibliographies of Lee's work by Phyllis F. Manocchi and Carl Markgraf, which, so far, give the most complete overview of Lee's books and their reviews. The interest they spurred in Lee was limited to a series of short articles, mostly in the *Colby Quarterly*. Gunnar Schmidt's strangely belated New Critical study of 1984, *Die Literarisierung des Unbewußten: Studien zu den phantastischen Erzählungen von Oliver Onions und Vernon Lee,* completely ignores her biography and history. His perfunctory and unreflected application of Freudian terms (neurosis and hysteria) gives an interesting example of new critical literary approaches but provides little new insight into the study of Vernon Lee. Unlike Schmidt, Peter Christensen in his 1989 essay, "The Burden of History in Vernon Lee's Ghost Story 'Amour Dure,'" integrates psychology and historical context, but equates gender and oppression too readily.

More recent studies, under the impact of cultural criticism, have both emphasized Vernon Lee's innovative creative potential and correlated her literary and sexual ambivalence for a different approach to the story of aestheticism. Before feminist-lesbian critique paid greater attention to Lee, two interesting studies centered Lee's critical female voice in a philosophically, politically, and culturally more complex aestheticism than previous literary history had allowed for: Ruth Robbins's cultural feminist approach, "Vernon Lee: Decadent Woman" (1992); and Carlo Caballero's erudite and psychologically intriguing study, "'A Wicked Voice': On Vernon Lee, Wagner and the Effects of Music" (1992). It seems odd, however, that Caballero would still speak of Lee's "emotional handicap." This has changed. In the course of "gaying" late-nineteenth-century studies, as Richard Dellamora puts it (*Victorian Sexual Dissidence,* 1), desire between women has become a more affirmative trope that is seen as shared by male and female writing traditions. Martha Vicinus's "The Adolescent Boy: Fin de Siècle Femme Fatale?" (1994)[28] and Kathy Psomiades' "'Still Burning from This Strangling Embrace': Vernon Lee on Desire and Aesthetics" focus on Lee's "queer" interaction with fin-de-siècle cultural politics. Moving away from the concept of a self-contained female literary tradition, both studies show how (in different texts) Lee's use of decadent iconology evokes and draws attention to something we now describe as lesbian desire. These and other more recent studies have placed Lee in the newly validated context of female aesthetes and New Women novelists, instead of keeping her in the minor league, second to Ruskin, James, Pater, and other "great men." Two recent books, *The Forgotten Female Aesthetes* by Talia Schaffer (2000) and *Women and British Aestheticism,* edited by Schaffer and Kathy A. Psomiades (1999) have shown how a significant group of women aesthetes challenged and expanded the familiar story of aestheticism, formerly conceived exclusively as a masculine tradition. Schaffer and Psomiades can be credited for designing new criteria that give the female aesthetes their own share of innovative, experimental techniques, usually associated with modernism. Their critique of literary history shows how female aesthetes have "fallen through the cracks," first, of male-centered aestheticism and modernism and then of feminist studies of the New Woman. As Schaffer points out rightly in *The Forgotten Female Aesthetes,* "In hunting for feminists, non-feminist genres get erased so completely that readers may not even know they are missing" (11). Schaffer's and Psomiades's analysis of the relationship between female aesthetes and New Women may also help explain why writers like Vernon Lee have been omitted by such groundbreaking works as Ann Ardis's *New Women, New Novels.* The fact that Ardis did not come across Lee's name in her encyclopedic research should be an indication of just how little Lee participated in the contemporary "Woman Question," while being an exemplary New Woman herself.

Although Lee is still not a widely known author today, her inclusion in the scholarship of the New Woman and female aesthetes has begun to alter our understanding of the fin de siècle and the roles of male and female writers. Unlike earlier studies, these recent discussions have significantly placed Lee in a greater cultural context, if not into a more central position of literary history. However, as this study will show, we need to connect Lee with even broader literary networks beyond New Womanism and Aestheticism. The concept of the public intellectual, for instance, investigated in chapter 2, will be more suitable to encompass her multiple roles as critic and writer.

## READING LEE TODAY

Reading Vernon Lee today reveals as much about her critics as it does about herself. In the modern marketplace, commentaries on individual authors become verifications for literary history and cultural trends—past and present. While individual figures cannot become the sole endorsement for larger narratives or structures, their individual lives, with all their contradictions and inconsistencies, afford the corrective for easy and exclusionary generalization. Since the "framing" of a writer is an integral part of his or her work, special attention has to be paid to the way we associate writers with certain movements or traditions. While Lee's interest in aesthetics and art places her somewhere between John Ruskin, Walter Pater, and Henry James, the range of her subjects extended to social and political issues including woman's rights, economic justice, theories of evolution, vivisection, international relations, war, and peace. None other than George Bernard Shaw elevated her to the ranks of "the old guard of Victorian cosmopolitan intellectualism,"[29] in other words, an emblem of the kind of British liberalism he believed to have vanished with World War I.

To reevaluate Vernon Lee's texts beyond short-range or special interests, we also need to investigate how she was commandeered by literary history. In the decades around the turn of the century, Vernon Lee emerged as one of the most respected and prolific female intellectuals. Her oeuvre comprises well over forty books, some of which reached fourth and fifth editions. But hers was not a household name, and often she was mentioned only as a backdrop to more famous writers.[30] Lee's absence from the literary canon today is in part the result of fading interest in Victorian texts throughout the twentieth century. She also fell victim to the complex relationship between aesthetic traditions and social and political powers. Arguably, her distance from the British market proved a disadvantage at a time when it was considered requisite for writers to maintain close contact with their publishers. Her failure to secure "monumentality" through collected works or autobiographies (like Arnold or Ruskin), her inexperience with the book market, and not least, her "un-British" stance and lack of diplomacy did not help accelerate her literary career.

The traits that make her interesting for us today—her contradictions, her national transcendence, and her interdisciplinarity—were held against her in literary history. Thus, we must subject her works to questions and inquiries that simultaneously challenge the claims we make about our own traditions. With the advent of cultural studies, modern scholars of the nineteenth century increasingly attend to the discursive interplay between different texts, sexualities, and disciplines to expose the artificiality of boundaries like those between fiction and nonfiction. In this revisionary context, critical studies have already reevaluated a large body of prose texts, many of them by "minor" writers:

> Alongside the monumental figures of the period—Coleridge, Newman, Arnold, Ruskin—appear an array of more modest but nonetheless important writers—women, working-class authors, and writers who have simply been cast into the shadows by the conventional literary historical practice of highlighting a "great tradition." . . . Such research has tended to contest the very concept of canonicity, and has led to the critical rehabilitation of a great body of non-fiction prose that previously only had the status of background material. (Fraser andBrown, viii)

Since Vernon Lee's literary standing has been adversely affected by the same canonical mechanisms that have kept so many women writers out of our view, reading her works within a feminist frame seems an obvious choice. But since feminist criticism has its own historical limitations, we need be cautious not to pigeonhole Lee in facile terms of female oppression or too narrowly defined women's issues. To be studying in today's climate a late-nineteenth-century writer who was cognoscent of but strove to look beyond gender polarities requires a careful examination of the historical dimension. When asking how Lee changes the familiar story of aestheticism and decadence from a woman's point of view, we need to attend to the changing roles of art and criticism as well as to the question of intellectual authority in a cultural atmosphere that bristled with loaded polemics. It was a time when public discourses were being reshaped by an ongoing process of institutional restructuring that also reflected the way social and intellectual authority interlocked with the aspects of sex and gender. Women were clearly at a disadvantage as intellectual authority became increasingly defined by academic institutions run by men.

Even without any institutional or organizational affiliation, Vernon Lee was a prominent figure in late-nineteenth-century intellectual circles. She was an audible and reasonable public voice, especially as a pacifist against the rampant and bellicose patriotism around the time of World War I.[31] Lee was aware of the prevailing prejudice against women's ability to think creatively *and* rationally. She did not employ political agitation, however, to combat discriminatory practices against her sex. Before her article "The Economic Parasitism of Women" (1902), Lee had kept a low profile on the Woman Question because she was skeptical of (but scarcely unsympathetic toward) the suffragists' agenda. She chose not to adopt an explicitly gendered viewpoint, but continued to speak as an intellectual whose gender was a matter of coincidence, not determination.

For this study, feminist, lesbian, and queer theories have been consulted selectively and with a critical awareness of their historical conditioning. Although Lee avoided any references to her sex as a writer, her decadent stories are inundated with sexual implications that often mock traditional heterosexual assumptions. These images can serve as important clues to her use of sexuality as manifestation of alternative identity on the borderlines of symbolic conventions. Lesbian theories have proven particularly helpful in discussing the correlation between sexuality and alternative female identity, which becomes an issue in Lee's shift from a male-identified subjectivity in her first book of dialogues, *Baldwin* (1886), to a male-surpassing subjectivity in *Althea* (1894). The question remains: How could Lee establish an alternative female subject position in an aesthetic discourse that structured difference in binary terms and privileged masculinity?

Arguably, in Lee's time, male subjectivities were construed as universal or integrated selves whose opposite was not the female subject but rather a simulacrum, that is, an imperfect double of masculinity. Since language constitutes consciousness, female consciousness of self could be likened to (in Eileen Schlee's terms) "hand-me-down clothes." As for "the new fashions of language, . . . we can only borrow [them] anyway" (71–80). Incidentally, Vernon Lee, too, uses the trope of second-hand clothes in *Euphorion* to explicate the passing on of cultural texts from leading groups to subclasses. She saw herself as "wearing" but constantly altering the texts of different contemporary models, for instance, in *The Handling of Words.*

> I can recognize long preliminary stages of being not oneself; or being not merely trying to be, an adulterated Ruskin, Pater, Michelet, Henry James, or a highly watered-down mixture of these and others, with only a late, rather sudden, curdling and emergence of something one recognizes . . . as oneself. Whether that oneself is better or worse is neither here nor there. What I am driving at is only the fact that writers learn most from what they read, because the mind is not a Pallas Athena bursting full grown and in full dress from even the most Olympian brain, but takes its substance and shape mainly from what it feeds on. (296)

Lee's indebtedness to her literary "fathers" suggests an intertextual approach to the way she employs the language of her peers while creating new conceptual space for herself. For instance, she challenges ideological premises by introduc-

ing an alternative context for a familiar trope. Her female characters who superficially resemble the decadents' femmes fatales are either "women not made
for men" (*Miss Brown*) or women leading a rich and productive life outside the
narrow definitions of their gender ("Prince Alberic and the Snake Lady"). Lee
recreates "unwomanly" figures as parody and irony, trying to expose masculine
egocentrism and sexual obsession under an aesthetic veneer ("Amour Dure,"
"Dionea," *Miss Brown*).

With the help of parody, Lee expressed her difference within a language
based on gendered opposition. As contemporary comments on the New Woman
reveal, any viewpoint outside the hetero-patriarchal decorum was culturally unintelligible and often labeled as "unwomanly" or "deviant." The question of cultural recognition is crucial here. Lee's overly invested male image in the public
realm and her personal preference for women often spun off conflicting images
in her fiction. But messages that could not be attributed to the accepted forms of
identity became unintelligible or invisible in mainstream culture.

Various critical schools have investigated the cultural invisibility of lesbian
or homosexual writers and subject positions. Any critical accounts of Vernon
Lee's lesbian orientation call for cautious attention. As pointed out, Burdett
Gardner's monumental study of Vernon Lee's lesbian "handicap" reveals the
historical limitations of any approach based on too narrow definitions of sexual
identity. While we may consider Lee's sexual orientation as a constituting factor
of her cultural perception, we need to be aware of the limitations of "lesbian" as
an analytical category that induced critics to marginalize her achievements. Instead of predicating Vernon Lee's life on a singular category, we need to see her
lesbianism "not [as] necessarily dependent on modern conceptions of homosexuality as a particular sexual identity" (Stevens, 123), but as one of the many contin-
gencies that shape her "difference" as a writer and critic. Even if Lee's alternative
subjectivity derives its potency from her same-sex orientation, it is embedded in
the language of fin-de-siècle aesthetic culture, which revelled in multifaceted or
blurred sexual identities. Predicating Lee foremost as a lesbian would too easily
displace the interesting contradictions in this writer. Therefore, when I use the
term "lesbian" here, it is to be understood more broadly as an abstraction for the
set of differences in her persona. In fact, accepting the "queering" of the theories
of sexuality and desire in the 1990s, I try to unsettle distinctions between femininity and masculinity when they appear too restrictive. The advantage of a queer
reading in the sense used, for instance, by critics of Henry James is that one can

read the demonstrable eroticism in Lee's text as libidinal relationships without having to reduce them as dichotomies of sexual identities. Gert Buelens's recent study of queer desire in Henry James's *The American Scene* reveals a striking relevance for Lee's use of erotic attachment. By showing how physical desire between identities can be "rechanneled" into an identification with the scene or place of desire, Buelens demonstrates how a queer reading (of Henry James) can work even outside any necessary relationship between two individuals. Given Lee's erotic endowments of places and scenes, Buelens's concept of the "spatiality of desire" (301) is particularly helpful. As this study shows, Lee often connects sexual desire with places to create transcending subject positions beyond the boundaries of sex and gender.

# 2 History and the Female Voice

Contemporary historiography was troublesome for Vernon Lee. To her, the past was often treated as "a thing so utterly dead as to be fit only for the scalpel and the microscope" (*Euphorion,* 1:12). The "European Barbarians," it seemed, who had ransacked Renaissance Italy in the sixteenth century, were about to pillage it again. This time the threat came from "this very modern scientific vandalism" of historical pedants like Herman Grimm or Mommsen, who dissected and filed history under abstract encyclopedic categories. Or worse, it came from the "laborious bookworms"[1] who assembled from history nothing more than antiquarian detail. Likewise, she was skeptical of historians who narrowed down past civilizations to the "germs" they contained for the present—either as "puritan contemners" or "decadent defilers." In general, Lee was skeptical of any historiography that catalogued public events from a universal or seemingly objective perspective but ignored lived experiences. She praised the "marvels of historic mapping," but reminded the reader that systematic historiography, "the whole topography, geological and botanical of an historic tract" could never represent the past completely and that "there are yet other kinds of work which may be done" (*Euphorion,* 1:9). Lee found these "other kinds of work" in what has now been designated as "Kulturgeschichte" (cultural history). An early example is her first book, *Studies of the Eighteenth Century in Italy* (1878), a collection of essays on literature and music treated in the context of Italian society of that century. Today we may say that Lee followed a course similar to Jacob Burckhardt—recently acknowledged as the founder of "Kulturgeschichte"—who had substituted for the history of political events the history of culture and civilization.[2]

Burckhardt abandoned high politics and chronological narrative in favor of a topical methodology that focused on the relationship between individual artifacts and larger political structures. Similarly, Lee organized her approach to history thematically and individually. In her first book-length study of the Italian Renaissance, *Euphorion* (1884), she thematizes her personal confrontation with the past, finding it no easy matter since our impressions of the past are "quite interwoven with our impressions of the present." To her, a subjective approach has more reality than a scientific, objective search for "truth," because it better reveals the relationship between past and present for the individual and does not attempt to make historical evidence fit the grid of "cunning abstractions." Lee illustrates her point by comparing historical narrative to a viewer's varying impressions of a landscape: "like a real landscape it [history] may also be seen from different points of view, and under different lights" (*Euphorion,* 1:10). Historiography can reveal only partial or relative truths and, like any other discipline, it is subject to change over time. Lee foresees that future historians would reveal what contemporary methods could not yet survey. So she warns historians not to "throw away noble ore for lack of skill to separate it from a base alloy" (*Renaissance Fancies,* 251). In other words, she pleads for a less exclusive selection of historical material and for a reconsideration of what constitutes historical relevance.

Lee's request for new perspectives is not singular but reflects the trend in contemporary historiography to search for "alter-narratives" (Smith, 716). As early as 1832, Thomas Carlyle had predicted a time "when History will be attempted on quite other principles; when the Court, the Senate, and the Battlefield, receding more and more into the background, the Temple, the Workshop, and the Social Hearth will advance more and more into the foreground" (Carlyle, 183). Later in the century, Carlyle's prediction was transformed into historical method by social history's portrayal of the quotidian and the conditions of the classes not usually noticed by those whose names live in historical remembrance. As the century was coming to a close, cultural pessimism and a growing awareness of social injustice prompted anthropologically minded historians to search for an alternative past. For many, that other past could be found in the hitherto uncharted history of women and other marginalized subjects—not necessarily with a feminist purpose, but distinct from mainstream historical scholarship that focused on "great men."

Female historians, in particular, delved into areas that had not received much attention from general historical scholarship. Taking advantage of new trends in the organization of historical knowledge—such as the turn to social history—they could assert their presence, as Rohan Maitzen has shown,[3] even though they first offered their work hesitantly and merely as supplements to historical master narratives. Margaret Oliphant's biographical history of Italian craftsmen; Vernon Lee's unearthing of little-explored eighteenth-century Italian music and literature; and Mrs. Humphry Ward's expertise in the equally neglected field of early Spanish history are examples of women's supplementary work that helped broaden the field.

Women's typical disavowal of poaching on male territory has often misled critics to adjudge their work as secondary or amateurish before giving credit to their fresh views. More recent scholars have recognized that women writers' emphasis of social and cultural aspects prefigures the evolution of "Kultur- und Sozialgeschichte" as different from political history. Margaret Oliphant's *Makers of Florence* (1881) is an example of women's alternative research seeking to prove that beyond the political battles, there coexisted "in strange serenity, another life in the very heart" of the prescribed historiographic mainstream, the life of "the chippings of the mason's chisel, and the finer tools of the wood-carver, and the noiseless craft of brush and pigment" (iv).

Today we know that women historians' devising of "alter histories" is at the beginning of the twentieth-century trend toward adopting more diversified perspectives from which the past might be told.[4] But in what way could historians like Vernon Lee or Margaret Oliphant help broaden the basis of historical scholarship? Rohan Maitzen suggests the possibilities:

> Participants in the ongoing discussion aligned themselves with or attempted to establish definitive distinctions between possible configurations of gender, genre, and history. . . . The result was not coherence and hegemony but incoherence, discord, even some confusion—and a tremendous expansion of possibility as the definition and the face of history changed and changed again to fit different conceptions of what a story of the past should look like, aesthetically, formally, and substantially. (*Gender, Genre,* 26)

At least theoretically, there was a desire for greater inclusiveness and diversity of historical texts in the late nineteenth century. Confronted with an explosion of knowledge, historians anxiously asked what should be included and how it should be ranked. On the one hand, they sought more energetically for generalizing perspectives and avoided texts cluttered with too much detail. On the other, they came to understand detail and the particular, as Carol Christ has shown, in a new way. Detail was not always discounted as trivial and unfocused, but came to represent the individual and, thus, an assertion of difference. The new challenge was to find the right balance between trivial or insignificant detail and important historical facts. By elevating into history everyday detail and the "common man," social historians, such as Macaulay, redefined the notions of historical agency: if all classes were participating in history, it became increasingly harder to justify history as the arena for "great men." To be sure, the advocates for expanding the field seldom mention women explicitly; but the turn to domestic detail helped put women's lives into a more central viewpoint (Maitzen, *Gender, Genre,* 23).

The quest for "feminization," as Mary Beard would call it, resonated in an intellectual environment that combined its opposition to a universalizing, hegemonic world view with a critique of patriarchal capitalist society. Social philosophers like Edward Carpenter in England or Georg Simmel in Germany reacted against a cultural narrative shaped by Hegelian concepts of unification and objectification. Interestingly, the assumed connection between objectification and the male character—often ranked as superior in contemporary criticism—is here turned against itself. Simmel's critique of capitalist patriarchal culture, for instance, is based on the assumption that it reduces the plurality of forms in human experience to a single model of explanation. Typical of the time, such anti-reductionist philosophy was conceived in notions of gender that declared the female to be something distinctly different and inexpressible in the terms of a (normative) male culture.

> The[se] expressions of the male nature claim normative significance on the ground that they exhibit the objective truth and rectitude that are equally valid for everyone, male or female. The fact that the masculine is absolutized in this way as the objective simpliciter and the impartial standard of authority applies not only to the empirically given actuality of the masculine. On the contrary, it also has the result that the ideas . . . that develop both from

and for the masculine acquire the status of trans-sexual absolutes. This has
fateful consequences for the valuation of women. (104)

Almost certainly, such consideration of the female was meant as a conceptual
rather than a practical encouragement. However, by advocating their cultural
critique in gendered terms, thinkers like Simmel indirectly paved the way for
an expansion of historical views and subjects.

## Nineteenth-Century Renaissance Studies and Changes in Historical Scholarship

For the Victorians, historiography became an important discipline for reading
and critiquing their perplexing present. The (Italian) Renaissance, then first
emerging as a distinct historical epoch, was the period they deemed most akin to
their own. Victorians mirrored themselves passionately in the Renaissance, but
not always for the same reasons: while some celebrated its strong and independent individualism, others deplored its moral decline. Renaissance studies became more and more contentious in proportion to the Victorians' growing
identification with this period: the Renaissance "was affected by factors which
had more to do with current intellectual interests than the facts of history, and it
engaged many writers who were not historians in any conventional sense of the
word" (Bullen, 2).

During the first half of the nineteenth century, the Italian Renaissance was
considered a high point in the development of Western art, and pilgrimages to
Florence and Rome had been a "must" for the educated tourist. Ruskin's *Lectures
on Architecture and Painting* in 1854 modified this view. He saw the medieval
gothic as a more genuinely English form in contrast to the depraved Italian culture of the Renaissance. His negative definition of the Renaissance emphasized
its malevolent, decadent force against the moral superiority of the Catholic Middle
Ages. To Renaissance zealots as diverse as Swinburne, Symonds, and Pater, the
period's art and culture supplied timely models of emotional and intellectual liberty. To retrieve the "modern" spirit of the Renaissance, Pater and Symonds were
drawn to "forms of sentiment which at first sight seem incompatible" (Pater, *The
Renaissance,* 37). Pater saw in the Renaissance a collision between an emerging
sense of difference (a condition for the modern self) and the less differentiated

religious identity of the Middle Ages. He discovered in Renaissance art an anal-
ogy to his own aspirations of constructing historical subjectivity through aesthetic immediacy. The Renaissance was also Vernon Lee's preferred historical
period chiefly because of its wealth of aesthetic expressions that sent mixed messages to high Victorian morality. Lee felt acutely this pull in opposite directions.
Like her contemporaries, she felt drawn to the era as a time of transition in which
a richness of cultural styles provided multiple forms of identification for modern
intellectuals.

Political historians, beginning with Michelet and his *Histoire de France*
(1855), viewed the Renaissance predominantly as a period of spiritual and intellectual rebirth. Vernon Lee half mocks this obsession in her fantastic story,
"Amour Dure," in which an accomplished but dangerously attractive Renaissance woman returns from the past, a feat that requires the murder of a modern
(male) historian. True to the genre of the ghost story, her actual rebirth is never
resolved. Lee was less enigmatic in her historical essays. In *Euphorion,* written
under the influence of Michelet's impassioned rhetoric and Symonds's dramatic
personifications, she presents an emotional defense of the Italian Renaissance,
which was "cut off pitilessly at its prime; denied even an hour to repent and
amend; hurried off before the tribunal of posterity" (*Euphorion,* 1:54).[5]

Eager to disprove what Ruskin called the infamous depravities of the Renaissance, Lee refused even to consider moral or religious judgments on art. She
was not unmindful of its political intrigue and unhampered individualism, but
her immense attraction to the period's aesthetic forms prompted her to devise a
different explanatory model. To her mind, nineteenth-century historiography
was not fit to account for the "apparent anomaly" of the Renaissance, by which
she meant the incongruity between the period's advanced culture on the one
hand and its moral corruption on the other: "the picture of a people moving on
towards civilization and towards chaos" (29). To accommodate this contradiction, she resorts to Ranke's historicism (otherwise an unlikely ally), which requires that each period be judged on its own terms, often incomprehensible to
later generations. Lee resolutely denies the contemporary adage of a kinship between the Renaissance and the Victorian age, proclaiming that "the moral atmosphere of those days is as impossible for us to breathe as would be the physical
atmosphere of the moon: could we, for a moment, penetrate into it, we should die
of asphyxia" (22).

The Renaissance conveyed to her the sense of something essentially new, a time of transition in which the people had "cast away all faith in traditional institutions; they had destroyed and could not yet rebuild" (47). Because of her empathy for the Renaissance, she found unacceptable the cultural pessimism that some contemporaries projected onto it. She criticized Ruskin as among those "who tell us that in its union with antique art, the art of the followers of Giotto embraced death, and rotted away ever after." But she did not readily join forces with those, such as Swinburne, who praised what Ruskin condemned: "There are others, more moderate but less logical, who would teach us that in uniting with the antique, the medieval art of the fifteenth century purified and sanctified the beautiful but evil child of Paganism" (213–14). After proclaiming that "both schools of criticism are wrong," Lee offers her own reading of the Renaissance, which melds aesthetic disinterestedness with an odd mix of accident and evolution. She defines historical change as a process of "natural" forces rather than the product of moral (or immoral) interference. Therefore, history resists our attempts to find in it meaningful messages for our own lives and has to remain ultimately unknowable to modern interpreters. Consequently, if history does not *mean* anything, we must not seek in it any value judgments, but instead must try to read it aesthetically, as a series of changing impressions.

How then has Lee's approach helped shape the image of the Renaissance? To determine the full extent of her historical method requires considering it not merely as an intellectual concept but as a discursive field that interacts with political and social forces, including the position of the female critic. A study of Lee's contribution to modern historiography cannot be separated from the question of her intellectual authority, which in the cultural context of her time was inextricably linked with gender. In other words, we need to ask how the nineteenth-century female historian could use the conceptual and rhetorical practices of the discipline to validate her different views.

Lee's historical argument ties in with innovative trends in historical scholarship from the second half of the nineteenth century: first, the breaking up of historical universality into individual and relative standpoints; second, the preference of descriptive (aesthetic) over normative approaches; and third, the attempt at diversifying the concept of historical subjectivity. Lee first developed a conceptual framework for an individual approach in *Euphorion,* which was honored by the *Spectator* for its "fresh and original" contribution to historical scholarship (12 July 1884, 216–18). Although *Euphorion* was not given the same credit as Pater's and Symonds's influential studies, it was widely read and admired.

In *Euphorion,* Lee argues against Ruskin's endeavor (as in *The Stones of Venice*) to correlate art history with the moral evolution of a culture, but her undertone reveals her reluctance to forsake moral aspects altogether. One reason for this might have been her suspicion that other contemporaries' ill-assimilated worship of Renaissance personality evoked coarser passions under the supposedly liberal and humanistic surface. We sense a certain indignation in her voice when she blames the Elizabethan dramatists, especially Webster and Ford, for having created a perverted picture of the Renaissance that still affects nineteenth-century historiography. Behind their mask of horror, she discovers hidden lust and morbid voyeurism of "gigantic villains" and atrocious evils. What nineteenth-century historiographers see as the Italian Renaissance, she argues, is for the most part its representation in sixteenth-century English drama. Lee assumes here what Roland Barthes calls the reduction of the real to "the effect of the real," implying that history is already structured according to ideological, cultural, and literary conventions of the language in which it is written. What historians provide as evidence, Lee claims, promotes only a particular version of their own period. "Is not what we think of the Past," she asks later, in *Hortus Vitae* (1904), "a mere creation of our own?" (196). The historian, she assumes, creates "a mere fiction," which serves as an explanation of the past. Modern critics of historical methods from Roland Barthes to Hayden White and J. B. Bullen would agree: even though historical scholarship can make certain truth claims about events, it is limited by its own historicity since explanations depend on the rhetorical and literary devices of the time. Bullen has further explained (in *The Myth of the Renaissance*) that historical consciousness had myth-like qualities in the nineteenth century because of the close interaction of fictional and nonfictional texts:

> Many of the texts which communicated powerful if partial views of the Renaissance were themselves confessedly fictions—Browning's Renaissance monologues and George Eliot's historical novel *Romola* for example—but even a work like Walter Pater's *Studies in the History of the Renaissance,* which appears at first sight empiricist and positivist, is only nominally so. (3)

Lee repeatedly draws attention to the relationship between past events and the myths created in their written record. In her *Euphorion* essay "The Italy of the Elizabethan Dramatists," she argues that the Elizabethans have created the prevailing negative image of Renaissance Italy. To her, Renaissance men and women were motivated solely by success, a value which was not recognized by the moral strictures of the English mind. As the English dramatists could express their reaction to Machiavellian practice only in their own moral terms, they designed a Renaissance picture that was not "true."

> Success was the criterion of all action and power was its limits. Active and furious national wickedness there was not: there was mere moral inertia on the part of the people. The Italians of the Renaissance neither resisted evil nor rebelled against virtue; they were indifferent to both, and a little pressure sufficed to determine them to either. (*Euphorion* 1:88–89)

In other words, what Lee considers the "real" Renaissance is at several removes from its image in Elizabethan drama and, likewise, from nineteenth-century historiography.

To impart her acute sense of historical difference between time periods, Lee assumes an extreme standpoint which has to be understood as a rhetorical position rather than a claim for truth: "The blindness to evil which constitutes the criminality of the Renaissance is so great as to give a certain air of innocence." It takes a rhetorician like Vernon Lee all of fifty pages to transform ruthlessness and corruption into its opposite. We may not agree with the extreme stretches of her theory. But her rhetorical intent was clearly misrepresented by a polemical Wyndham Lewis, almost fifty years later, when he attacks her in "A Lady's Response to Machiavelli" (*The Lion and the Fox*):

> We are provided in the work of a lady (the *Euphorion* of Vernon Lee) with the best indication, perhaps, of the attitude of the anglo-italian resident of the more correct type to the lingering renaissance they have settled amongst. To read her pages is like watching a person of some intelligence administering electric shocks to herself. (111)

The abusive tone of Lewis's diatribe against Lee's nonchalant attitude toward Renaissance evils has to be read in the context of his general condemnation of fin-de-siècle aestheticism as "incurably gothic, diabolic and medieval" (110). Without condoning his unfair personal criticism, we have to admit that Lee's charge against the Elizabethan Dramatists does at times sound overblown:

> The Italy of the Renaissance was, of all things that have ever existed or ever
> could exist the most utterly unlike the nightmare visions of men such as Web-
> ster and Ford, Marston and Tourneur. . . . These frightful Brachianos and
> Annabellas and Ferdinands and Corombonas and Vindicis and Pieros of the
> "White Devil," or of the "Duchess of Malfy," of the "Revenger's Tragedy,"
> and of "Antonio and Mellinda," are mere fantastic horrors, as false as the
> Counts of Udolpho, the Spalatros, the Zastrozzis, and all their grotesquely
> ghastly pseudo-Italian brethren of eighty years ago. (*Euphorion,* 1:80–81)

Lee does not resolve the discrepancy between the sinister reputation of the Italian Renaissance and the "serene beauty" of its art, but explains it as the result
of modern historical consciousness, that is, as the result of viewing the past
from a cultural perspective different than that of the people who lived in it. Instead of aiming at a unified historical picture, she explores the nature of the
historians' relationship to their subject and their methods to define it, in other
words, their awareness of the cultural gap between past events and their historiographic accounts for it.

> And thus the Italians of the Renaissance walked placidly through the evil
> which surrounded them; for them, artists and poets, the sky was always blue
> and the sun always bright, and their art and poetry was serene. But the Eng-
> lishmen of the sixteenth century were astonished and fascinated by the evil
> of Italy: the dark pools of horror, the dabs of infamy which had met them
> ever and anon in the brilliant southern cities, haunted them like nightmare,
> bespattered for them the clear blue sky, and danced, black and horrible spots,
> before the face of the sun. (107)

Lee's colorful representation of two fundamentally different mindsets is a serious attempt to confront the limitations of historical writing, namely, its inability to express the whole "truth" of an epoch. Opposing the Victorian view
of history as a regime of truth, she construed history as the genealogy of its own
interpretations. Likewise, she dismissed the worship of "facts," not only because of the historians' limited views, but because what they see has already
been predetermined by previous readings. In *Euphorion* and *Renaissance Fancies and Studies,* Lee demonstrates that the Italian Renaissance was constructed
severally: first by Elizabethan dramatists, next by "the grim and ghastly ro-

mances of the school of Ann Radcliffe" (*Euphorion,* 1:79), and last by her contemporaries who looked to the Renaissance as an epoch congenial to the
nineteenth century. By pointing to the constant remaking of the past, Lee
draws attention to the relativity inherent in historical judgment and thus refutes the scholarly axioms of objectivity and truth.

Few critics have given Vernon Lee her due as an earnest historiographer;
one who has, Hilary Fraser, recognizes her "serious attempt to confront questions relating to cultural and historical relativism which many of her contemporaries chose to ignore" (229). According to Fraser, Lee eschews the questionable
alternatives of "doctrinaire objectivism versus doctrinaire subjectivism," but is
interested in finding a new narrative form for the ongoing dialogue between historian and the past, scholar and subject (7).

Historical scholarship at the fin de siècle was a contested field that became
increasingly the province of a highly specialized group of professionals determining who had the authority to speak on historical matters. The study of the
past was turned into a scientific discipline supervised by the universities, which
organized the field in terms of Symonds's universal and systematic survey,
emancipating it from Carlylean literariness (Bann, 102–4). Historical methodology relied on fact and objectification as the guarantors of truth, dismissing alternative forms of cultural accountability. What counted as history was determined
by those who constituted the field: educated middle-class men who controlled
the present and possessed the past. A universal perspective produced an abstraction of "man" that excluded the unhistorical and the particular, most conspicuously: women. Their invisibility as historical subjects was rivaled only by the
poor, the savages, and all "primitive" people who were equally displaced by a history written "from above" (Crosby, 151). As the contemporary controversies, for
instance, over Jacob Burckhardt's "Kulturgeschichte" reveal, mainstream scholarship was reluctant to accept alternative historical accounts.

Burckhardt's method "earned" him the epithet of a clever dilettante, a description which fits Vernon Lee—and actually any nineteenth-century female
historian—just as readily. But whereas Burckhardt countered grand historical
schemes with a concept of the free, autonomous individual anticipating the
Nietzschean superman, Lee's historical subjects spring from a less ambitious
plan: a living community of rather ordinary people, brought in contact by accident and evolution (*Belcaro*). History to her is not the result of cause and effect, but of individual "coincidences," which are shaped only retrospectively

through the application of abstract models (*Renaissance Fancies,* 252). Adapting Darwinian theories of evolution, she sees individual and general historical development in a paradigmatic relationship. Therefore, she feels justified to derive historical insight even from her own individual history, which she describes as an "accident of education" and an "accident of family circumstances" (*Baldwin,* 5). But the accidental and the particular did not meet mainstream standards, which favored more systematic categories. Consequently, traditional scholars saw Vernon Lee as an "exotist," unable to create a lasting, universal Renaissance picture as the "Urgrund" of the modern European spirit. The Swiss historian, Max Bräm, for instance, finds that unlike Pater or Symonds, she can elucidate singular aspects of the Renaissance but is incapable of reading into it an overarching cultural ideal (97–98).

Ruskin's *Lectures* (1854), Pater's *Studies in the History of the Renaissance* (1873), and Symonds's *Renaissance in Italy* (1875) were key texts in Lee's historical training. Although her communal focus and her evolutionary models were clearly derived from Ruskin, she went out on a limb to show that his value judgment could not accommodate the difference of Renaissance aesthetics. Lee admired the way Symonds drew individuality closer into Renaissance culture and politics, but the language of his more systematic historiography suggested historical positions with which she could not identify. To keep "the spontaneity and wholeness of personal impression," as she puts it, she even denied herself "the pleasure and profit" of reading Symonds's important volumes on Italian literature: she feared finding herself "doubtless forestalled by him in various appreciations" (*Euphorion,* 2:238). Her decision to forego this pleasure was promptly criticized in the *Saturday Review* (1884): "She should have read Symonds, whom she says she has avoided, for his *Italian Byways* and *Italian Literature* have preceded her and might have aided her" (318). Lee's circumvention of Symonds had other reasons. His letters to her vacillate between envy of the "freedom of [your] method" (20 June 1884) and anger at her audacity of assuming to know as much as a revered authority.[6] The contentious correspondence between Lee and Symonds reveals not only high personal tension but also strong disagreement in their views of history and art. But Lee—other than ignoring his Renaissance studies—did not take issue with Symonds publicly, as she did with Ruskin. In fact, her quibbles with Ruskinism as late as 1884, after Ruskin had long modified his view of the Renaissance, makes us wonder if her belligerence was not actually directed toward her more immediate contemporary, J. A. Symonds.

Lee's interest in individual experience and random impressions drew her closer to Pater's impressionist approach, which gave the study of individual consciousness and sentiment new historical significance. Like Pater, Lee believed that "the past can give us, and should give us, not merely ideas, but emotions" (*Euphorion*, 1:12), which could never be grasped by "the cynical skepticism of science." The language of emotions, however, demands an expression more individual than that offered by the universal zeitgeist: "No allegory, I well know, and least of all no historical allegory, can ever be strained to fit quite tight—the lives of individuals and those of centuries" (*Euphorion*, 1:7). Aware of the insufficiency of historical discourse as a means to record the intangibles of individual change, Lee turned to Pater for her own dialogue with the past. He had construed the historian as one who "amid the multitude of facts presented to him must needs select, and in selecting assert something that comes not of the world without but a vision within." This "vision within" shapes all of Pater's historical writing. Dismissing the traditional apparatus of historical reference, Pater sees his first duty not in representing history as a sequence of exterior events, but in finding a legible form for his impressions. And therefore, history is to him not a matter of scientific truth but a piece of art made up of layered impressions. As Pater puts it, "Gibbon, . . . Livy, Tacitus, Michelet . . . each, after his own sense, modifies— who can tell where and to what degree? and becomes something else than a transcriber . . . he becomes an artist, his work fine art" (*Appreciations*, 5–6).

By turning history into artistic composition, Pater created a meta-text, that is to say, a text that arises between the artifact or historical object and its verbal representation. The role of art here is twofold: first, to "act as the paradigmatic mode[s] of perception of the subjects of the essays" and, second, to serve as "the expression of Pater's own consciousness" (Bullen, 160). Pater illustrates this aesthetic process best in "Winckelmann," the master text from which he spins off his individual portraits of artists. Pater's use of artworks resembles what Michael Riffaterre in *Textproduction* has called "paragram" in Symbolist poetry. The images in a text form a subcode or paragram which makes it possible for the text to control its own decoding. "What happens," Riffaterre asks, "when a literary tradition is forgotten and cultural changes wash away the paragram?" And in Pater's case, we may ask, what happens if the audience is not familiar with pictures he discusses or no longer shares a stable concept of art? Such epistemological gaps—according to Riffaterre—do not alienate the audience but create different levels of access to the text:

The text is the starting point of the reader's reactions, not its paragrams. Obviously the reader who shares the author's culture will have a richer intertext. But he will be able to draw on that wealth only when semantic anomalies in the text's linearity force him to look to nonlinearity for a solution. And the reader who is denied access to the intertextual paragram still sees the distortion, the imprint left upon the verbal sequence by the absent hypogrammatic referent. (87)

In Pater's text, the readers' degree of familiarity with the artworks and their interpretation determines the degree of immersion in the text. His unconventional selection of impressions amounts to his idea of "strangeness," which stands for the emergence of a new consciousness linking artwork and interpreter. Pater coerces his audiences into recognizing his texts as "sacred representations or interpretation of the whole human experience, modified by the special limitations, the special privileges of insight or suggestion, incident to their peculiar mode of existence" (*Greek Studies,* 100). Pater thus creates a bond between himself and those readers from the same cultural elite who are not only familiar with the symbols but also share his different use of them.

Why this excursion to Pater? In general, Vernon Lee's texts appeal to a similar audience: educated middle-class readers who partake in the intellectual debates about art and literature. But Lee addresses a less esoteric, academic readership than does Pater. Whereas he restricts the circle of his implied readers, she broadens it. His lens is that of the sensitive artistic individual; Lee's resembles that of the communal chronicler who wanders casually through the landscape.

## LEE'S RECONFIGURATION OF PATER

Pater's philosophy gave Lee the justification to explore history individually, through her own impressions of the past gathered when she was growing up among the relics of Italian history. She was convinced that this experience made her superior to the "bookish" historians who were writing at a distance from their subject of inquiry. Lee's identification with a place became a textual strategy, a trope for her perceiving consciousness which, as she tells us in *Baldwin,* "hangs flakewise like the wool of sheep" on her surroundings. To her, the immediate impressions of landscape and architecture convey a more real presence of history than the studies of written texts.

> Impressions are not derived from description, and thoughts are not suggested by books. . . . You find everywhere your facts without opening a book. The explanation which I have tried to give of the exact manner in which medieval art was influenced by the remains of antiquity, came like a flash during a rainy morning in the Pisan Campo Santo; the working out and testing of that explanation in its details was a matter of going from one church or gallery to the other. (*Euphorion,* 1:19)

Lee literally *walks* the readers through her argument, which becomes a matter of showing rather than telling. Through the palpable contact with historical settings, local stories, and legends, she sees herself more directly in touch with the past than the mere theoretical writer whose knowledge is always mediated.[7] Lee sees her personal history as a special opportunity to construct "world" history in certain corners of Italy, conflating present and past, microcosm and macrocosm.

> I can remember all this, and the effort to construct myself a universe out of this tiny spot [a small Italian village]. The same happened with a more mature myself, greater wants and richer surroundings here; the same making out of this place my microcosm of the world. . . . As with nature, so with associations. I had to make up the Past out of this place. (*Baldwin,* 10)

The Italian Renaissance was a place to her (rather than a period) from which she could respond to cultural processes from "within." Through her life in Italy, she saw herself organically linked to the Renaissance, believing herself to be free from theoretical impediments and thus superior to contemporary scholarship.[8] Lee tried to evoke historical "moments" in a place or an area, in which "the smallest trifle carried value." Strolling through historical landscape, she discovers the "trifles" of history, meaning all those aspects that are not usually elevated into its narrative: "There are things about which certain historic epochs are strangely silent" (*Euphorion,* 1:116–17). She finds that "according as you stand, the features of the scene will group themselves—this ridge will disappear behind that, this valley will open out before you, that other will be closed" (10). Looking at a scene in perspective—accidentally one of the artistic achievements of the Renaissance—implies that every standpoint reveals slightly different views, none of which can convey absolute, universal or essential knowledge (10–12). History resembles "an extended landscape" in a picture canvas which we cannot really enter; all we can do is describe our impressions, "from different points of view, and under different lights. . . . [A]ll the rest is the result of cunning abstraction" (10).

Since, to Vernon Lee, history is a series of individual experiences, she questions any claim to reconstruct a historical setting as "wie es eigentlich gewesen ist" in the abstract and universal language of the discipline:[9]

> Yet it is nevertheless certain that the past, to the people who were in it, was not a miraculous map or other marvelous diagram constructed on the principle of getting at the actual qualities of things by analysis; that it must have been, to its inhabitants, but a series of constantly varied perspectives and constantly varied schemes of colour, according to the position of each individual, and the light in which that individual viewed it. (11)

Like Pater, Lee locates the realization of history in the persona of the historian, who becomes the site where the merging of past and present occurs. But she acknowledges that there are blind spots and personal colorations as we

> see only very little at a time, and that little is not what it appeared to the men of the past, if not the same thing, yet in the same manner in which they saw, as we see from the standpoints of personal interest and in the light of personal temper. (12)

What is most concealed from the historian's conscious inquiry are so-called "unconscious analogies" (*Renaissance Fancies,* 251), by which she means historically determined habits of identification and perception which partake in the construction of the historical text.

We may ask to what extent she herself might have been subject to such unconscious identifications. For instance, the strong influence of Pater on *Euphorion* can hardly be overlooked, not only because she dedicated the book to him, but because she uses the same key concepts, such as the privileging of impressions over facts. However, if Lee uses Pater as methodological reference, she still has to rid herself of his exclusive, male-centered design. Because a certain degree of misogyny was built into aesthetic discourses, as Elaine Showalter and other feminist critics have argued, Lee had to maneuver circumspectly. Even though we may agree that Pater's aesthetic approach could devise new discursive possibilities and "conditions in which groups—of women, of homosexuals, of industrial and agricultural workers, of colonial others" (Dellamora, "Critical Impressionism," 136), Paterian language was limited as an expression of female experience since it formed itself around the male subject. Pater meant to challenge established literary traditions in the academy by introducing alternative notions of difference into a cultural system that assumed masculine dominance and precluded woman's agency. His representation of masculine difference through the aesthetic took place within patriarchal structures defined by the subordination of women to men. Although his new conception of masculinity could spin off reconsiderations of other social hierarchies, such as the structure of male-female relations, there is a crucial difference: Since women did not have an equal share in academic discourses in nineteenth-century Britain, Lee's use of Pater's aestheticism could not have the same effect.

Pater's aesthetic language accentuated sensitive and impressionist styles generally associated with the feminine but without granting actual women a voice. If Lee were to have identified with this perspective, she would have run the risk of marginalizing herself. Using Paterian discourse to oppose traditional historical writing meant to her creating a different subject position *and* validating it with intellectual authority. Because of her exclusion from academic and professional institutions as a woman, her publications alone had to establish her expertise in historical scholarship before she would be heard at all. So Lee had to find a language that expressed her experience in other than woman's terms to give credence to her different voice. To put it differently, she had to write from a highly self-conscious position, desiring inclusion among the experts while undermining the terms of their expertise.

A careful study of Lee's voice shows that she did not adopt Pater's style uncritically. His "fairy-land idyls" left in her "a sense of caducity and barrenness" (*Renaissance Fancies,* 253) that could not accommodate her keen sense of social realism, as she demonstrates in her own version of "Aucassin et Nicolette."

> In his beautiful essay upon that story, Mr. Pater has deliberately omitted this
> episode, which is indeed like a spot of blood-stained mud upon some perfect

tissue of silver flowers on silver ground. It is a piece of the cruellest realism, because quite quiet and unforced, in the midst of a kind of fairy-land-idyl of almost childish love, the love of the beautiful son of the lord of Beaucaire for a beautiful Saracen slave girl. (*Euphorion,* 1:133)

Lee's subtle criticism turns into sarcasm in *Renaissance Fancies and Studies.* Her mockery of Pater's aesthetics, which captures only "pleasurable" aspects from the viewpoint of the "leisurely traveller," leaves no doubt that Lee has left behind the early aesthetic, or as she calls it, "hedonist" school. But the reader should be careful not to read too much into her rhetorical pose since she mimics the indignation of Pater's critics with equal sarcasm: "What! become absentees from the poor, much troubled Present; turn your backs to Realities, become idle strollers in the Past." "And why not, dear friends?" she asks in her new sanguine tone, "why not recognize the need for a holiday?" (238).

Lee developed her independent historical voice steadily and subtly. She spoke from her own intuition but was careful to substantiate her views by authorized intellectual voices, such as Michelet's, to avert the contemporary bias against female historians—especially when they ventured into subjects outside the domestic space. But she also acknowledged her "masquerade": "How much I am indebted to the genius of Michelet; nay, rather, how much I am, however unimportant the thing made by him, every one will see and judge" (*Euphorion,* 2:237). Her search for an alternative historical language occurred within a male discourse which she had to wear like a borrowed garment—a pervasive image in her texts—to make herself visible. The "garment" had to come off piece by piece as she felt "its" interference with her evolving historical consciousness. Soon enough, she could adjust her readers' view to the female subject underneath. Between *Euphorion* and *Renaissance Fancies and Studies,* Lee developed a unique and independent historical method that connected the individual with the general, thus expanding the notion of historical subjectivity.

Lee's first historical book, *Studies of the Eighteenth Century in Italy,* reveals most authentically her method of unmediated response to pedantic scholarship. She claimed the study of this period in Italian history for her own because it had not yet been "exhumed and examined and criticized and classified," and because its artifacts still bore "the dust of their own day" (293). In contrast to traditional theoretical scholarship, Lee claims to have "felt" the reality of Italy's historical sites even *before* she learned the scholarly terms.

> I have seen the concrete things, and what I might call the concrete realities of
> thought and feeling left behind by the Renaissance, and then tried to obtain
> from books some notion of the original shape and manner of wearing these
> relics, rags and tatters of a past civilization. (*Euphorion,* 1:16)[10]

The image of clothing here is carried over into the next paragraph to an "Italy
... [who] was never able to weave for herself a new, modern civilization," where
it creates a metonymic relation between Lee's writerly self and Renaissance Italy.
She weeps over the century-old "victimization" of Renaissance Italy, whose garments were worn and torn through "the rough usage of other nations ... their
utter neglect by the long seventeenth century, their hasty patchings up ... by the
happy-go-lucky practicalness of the eighteenth century and the Revolution."
Lee's identity as a historian is metonymically linked with her subjects, but it also
is detachable, like a piece of clothing. The patched-up garment suggests the
humbleness of "her" Renaissance, especially in comparison to those modern historians who dress the Renaissance in the "garments of modern civilization." Yet,
"her" ragged Italian Renaissance has been strong enough to impress the other
European nations so much that they believed "it must be brand new, and of the
very latest fashion" (17).

In this allegory, Lee slights contemporary Renaissance studies for attempt-
ing to find in the period the predecessors of the modern individual. She criticizes
the scholars' failure to open other dimensions of the Renaissance because they
have neglected the seemingly insignificant details of everyday life that are still
present in the "seams of battered bricks of the solid old escutcheoned palaces" or
the "broken tiles and plaster" (18). In her mind, historiography has failed to develop methods to discriminate such detail because it has blindly followed the
modernist propensity for stylistic cleansing. Lee, however, *includes* all the debris:
"mere useless and befouled odds and ends, like the torn shreds which lie among
the decaying kitchen refuse" (18). These "unpractical and old-fashioned things"
are for her an organic and vital part of the historical landscape. She does not select
her materials from among "a series of elevated points" (Pater, *Renaissance,* 159),
but rather looks at "things of little weight, mere trifles of artistic material,"
though "equally fascinating" (*Euphorion,* 1:8).

Lest the historian miss the "noble ore," Lee maintains, history should be
approached like a "historic habit," with the constant inclusion of even periph-
eral aspects of the past in the present. Such habit, she claims with Hegelian

conviction, creates historical consciousness.[11] To her, history writing is composed as much of unconscious habit as it is of conscious thought. The habitual memory in history is not to be found in its choice masterworks, but in the less outstanding and more repetitive examples of traditional workmanship.

> This is one of the peculiarities of rudimentary art . . . of every peasant potter
> all through the world: that, not knowing very well its own aims, it fills its im-
> perfect work with suggestion of all manner of things which it loves . . . and
> lays hold of us, like fragments of verse, by suggestiveness, quite as much as
> by pictorial realisation. And upon this depends the other half of the imagina-
> tive art of the Renaissance. (*Renaissance Fancies,* 95)

Literally, we find the habitual memory recorded in the patterns and decorations, which were carried out by the multitude of artisans, craftsmen, or dilettante artists—in other words, by the concrete manifestations of Michelet's more abstract "peuple."[12]

Not unlike Margaret Oliphant in *The Makers of Florence,* Vernon Lee finds a luxuriant alternative past of artists and artisans in need of restoration. Lee sees herself as the biographer of the neglected or displaced "simple people," including the popular bards whose art of storytelling she means to salvage from oblivion. Aware of the contemporary distinction between "high" art and popular art, she repeatedly makes a case for the latter, which to her often just means nonacademic art. She dramatizes this difference in her portrayal of two poets from the High Renaissance, Ariosto and Boiardo. In "The School of Boiardo," she compares Ariosto's academic style with the amateurish verses of Boiardo.

> Ariosto is a man of far more varied genius; he is an artist while Boiardo is an
> amateur; he is learned in arranging and ornamenting. . . . Moreover, he is a
> scholarly person of a scholarly time: he is familiar with the classics, and, what
> is more important, he is familiar with the language in which he is writing.
> He writes exquisitely harmonious, supple, and brilliant Tuscan verse . . .
> while poor Boiardo jogs along in a language which is not the Lombard dia-
> lect in which he speaks, and which is very uncouth and awkward, as is every
> pure language for a provincial. (*Euphorion,* 2:103)

In this comparison of two Renaissance poets, Lee explicitly circumvents an objective or systematic approach: "I personally prefer Boiardo. . . . My preferences, my impressions, I have said, are in this matter much less critical than personal" (104–5). Notwithstanding her protestations, her "personal" preferences are well sustained by a series of arguments which, at times, disparage Ariosto's stilted learnedness of which she yet seems to be envious. When she ridicules Ariosto, her tone reminds us of her critique of Pater's imagery in "The Outdoor Poetry:" "I confess that I am bored by the beautifully written moral and allegorical preludes of Ariosto's cantos; I would willingly give all his aphorism and all his mythology to get quickly to the story" (104). The gist of her criticism: "The picture painted by Ariosto is finer, but you see too much of the painter."

We may wonder to what extent Lee identifies her own amateur status with "poor Boiardo," against the more refined and academic Ariosto. Does she assert herself through Boiardo against academically trained male historians whose language she still must borrow?[13] She smugly asserts her awareness of the prevailing standards: "Comparing together Boiardo and Ariosto, I am of course, aware of the infinite advantage of the latter" (*Euphorion,* 2:105). But she immediately adds how "amused" and "delighted" she is by Boiardo's poetry: "this is the real Fairyland this Boiardo ... the wonderland of medieval Romance ... the fairyland of the Renaissance" (106). To her the folklorist fairy-tale side of the Renaissance has more cultural relevance than the revival of classical culture generally celebrated by nineteenth-century critics. Lee shares their fascination with the rebirth of a kind of paganism, with the difference that she believes it springs from and is alive among the locals.[14]

The folklorist art, which she would expand into "Persia and India, of Constantinople, of every peasant potter all through the world," to her represents "the other half of the imaginative art of the Renaissance, the school of intellectual decoration" (*Renaissance Fancies,* 94–95). It is Lee's identification with the "pagan fairyland" of the painters and the peasants of the early Renaissance which marks her position as distinct from academic historians who identified with the intellectual and cultural elite. For Lee, what mattered in Renaissance culture was not only the taste for "platonic philosophy, classical erudition, religious hymns, and Hebrew Kabala," but also a sense of "a certain kind of realism, [for] the language and mode of thinking of the lower classes, as a reaction from Petrarchesque conventionality" (*Euphorion,* 2:90).

Poets whose social reality and poetic expression were vastly remote from chivalrous high culture became suitable candidates in Lee's promotion of the popular element in the Renaissance. Next to Boiardo, she enlists Luigi Pulci, a popular poet of the early Renaissance, who adapted the chivalric texts to the language of "Florentine wool-workers, housewives, cheese-sellers, and raga-muffins, crammed with the slang of the market-place" (*Euphorion,* 1:92).

> As the Magnificent Lorenzo had the fancy to string together in more artistic shape the quaint and graceful love poem of the Tuscan peasantry; so also Messer Luigi Pulci appears to have been smitten with the notion of trying his hand at the chivalric poem like those to which he and his friends had listened among the butchers and pork-shops, the fishmongers and frying booths of the market. (90)

In a s(n)ide remark she corrects historical scholars for not recognizing Pulci's relevance in the way his contemporaries did: "For the men of the Renaissance, no matter how philosophized and cultured, retained the pleasure in mere inci-dent which we moderns seem to have given over to children and savages" (91). Again, Lee derides the separation between high and low culture which has narrowed the scope of historical studies and excluded certain groups by lend-ing them the invisibility of the "uncultured."

Lee's patronage of everyday culture and realism was not only meant to bring into view marginalized cultural traditions. She goes so far as to claim that all major artistic figures "cannot be well understood unless we previously reconstruct the so-ciety in which they lived, and unless we reassemble around them those men who, though seemingly indifferent or insignificant, yet indirectly influenced their lives, their art, and their fame" (*Studies,* 6). Lee's argument about the role of the lower classes as promoters of the zeitgeist is often directed against Pater's ideally defined image of an elite culture. In "The Outdoor Poetry," she locates the emergence of the modern spirit in Lorenzo dei Medici's "realistic" songs of peasantry and na-ture, whereas Pater had seen the beginnings of the Renaissance in the courtly ro-mances of France.[15] Lee finds that Lorenzo dei Medici breaks the "silence" about the quotidian in history by making visible the realism of the peasant culture, which had been concealed under the conventionality of French medieval poetry:

> this medieval spring . . . neither of the shepherd, nor of the farmer, nor of any man to whom spring brings work and anxiety and hope of gain; it is a mere vague spring of gentle-folk, or at all events of well-to-do burgesses, taking their pleasure on the lawns of castle parks. (*Euphorion,* 1:123)

Lee derides the dainty images of courtly poetry as pastoral "trappings," which conceal social difference. Courtly poetry suppresses the plight of the serf by employing images borrowed from the antique bucolic tradition. Over several pages, Lee demonstrates that the somewhat schematized and idealized image of the peasant, perpetuated through medieval poetry and art, is only a projection of upper-class desires. The aesthetic conventions separated an idyllic image of the peasantry from their social reality so that the "serf" became synonymous with "the bruitishness, the cunning, the cruelty, the hideousness, the heresy of the serf" (131). Thus medieval French poetry conserved under its aesthetic artifice a diminished and derogatory image of the peasant. What we can study in courtly poetry, Lee argues, is only an aesthetic form that was designed to conceal the gap between upper and lower classes.

Lee complicates her argument on art as a means of social oppression by adding a gendered dimension. In an overlong footnote—one of only two footnotes in the 450-page work—she demonstrates that the courting of lower-class women by knights in the thirteenth-century Provençal *Pastourala* denigrates rather than elevates women: the "courting, by the poet, who is of course a knight, of a beautiful country-girl, who is shown us as feeding her sheep or spinning with her distaff" does not place the woman in a higher class. On the contrary, the "extremely insincere and artificial" tone of the idylls is proof to Lee that these poets "never looked a live peasant in the face." The aristocratic pastorals depicting an homage paid by upper-class men to lower-class women "conceal beneath the conventional pastoral trappings the intrigues of minnesingers and troubadours with women of the small artizan or village proprietor class." But such aesthetic reverence, Lee assures us, had no social consequences: "The real peasant women would scarcely have been above the noblemen's servants" and therefore not have been noticed, let alone "offered presents and fine words" (131–32n).

Lee's ideological text critique is also an ironic jab at Pater's socially restricted view in, for example, his too "beautiful" representation of the thirteenth-century French tale "Aucassin and Nicolette."[16]

> I can recall one, though only one occasion in which medieval literature shows us the serf. The place is surely the most unexpected, the charming thirteenth century tale of "Aucassin and Nicolette." In his beautiful essay upon that story, Mr. Pater has deliberately omitted this episode, which is indeed like a spot of bloodstained mud, . . . the episode which I am going to translate. (133–34)

Here her unusually explicit criticism of Pater becomes more salient through the qualifier "deliberately." Pater's omission appears even more serious because she declares this passage to be unique in its representation of the lower classes. Her triumphant announcement, "which I am going to translate," gives her the last word. The little episode in which a poor serf looking for his cow meets Aucassin plays a central role in Lee's argument that medieval court poetry aestheticizes "the classes for whom poetry was not written," thus dismissing them from history. But she goes even further, showing a connection between the historical text (courtly poetry) and the historian's interest (Pater's "idyl of lovely things" [132]). Pater's text, by implication, helps perpetuate a timeless, elitist perspective which distances itself from social reality. Lee's different awareness puts on the map what Pater has to omit. In her version of "Aucassin et Nicolette," Nicolette is construed as a women of unknown parentage, "a woman of lower degree ... bought of the Saracens" (with all the racial and sexual implications of this phrase), in any case enough to make her déclassée for her suitor's father. When Lee describes Pater's reading of the passage in *Renaissance Fancies and Studies,* she makes him sound almost hypocritical:

> These adventures are of the simplest sort, *adventures which seem to be chosen for the happy occasion they afford of keeping the eye of the fancy, perhaps the outward eye, fixed on pleasant objects,* a garden, a ruined tower, the little hut of flowers. . . . All the charm of the piece is in its details, in a turn of peculiar lightness and grace given to the situations and traits of sentiment, especially in its quaint fragments of early French prose. (15; my emphasis)

Pater saw in the Renaissance mainly a renewed pursuit of intellectual freedom in secular and religious life, and newly located these qualities in France's thirteenth-century romances and sixteenth-century court poetry. "The history of the Renaissance ends in France, and carries us away from Italy to the beautiful cities of the country of the Loire. . . . But it was in France also, in a very important sense, that the Renaissance had begun" (*Renaissance,* 1). Lee's emphasis, however, is on Italy and its medieval communities: "the upper classes ... quite different as much from the upper classes of feudal countries ... were ... constantly in contact with the working classes" (*Euphorion,* 1:142). While idealizing the more democratic structure of Italian communities as being more conducive to Renaissance culture than were the feudal and more hierarchical systems of France and the northern countries, Lee also points at the limitations of "high" aesthetic art as a method for historical inquiry. Her ideological analysis of upper-class aesthetics strikes us as an early form of criticism now prevalent in modern cultural studies. By attributing aesthetic relevance to a neglected social class, she occasions the configuration of a new historical subject, questioning the aesthetic discourse that had enabled this subject in the first place. Lee raises less-privileged groups to historical subjects by construing them as bearers of historical continuity. According to this model, vagabond balladeers and storytellers gradually picked up medieval romances, patching up the foreign materials (note the clothing metaphor) "with rustic ideals, feelings, and images," and making them the subject of Tuscan folk legends and songs.

> I feel that the adoption of Courtly medieval poetry by the Italian peasantry of the Renaissance can be compared more significantly than at first seemed with the adoption of a once fashionable garb by country folk. The peasant pulled about this Courtly lyricism, oppressively tight in its conventional fit and starched with elaborate rhetorical embroideries; turned it inside out, twisted a bit here, a bit there, ripped open seam after seam, patched and re-patched with stuffs and stitches of its own; and then wore the whole thing as it had never been intended to be worn. (*Euphorion*, 1:150–51)

Literature from "high culture" trickled down to the lower classes, even across national borders; the recipients adapted these materials to their own lifestyles, thus becoming simultaneously perpetuators and innovators of history.[17] Lee tops off her argument by showing that courtly poetry became pleasurable to nineteenth-century audiences only *because* of its translation into more popular expression:

> And indeed, it appears to me that one might say, without too much paradox, that in these peasant songs only does the poetry of the minnesingers and troubadours become thoroughly enjoyable; that only when the conventionality of feeling and imagery is corrected by the freshness and straightforwardness, nay, even the grotesqueness of rural likings, dislikings, and comparisons, can the dainty beauty of medieval Courtly poetry ever really satisfy your wishes. (150)

Yet Lee was too much of a nineteenth-century liberal to let the lower classes become historical agents on their own. Their collective cultural achievements still had to be recognized and recorded by an outstanding individual, who was in touch with these traditions. That task fell on Lorenzo dei Medici because he "has sung no longer of knights and of spring" and therefore has "broken the long spell of the Middle Ages" (165). She leaves no doubt about her identification with Lorenzo whom she stylizes as both "true" Renaissance man and ideal aesthete. He is a "man of impressions" and also has an "extraordinary temper of art for art's sake." But his best quality for Lee is that he "is naturally attracted most by what is most opposed to the academic." She shares Lorenzo's preference for realist styles, which drew him "towards the classes where realism can deal with the real; and not the affected, the self-conscious, the deliberately attempted" (154).

Lee's portrayal of Lorenzo dei Medici is a clever piece in that it reorganizes the existing studies without dismissing any of them, while plausibly promoting her own. She features not the politician but the artist whose main achievement is the recording of rural poetry for posterity.

> Well; for many a year did the song of the peasants rise up from the fields and oliveyards unnoticed by the good townsfolk taking their holiday at the Tuscan villa; but one day, somewhere in the third quarter of the fifteenth century, the long-drawn chant of the rispetto . . . did at least waken the attention of one lettered man, a man of curious and somewhat misshapen body and mind, of features satyr-like in ugliness, yet moody and mystical in their very earthiness. . . . The man was Lorenzo dei Piero dei Medici. . . . It is the fashion at present to give Lorenzo only the leavings, as it were, of our admiration for the weaker, less original, nay, considerably enervate, humanistic exquisite Politician; and this absurd injustice appears to me to show that the very essence and excellence of Lorenzo is not nowadays perceived. (153)

Through Lorenzo dei Medici, Lee reinforces her advocacy for the neglected. She supplements the historians' one-sided emphasis on the despot and "exquisite Politician" (as Sismondi has represented him) and promotes instead "the most versatile poet of the Renaissance." Lorenzo dei Medici is "new" and "modern"; he appears as the most perfect link between the Renaissance and her own age, "because he is so completely the man of impressions" (153).[18] And although Lee

echoes Pater's diction here, the implications are slightly different in that she sets
Lorenzo apart from Pater's refined artists—and particularly from Pater himself.

> [Lorenzo] is naturally attracted most by what is most opposed to the aca-
> demic, Virgilian, Horatian, or Petrarchesque aestheticism of his contempo-
> raries; he is essentially a realist.... Instead of seeking, like most of his
> contemporaries, to be Greek, Roman, or medieval by turns, he preferred try-
> ing on all the tricks of thought and feeling which he remarked among the
> unlettered townsfolk. (154)

With unconcealed delight, Lee describes the quaint picturesque details in his
poem, "Nencia da Barberino," so "that we almost forget verses and song, and
actually see the pulling, twisting, and cutting of the gold-threads" (155). Compared with Dante's work, she concedes, Lorenzo's poem is not beautiful or
even poetic; other critics may not see this poem as a work of art because it lacks
formal perfection, but "the construction, which appears to be nowhere, is in reality a masterpiece." In her mind, Lorenzo's poem is a piece of historical reality
which still reaches beyond its time because "he has given us a peasant's
thoughts, actions, hopes, fears; he has given us the peasant himself, his house,
his fields, and his sweetheart, as they exist even now" (159).

Lorenzo dei Medici's art, Lee admits, is not that of a genius, but actually
rather commonplace. His creation is only "the result of those Tuscan peasant
songs," and yet his work is more than "the poetry of the Renaissance peasant;
it is the poem made out of his reality" (155).[19] Lorenzo is Lee's model artist, the
mediator between high and popular culture in the service of the community.
As a communal artist, however, he has little in common with Pater's artistic
individuals who appear alienated from the community or even threatened by
the "mob," as in "Apollo in Picardy" or in "Denys L'Auxerrois."

Eventually, Lee finds all "high" art transitory and ephemeral, whereas
communal art creates historical continuity and permanence. "Lorenzo is
gone," but what endures is our impression of the peasant: "everything changes,
except the country and the peasant." At this point, Lee closes the circle that
connects the impressionist historian Vernon Lee with the impressionist
Lorenzo by describing her own contact with the Italian peasants of her time
and their farms in her neighborhood: "all about Florence; farms which I pass
every day" (160). She raises the peasants to historical agents, and eventually,

not only a neglected social group, but the historian Vernon Lee herself emerges visibly from the text.

In her portrayal of Lorenzo dei Medici, Lee praises the humanist, whose "heart for the simpler, ruder, less favoured classes of mankind" marks the real beginning of the Renaissance and, therefore, of modernity: "modern times have begun, modern sympathies, modern art are in full swing" (166). In *Renaissance Fancies,* she further develops the connection between the Renaissance, the people's art, and the modern spirit, notably in the essay "The Imaginative Art of the Renaissance" (67–133), which reads almost like a sequel to "The Outdoor Poetry." In the later essay, she aligns herself with those who record the history of the "sufferers" in a genealogy from Lorenzo dei Medici to sixteenth-century German engravers, whose

> expression [was] not for the multitude at large, fresco or mosaic that could be elaborated by a skeptical or godless artist, but a re-explanation as from man to man and friend. . . . The Virgin, they have discovered, is not the grandly dressed lady, always in the very finest brocade, with the very finest manners . . . but a real wife and mother with real milk in her breasts. (*Renaissance Fancies,* 116–17)

Like Lorenzo's poetry, this "Teutonic" art represents the reality of everyday people, with the modern difference that their reality is given back to them in the new commodity of the print, which makes art accessible to everyone. At the same time, she is skeptical of this kind of mass art. "We get the benefit of the fancy and feelings of this individual, but we are at the mercy, also of his stupidity and vulgarity" (122).

Among her "people's" artists, Lee also includes Goya, which comes as a surprise, because one would not necessarily connect this painter of the most ruthless aspects of human misery and torture with her aesthetic professions. However, from her conception of the artist-historian as the recorder of the neglected, the "sufferers," in history, Goya has a legitimate if not the most prominent place.

> Like Dürer and Rembrandt, the great Spaniard is at once extremely realistic and extremely imaginative. But his realism means *fidelity, not to the real aspect of things, of the thing in itself, so to speak, but to the way in which things will*

*appear to the spectator at a given moment.* He isolates what you might call a case, separating it from the multitude of similar cases, giving you one execution where several must be going on, one firing off of canon, one or two figures in a burning or a massacre. (131–32; my emphasis)

What Lee describes here of Goya's technique follows precisely Pater's outline of aesthetic criticism in *The Renaissance*. Purposefully swerving from Arnold's doctrine, Pater had declared "'To see the object as in itself it really is' . . . is to know one's own impression as it really is, to discriminate it, to realize it distinctly" (xix). For Lee, too, aestheticism means truthfulness to one's impression, but the difference is that she wants to see the aesthetic method applied to the views and emotions of the neglected.

[T]hese scenes are not merely rather such as they were recollected than as they really were seen; they are such as they were recollected in the minds and feelings of peasants and soldiers, of people who could not free their attention to arrange these matters logically, to give them their relative logical value. (*Renaissance Fancies*, 132)

Like Lorenzo dei Medici, who does not let poetic form overshadow reality, "Goya does not for a moment let us suspect the presence of the artist, the quasi-writer." Like Goya, Lee also does not look at history from a point "as safely separated as [are] those who look on from the enfuriated bulls in an arena" (*Euphorion*, 1:13), but as an active participant in historical reality. It is the aspect of participation or partaking which forms an important link between the historian Vernon Lee and "the sufferings, real and imaginative, of the real sufferers" (*Renaissance Fancies*, 133).

Lee's increasing empathy with social issues in her writing inflects her aesthetics with an alternative and, in some sense, a female version. Although she still "wears" Pater's aesthetic garment in the 1890s, she has marked her position as different from his by aligning herself with the reality of neglected social groups, among which she could include herself. She does not explicitly identify with the woman's position; it would take another decade for her to speak on behalf of feminism. But the consistency with which she pursues the history of overlooked subjects resembles the manner in which she often describes herself.[20] The dedication page of *The Handling of Words,* for instance, reads almost like a reminder of her existence to the audience. "To the many writers I have read and the few readers who have read me."[21]

We have seen that Lee draws on Pater to express her different historical experience as a woman. By claiming to arrange impressions randomly, she manages to open new cultural spaces for historical inquiry. In her portrait of Lorenzo dei Medici, Lee applies one of Pater's leading questions in *The Renaissance* ("In whom did the stir, the genius, the sentiment of the period find itself?") but redefines it by widening the social basis of her inquiry to the community. Pater also identifies the age of Lorenzo as one of those happy eras in which "the many interests of the intellectual world combine in one complete type of general culture," but he speaks of the "exquisite" personalities who make up the volume of his Renaissance studies.

> Here, artists and philosophers and those whom the action of the world has elevated and made keen, do not live in isolation, but breathe a common air, and catch light and heat from each other's thoughts. There is a spirit of general elevation and enlightenment in which all alike communicate. (*Renaissance,* xxiv)

In Pater's description, the sense of communality also prevails, but this is the communality of "those whom the action of the world has elevated"—in other words, an elite.

We may say that Pater and Lee differ in their implied subject positions, in spite of the similarities in their aesthetic approach. Pater selects historical moments to express the "temperament" of the author metonymically linked to the Renaissance. His "moments" arrange themselves along an imaginary sentiment that he shares with his subjects. Lee also collects impressions subjectively, but through her view from below. By locating intellectual authority in a writer's attachment to the community, she proposes a public role for (women) historians even outside academic scholarship.

Lee's historical text divulges growing self-confidence, and she is aware of it, professing "the knowledge has grown on me that I was saying farewell to some of the ambitions and to most of the plans of my youth" (*Renaissance Fancies,* 235). Her assuredness—which annoyed ambitious men like Symonds—came not only from her solid knowledge of historical scholarship. It also reflects the changed intellectual climate in the 1890s when the Renaissance had become an "accomplished fact" (Pater) or, in Lee's terms, when "our conscience has become quieter, not because it has grown more callous, but because it has become more healthily sensitive, more perceptive of many sides, instead of only one side in life" (*Renaissance Fancies,* 249).[22] Her voice here suggests an independence that enabled the mature and far-sighted commentaries on twentieth-century European history and politics for which she became known in later decades.[23]

## LEE'S "NEW HISTORICISM"

For the promotion of her alternative views, Lee could take advantage of the general intellectual uncertainty in the 1870s and '80s which put into competition different epistemological models. The striving for intellectual authority was not only an issue for female historians but also became a central issue "for virtually all disciplines in the last decades of the century" to validate their critical practices (Small, 28). In this climate, Lee could nonchalantly sweep aside a portion of the historical canon: "good heavens! why should we sicken ourselves with the thought of this long dead and done for abomination?" (*Renaissance Fancies,* 250). Her expression of an independent, bold new historical consciousness anticipates strikingly Virginia Woolf's rhetorical sweep in *A Room of One's Own.* Like Woolf's invention of "Shakespeare's Sister," Lee's imaginary portrait of an artist introduces her last essay of *Renaissance Fancies and Studies,* "A Seeker of Pagan Perfection: Being the Life of Domenico Neroni, *Pictor Sacrilegus,*" as

> a certain story [which] has long lurked in the corners of my mind. Twenty years have passed since first I was aware of its presence, and it has undergone many changes. It is presumably a piece of my inventing, for I have neither read it nor heard it related. But by this time it has acquired a certain traditional veracity in my eyes, and I give to the reader rather as historical fact than as fiction the study which I have always called to myself: Pictor Sacrilegus. (166)

This passage combines two aspects of Lee's "new historicism." First, by refusing to distinguish between fact and fiction, she declares herself (the historian) as the site where knowledge is produced. She constructs her persona as the point of reference and authority from which the narrative derives method and meaning; in other words, Lee is the historical text as well as its commentator. In *Euphorion* she still took pains to locate her style within the polarization of fact and fiction; now she dismisses such differences as irrelevant, especially if defined in binary opposites as the only way to establish meaning. It is important to note that Lee does not blur or reverse the opposition of fact and fiction but simply ignores it, very much aware of its existence. By avoiding the code of inbuilt opposition she believes she is able to counteract hierarchization. At the same time, Lee mimics the imaginary effects of language in which certain modes of representation—like the discourse of "fact"—pose as real.

Second, Lee's historical subject is (again) the run-of-the- mill artist—not the genius, here embodied by Domenico Neroni, a minor sculptor during Savonar-ola's regime, whom Vasari mentions only in passing. Neroni "resembled in some respects his great contemporary Leonardo," but the former is obviously less dis-tinguished (socially and artistically), as his workshop is "full of cobwebs and dust, littered with the remains of frugal and unsavoury meals, and resolutely closed to the rich and noble persons in whose company Leonardo delighted" (*Renaissance Fancies,* 174).

Her emphasis on the imaginary quality of "A Seeker of Pagan Perfection" emulates Pater's narrator in "Denys L'Auxerrois," who asserts "the story shaped itself at last" based only on "a fancy in my mind" (*Imaginary Portraits,* 54). But Lee does not even bother to construct another narrator. She declares herself the historical source. The plot of Lee's tale resembles the narrative structure and content of Pater's "Denys L'Auxerrois," while it mimics his por-traits of artists in *The Renaissance.* We are explicitly reminded of Pater through Lee's reference to the same painters and her mocking imitation of Pater's aes-thetic formulas in Neroni's almost perverse delight in anatomy. Such cita-tional practice opens a space for alterity, which allows for critiquing Pater's aesthetical rhetoric and, at the same time, alerts us to her own ideological moves:

> And that St. John in the Wilderness—how beautiful are not his ribs, showing under the wasted pectoral muscles; and how one sees that the radius rolls across the ulna in the forearm; surely one's heart, rather than the statue, must be made of stone if one can contemplate without rapture the exquisite render-ing of the texture where the shinbone stands out from the muscles of the legs. Such must have been the works of those famous Romans and Greeks, Phidias and Praxiteles. (*Renaissance Fancies,* 179)

In Domenico Neroni, Lee attempts to recreate a late medieval mind, still un-scathed by the knowledge of the "superiority of antiquity." Neroni is basically a "good Christian" whose "unhappy mania" turned him into a fervent anato-mist who did not eschew "handling horrible remains." Most of all, he is "a mere handicraftsman, [who] had not learned from the study of Cicero and Plato to examine and understand the difference between reality and fiction" (210). Neroni is the "everyman" version of Pater's rarefied artist, who is led into some sacrilegious pagan ritual by a cunning humanist (Filarete) of "sinis-ter reputation." Their attempt to conjure up a pagan god is discovered; both are mutilated and burnt under Savonarola's rigid regime. Neroni's end seems overly cruel and unjust, but we cannot say that Lee displays much sympathy with him. Similar to the way she discovered rustic realism in Lorenzo dei Medici, Lee here tries to render a realist picture of the historical circumstances under which artists of the time carried out their work. The clear absence of some-thing like an antique or even "modern" spirit (in Pater's sense) and the lack of direction or time-transcending moments is a significant departure from Pa-ter's historical portraits. In fact, Neroni's search for pagan beauty is presented as not only naive and dangerous, but ultimately impossible.

Lee depicts a historical setting that is not yet shaped by the interpretation of later generations. She constructs her historical portrait not ideally (symbol-ized by Neroni's failure to evoke the pagan spirit) but materially. What the reader gleans from her text is a social study of the conditions of artistic produc-tion in the fifteenth century. This includes scientific developments, artistic pa-tronage, the life style of the moneyed classes, and, most of all, the mindset of the artist who comes across as an ambitious craftsman rather than as an artist of refined temperament with a time-transcending mystique. All in all, her study of Domenico Neroni is an exercise in "alter history," an attempt to ren-der history as a possibility—as Stephen Greenblatt put it recently, "that *it could all have been otherwise*" (60).

When Vernon Lee sought to negotiate a position among contemporary male his-torians, she applied a rhetorical convention common among women writers who offered their diffferent perspectives not in opposition but as supplement to dominant views. Like other female historians, Lee was eager to demonstrate her

knowledge of established scholarship—"already carried out with all the perfection due to specially adapted gifts, to infinite patience and ingenuity, occasionally
amounting almost to genius"—only to argue that there was still room for her
own projects: "besides such marvels of historic mapping as I have
described . . . there are yet other kinds of work which may be done" (*Euphorion,*
1:9). We should not be astonished by her remarks, for a woman venturing into
theoretical writing surely had to prove her intellectual authority. Not only were
the actual historians men, but their subject matter, too, had been shaped by the
experience of men so that the focus was on "great men" and high politics.

   To generate intellectual authority, Vernon Lee needed to be accepted in the
community of male historians, which meant that she had to speak their language. Since she was aware of women's marginal status, she avoided drawing attention to an explicitly female viewpoint. Nevertheless, Lee's historical texts
reveal what we may call a "second vision." They allow us to see a woman's view
underneath a seemingly unmarked text and the sometimes annoying flood of details. Once we begin to read Lee in her own terms and temporarily suspend our
expectation of academic scholarly discourse, her language forms a logic whose
meaning arranges itself around a different subject position.

   Lee configures her subjectivity in a constant struggle not only with contemporary intellectual positions but also with the difficulty of defining her own. Some
stretches of her essays read like repetitions of other historians, most notably Jules
Michelet, J. A. Symonds, and Walter Pater. The citational mode—typically employed by aesthetic writers—serves two functions.[24] First, by demonstrating her
familiarity with traditional scholarship, she can ward off accusations of "mere"
dilettantism while making her choice of style appear more original. Second, citations can operate as a kind of feminist doubling and open spaces of difference. As
Derrida claims, all terms are citational; it is the very repeatability of a term that
demonstrates its inscription in a system of meaning. Any repetition, no matter
whether it be identical, is always also a difference, and it is that space of difference
which allows for a feminist reading (Weed, iv–xxxi). As citation carries less content of its own, it helps the writer to resist her own ideological blind spots and to
use her strategic repetition as conscious participation in cultural formation.

   Often enough, Lee assumes the empathic view of the producers of art: accomplished craftsmen whose artistic expression she saw conditioned by task, materials, and skill, all in a communal context. Lee's concept of productive art
reflects the way she imagined her own working style as a female historian outside

the academy. In her historical texts, Lee forms a perspective around and through social groups that were in the background of the contemporary discourses on art and history. She does not offer a thorough analysis of social history, but jaunts through periods in the mode of an aesthetic impressionist. However, by including the standpoint of the neglected and elevating it to the level of historiography, she suggests other possibilities for historical identification.

Pater's language created the conditions for an alternative historical discourse; but Lee still desired to speak for herself. Her second book on the Renaissance achieves this independence: she is deliberately iconoclastic and no longer tries to legitimize her method. Demonstrating that habitual knowledge poses as historical truth but is nothing less than applied ideology, she dismisses the search for truth and construes history as "coincidence of contrary movements." Since she feels no longer obliged to address the questions from the period historians, she nonchalantly sweeps aside portions of the canon to speak about the subjects of her own choice.

In *Renaissance Fancies and Studies* Lee proposes to get in touch with the pleasures of the past, but such a venture depends on the individual investigator, for "every individual has in the Past affinities, possibilities or spiritual satisfaction differing somewhat from those of every other" (245). The "Valedictory" of this book, then, can be read as a positioning of her own subjectivity, in particular, in relation to Walter Pater. Her reassessment of his role as aesthetic critic is a rather balanced view of his innovations and limitations. Lee's stylistic finesse shows that she has outgrown the role of a youthful devotee and has become a self-assured writer. Her puzzling phrase from *Baldwin,* "my master, yet made by me," has a different ring here. The phrase deconstructs the relationship between master and pupil, subject and object and finally, turns hierarchy against itself: by putting choice at the center of her discourse, her master will cease to be one. For what kind of master is a master by choice of others? A representative of the people's will? Of Vernon Lee's will? A nice piece of logic or a trick of the mind? "Choose and understand," she says, "for I cannot."

> I am the pupil of Baldwin, the thing made by him, or he is my master, yet made by me . . . better far than I and wiser, but perhaps a little less human, you are not myself; you are my mentor, my teacher, my power of being taught; and you live, dear abstract friend on the borderline between fact and fancy. (14)

# 3  Between the Lines of Gender and Genre

Vernon Lee's complicated relationship to gender and sexuality has often been seen as standing at the center of her ambiguous and sometimes contradictory texts. While modern criticism has generally addressed with interesting results the connections between sexuality and textuality, these connections can easily create new limitations. As Virginia Blain puts it in her review of Burdett Gardner's psycho-sexual study of Vernon Lee, "The lack of value ascribed to women by her culture and reinforced tenfold by her upbringing did Violet Paget more damage than could ever have been undone by going to bed with one of her string of female admirers" (51–52). But how exactly did Lee's unique viewpoint emerge between her rejection of conventional female roles and her self-construction as a male writer? How did her lack of reverence for masculinity complicate her male identification or undermine her sense of self?

Lee's writing is the testimony of a woman who was passionately and primarily committed to her creative life in a culture that gave little credit to intellectual women. Vernon Lee's own statement at the time of her breakup with Kit Anstruther-Thomson supports the assumption that Lee's devotion to a career as a writer surpassed even the love of woman.

> Whether my work is worth anything or not, I must see to its being as good as
> it can possibly be made. . . . Again I say that short of hurting her very much

not twenty Kits would be worth losing my serenity and intellectual elasticity.
(VL to Mona Taylor, 1899, Colby)

Neither Gardner's pathological study nor Gunn's genteel repression of Lee's lesbian orientation does justice to the complexity of her writing. Gardner, by taking her images at face value, throughout the full 592 pages of his study neglects Lee's continual attempts to dismantle some of the most pervasive dualisms of her time, such as male-female, subject-object, fact-fiction. Ironically, his obsession with Lee's sexuality proves once more what Lee criticized among her contemporaries: the rating of women foremost as sexual beings. Lee's complicated relationship to representations of sexuality needs to be read less as her personal expression and more in the context of the prevailing aesthetic and iconographic trends of the fin de siècle, which also colored her literary language.

Only in the last few years have critics started investigating how feminist and lesbian theories can be connected with Lee's texts, or, in other words, how gender and genre, sexuality and textuality intersect. Martha Vicinus's essay, "The Adolescent Boy: Fin de Siècle Femme Fatale?" is an example of a reading that foregrounds such questions. Vicinus analyzes Lee's use of the boy image in "Prince Alberic and the Snake Lady" in the context of other lesbian writers, such as Michael Field or Renée Vivien. Her study throws new light on a whole network of lesbian metaphors, particularly in their relationship to male homosexual language which, as Terry Castle has pointed out, has always overshadowed lesbian discourses (16). Castle's attempt to retrieve the lesbian from her "invisibility" and bring to light her ubiquity even in the cultural mainstream opens a door for a broader understanding of lesbian writing. However, both critics have focused mainly on fictional texts. Obviously, the expository mode of nonfictional writing suggests different approaches. Virginia Blain's proposal to emphasize Lee's "over-invested male identification" rather than the repression of her (anomalous) lesbian tendencies presents a constructive venue. Blain's view also supports Lee's propensity to refashion male texts (namely those of her mentors) or to adopt male voices, all the while recasting traditional gender images. Her cultural redefinitions resemble Monique Wittig's textual lesbianization of mythological texts. By changing the primary signifiers, Wittig created openings for new readings of classical myths.[1]

Whereas Wittig is interested mainly in producing new poetic codes, Lee exposes the cultural construction of sexual images and their multiple origins in a discursive system that polarizes and unifies these images to hide their attachment to hierarchical power structures. By mocking familiar narratives about female figures in history and mythology, Lee questions any single definition of meaning as a manifestation of prevailing hierarchies.[2] In her fiction, snake ladies, femmes fatales, and pagan goddesses are dressed down and up again, to remain enigmatic; in her essays, Lee carefully layers and then reorganizes her subject positions to let us glean alternative aesthetic and historical texts. To arrive at a different form of self-representation, Lee contests the prevailing epistemic system and especially the conventional practices of "Stiltrennung" (separation of styles), which separated fact from fiction and prescribed clear argumentative structures. Through creative orchestrations and collages of discursive practices, Lee establishes an alternative subjectivity that ultimately undermines the very notion of the subject.

## Experiments in "Stiltrennung"

That the effects of "Stiltrennung" are still alive today becomes evident in the inconsistencies of common reference guides. The nomenclature for Vernon Lee ranges from "essayist, novelist, or short story writer," to "critic" or "aesthetician."[3] Elsie B. Michie, the author of the entry on Vernon Lee in the *Encyclopedia of British Women Writers,* has no problems supplanting the annoying genre description altogether by a no-nonsense Born-Died-Daughter-of-Wrote-under chart.

Vernon Lee wrote fiction and nonfiction, often in the same text, or, as Vineta Colby puts it, "in a sense almost everything that Vernon Lee wrote bore the stamp of fiction" (235).[4] At home in both argumentative essay and fictional narrative, Lee was torn constantly between different modes of representing and organizing knowledge. The overlapping of styles and genres in Lee's works often challenged contemporary assumptions about literary categories, so that she felt compelled to comment on her texts in extensive forewords and epilogues, thus drawing attention to her own literary discourse, if not discomfort.

Throughout her work, Lee finds triple fault with "Stiltrennung," mainly with respect to her own preferred medium, the historical essay: first, the essay's confinement to fact; second, the use of abstraction, which unjustly homogenizes subjects; and third, the built-in hierarchies in the symbolic system which automatically establish one view over another.

Differentiating between fact and fiction played an important role in late-nineteenth-century literary debates. The normative character of this dualism reaches beyond the functional "circulating library distinction" (Northrop Frye), a reference that reminds us also of the historical dimension. With the rise of science in the second half of the nineteenth century, the symbolic division between fact and fiction determined the way meaning was ascribed and authorized. As binary oppositions, fact and fiction then became mutually exclusive and, simultaneously, mutually dependent. Their dualistic framework distinguishes between different modes of making sense, each marking a different "fellowship of discourse" (Foucault) in the intellectual struggles over epistemic control.

Fact and fiction correspond to and are influenced by similar divisions including binary gender dimension. The twofold function of gender as a primary signifier for symbolic hierarchies and as a determining factor of social relationships based on perceived differences between the sexes makes it a crucial site for ideological formation.[5] Gender invades and determines *every body's* life and therefore is the general and the individual at the same time. Gender also marks the visible intersection of symbolic language and social reality which makes it an ideologically powerful sign. In the nineteenth century, the prevailing gender norms set by the heterosexual value systems of the middle classes increasingly invaded literary discourses and judgments. But heterosexuality, in the context of late-nineteenth-century Britain, was a male-defined value since, as Ruth Robbins puts it, "the institutions which support dominant discourses are bastions of male power . . . [and] an appeal to the mean, and to the only form of sexuality validated by Church and State" (145).

In "The Economic Parasitism of Women" Lee makes a similar argument to expose the hierarchy implied in the binary opposition of male and female in Western thought, although the terms are assumed to be complementary.

> [T]herefore, we have obtained a primitive human group, differing most essentially from the group composed by the male and female of other genera: the man and the woman, vir ac femina, do not stand opposite one another, he a little taller, she a little rounder, like Adam and Eve on the panels of Memling or Kranach; but in quite asymmetrical relation: a big man, as in certain archaic statues, holding in his hand a little woman. (*Gospels of Anarchy*, 270)

Here and elsewhere, Lee discusses the relativity of binary opposites in their different historical shapes by exposing them as social and intellectual conventions rather than as essential differences. In "Faustus and Helena" (*Belcaro*), for instance, she describes the division between the real and the fantastic—another powerful dualism —as symptomatic of a certain mode of perception in a certain time. To emphasize the mutability of such conventions, she shows that in earlier societies these distinctions were inconceivable because of their different concepts of reality, which did not privilege rational modes of representation to the same degree. Thus, Marlowe's "spirits" were read as realities, whereas Goethe's were not.

> In this story of Doctor Faustus, which, to Marlowe and his contemporaries, was not a romance but a reality, the episode of the evoking of Helen is extremely secondary in interest. To raise a dead woman was not more wonderful than to turn wisps of straw into horses. . . . Goethe's Faust feels for Helen as Goethe himself might have felt, as Winckelmann felt for a lost antique statue . . . the essentially modern, passionate, nostalgic craving for the past. (100–101)

Similarly, Lee questions contemporary assumptions about objectivity. She holds that the alleged truth value of "objectivity" is no more than a discursive pose, an aesthetic consensus, which reflects the interests of a certain community. Her epistolary novel *Louis Norbert* (1914), for instance, revolves around the relationship between (objective) scientific and (subjective) fictional methods of inquiry which, to her, as to Wilde or Pater, both describe different kinds of truth.[6]

In Lee's novel—a series of letters between a young professor of archeology and a middle-aged lady dilettante—different ways of knowing are aligned with contemporary gender stereotypes. Lee confronts the pedantic professor, who represents the masculine prerogatives of scientific rationality, with an enthusiastic amateur woman "whose imagination not only gallops but flies" (18), thus bringing to their project the feminine qualities of fancy and sentiment. As soon as the reader accepts the correspondence between gender and ways of knowing, Lee reverses the characters' roles. When their historical inquiry becomes mired, the professor implores Lady Vinetia to "invent." She is as outraged as if he had made an indecent proposal—a comparison with a grain of truth, since behind their historical correspondence unfolds a delicate love affair. In Lady Vinetia's eyes, the archeologist not only betrays scientific principles, but also ridicules her serious interest in historical research. He manages to allay her anger by interpreting "to invent" as "to discover" in the original

Latin sense: "for a hypothesis is a scientific invention" (118). At the same time, he invalidates the distinction between fact and fiction, history and romance, to expose the common ground of these dualisms. What their discussion demonstrates is that even scholarly inquiry is determined by individual interest and is therefore inflected by subjectivity. In more radical terms, history is "invention," and so, paradoxically, the concept of objectivity is a "fiction."[7]

In *Renaissance Fancies and Studies,* Lee already designed an interesting epistemic concept which challenges traditional assumptions about reality: she places the real and the imaginary in the same philosophical category as "things in our mind," which include impressions, emotions, habits, and beliefs.

> The things in our mind, due to the mind's constitution and its relation with the universe, are, after all, realities; and realities to count with, as much as the tables and chairs and hats and coats, and other things subject to gravitation outside it. It would seem, indeed, as if the chief outcome of the spiritualizing philosophy which maintains the immaterial and independent quality of mind had been to make mind, the contents of our consciousness, ideas, images, and feelings, into something quite separate from this real material universe, and hence unworthy of practical consideration. (239)

Lee attributes the dichotomy of mind and matter, or, likewise, of subject and object, to a purely idealist manner of thinking, which limits all accounts of history. In *Euphorion,* she rejects the abstract ideals of Hegelian philosophy by denying the validity of a universal "average" as too absolute and therefore unreal. To her, universality unjustly homogenizes differences, which should rather be represented in terms of relativity:

> [T]he art which deals with impressions . . . is the only truly realistic art, and it only, by giving you a thing as it appears at a given moment, gives it you as it really ever is; all the rest is the result of cunning abstraction, and representing the scene as it always is, represents it (by striking an average) as it never is at all. (*Euphorion,* 1:11)

Lee, like Pater, questions the authority of abstraction. To her, building one's judgment on such a precarious notion is like a false claim, a claim for universality from a merely human standpoint which has to be very limited as "we see only very little at the time" (*Euphorion,* 1:12). The habit of abstraction automatically suggests a tendency to categorize, rank, and judge a subject:

> This feeling is typical of our frame of mind towards various branches of the same art, and, indeed, towards all things which might be alike, but happen to be unlike. Times, countries, nations, temperaments, ideas, and tendencies, all benefit and suffer alternately by our habit of considering that if two things of one sort are not identical, one must be in the right and the other in the wrong. ("Tuscan Sculpture," *Renaissance Fancies,* 137)

Lee here reinforces her criticism in *Euphorion* wherein she faults scholarly methods of categorizing, contrasting, and comparing as too limiting since they "bring one side into full light and leave the other in darkness" (*Euphorion,* 2:224). In a shrewd argument bolstered by her remarkably detailed knowledge, Lee expounds that comparison does not clarify but rather obscures differences while automatically placing the compared subjects in a hierarchic relationship: "The act of comparison evokes at once our innate tendency to find fault; and having found fault, we rarely perceive that, on better comparing, there may be no fault at all to find" (*Renaissance Fancies,* 137). She dismisses such comparison as unhistorical. Why? To Lee, the implied value judgment that privileges certain civilizations or periods over others from an allegedly universal viewpoint "had the disadvantage of straining the characteristics of a civilization or of an art in order to tally with its product or producer" (139). Results obtained in this way have to be flawed since they omit all of those details that cannot be assigned to dominant categories and thus tell us less about the artwork itself than about the methods of modern scholars.

But how could she escape this epistemological closure in her own writing? For once, Lee constantly alerts her readers to the underlying assumptions in scholarly work, especially in the pervasiveness of binary opposites. Naturally, she cannot entirely avoid employing some of the most blatant ideological assumptions herself, yet she keeps pushing her readers toward an awareness of their own habits of thoughts. For instance, she enlists different intellectual positions, not merely to juxtapose them or to show the superiority of one over the other, but to let them modify one another in dialogues that are not arranged as arguments but as ongoing modifications, similar to musical rounds. With conversational ease she exposes what she considers to be faulty or limited positions without completely dismissing them. She moves through aestheticism, Darwinism, socialism, and Ruskinism in a citational manner, asserting her own voice through the dynamics of their frictions. Arguing for epistemological relativity, Lee questions the validity of absolutes.

Lee's nineteenth-century critics, however, misconstrued her intentions. Harriet Preston Waters, critiquing *Baldwin* (1886) for the *Atlantic Monthly,* called her method "backing away from victory" (59). Waters, a relentless and skeptical critic, describes Lee's technique accurately, but sees her departure from the rules as shortcoming rather than experiment: "Vernon Lee has not yet mastered the technique of synthesis. . . . [S]he enumerates, never unifies . . . giving no distinct idea or clear image to the reader."

Already in *Belcaro* (1881), Lee had borrowed different voices (from philosophy and science) to demonstrate that Ruskin's moral-theological reasoning of aesthetic questions was built on faulty assumptions. Using Kantian and Hegelian precepts, she disentangled moral and aesthetic to reveal the ideological limits of Ruskin's cause-effect theorem. She read Ruskin's evolutionary model of art and culture against itself, not necessarily to refute it, but to show the reasoning behind his judgment. She does not attack his argument at the outcome but at the construction level. By pushing back the assumed beginning ("germination") of the Renaissance into the Middle Ages, she removes the premise of Ruskin's reading of the degeneracy of the Renaissance against the morally superior Middle Ages. In this way, she can avoid the (in her eyes) incorrect antagonism of art and morality and frame the conflict as a question of origin, while at the same time holding on to her preferred evolutionary model of history. The uncertainty in the demarcation of time periods—Middle Ages and Renaissance—makes it difficult to regard them as absolutes, which is her point. Thus she can disagree with Ruskin's judgment without abandoning the evolutionary aspect, which she regarded as valid.

As this example shows, Lee was quite able to represent her different viewpoint convincingly even within the given structure of logical arguments. But she found it difficult to describe entirely new or less obvious perceptions and ideas in the available idioms. In the preface to her "idyll" *Ottilie* (1883), Lee complains about the writer's conventional confinement to particular genres for specific areas of inquiry, especially the "plight" of the essayist, "tied up in the narrow little stable of fact." Just like "the superior creature called a novelist," she claims, the essayist has "a certain love of character and incident and description, a certain tendency to weave fancies about realities," and yet, "essayists must not encroach on the novelist's ground" (8). Historical essays are not supposed to be written in a fictional manner if they are to be taken seriously. Yet she finds that imagination and literary invention can render history "all the more true for being imaginary":

> In studying any historical epoch, in trying to understand its temper and ways, there rise up before the unlucky Essayist vague forms of men and women whose names he does not know, whose parentage is obscure; in short who have never existed and who yet present him with a more complete notion of reality of the men and women of those times than any real, contradictory, imperfectly seen creatures for whose existence history will vouch. (*Ottilie,* 10–11)

In many of her historical portraits, Lee blends different narrative forms, with the effect that publishers put some of these "hybrid" pieces simultaneously among her historical essays and short stories. For instance, her sketch "Ravenna and Her Ghosts" was included in *Limbo and Other Essays* (1897) as well as in *Pope Jacynth and Other Fantastic Tales* (1904).

About two-thirds of Lee's oeuvre consists of essays—to use the term for preliminary convenience—but they vary so much in form, subject, and intention that the genre name becomes almost meaningless. Lee called her pieces anything from "fancy" to "dialogue" to "study." To group them, we might speak loosely of her historical essays as being distinct from her philosophical dialogues, which combine several viewpoints in a conversational tone. Lee's early essays, collected in *Studies of the Eighteenth Century in Italy, Belcaro,* and *Euphorion,* are modeled after continental and British historical writing from Michelet to Carlyle to Ruskin, while also reflecting Pater's impressionism. Lee, torn between the "scientific" demands of historiography and Pater's aesthetic approach, was never satisfied with her own writing. Her prefaces and afterwords reveal her self-conscious discontent with the limitations that form and method imposed on her intent.

"Neither fish, flesh, nor fowl," as she puts it in *Ottilie* (7), the essay has been considered a hybrid form in literary history. The handbooks direct us to its dual origins in Montaigne's philosophical "attempts" and Bacon's practical-utilitarian instructions. Seventeenth-century contributors, including Jonson, Milton, and Dryden, developed both formal and informal prototypes: sketch, dialogue, or argumentative address. In the late eighteenth century, with the expansion of journalism, the briefer periodical essay, designed to entertain as well as to inform, evolved alongside the formal "learned" treatise. Addison's terms "serious essay" and "occasional paper" mark the two poles of this development. The informal, autobiographically inclined essay played a significant role in the expansion of the periodical press that gave writers as diverse as De Quincey and Martineau a suitable forum for their witty, brief life sketches. The personal sketch could address a broad range of topics that did not require specialist training. It was therefore considered a "natural" medium for women writers. The essay's open-ended, non-linear, and often personal form—traditionally associated with the feminine—not only offered women new possibilities for writing, it also became the site for modernist experiments with new kinds of style.[8]

Surveys of the essay emphasize that its protean form was instrumental in opening and democratizing writing conventions in the nineteenth century. Fraser and Brown, for instance, describe the essay's "freedom from generic limits" as a natural expression of the intellectual anarchy of the time (12). They see its possibilities as "the Trojan horse that allowed women writers to enter the male preserve of professional writing" (20–21). Given that the genre had already become more versatile, it seems odd that Vernon Lee would advocate more flexibility for the essayist. Why, if the essay was such an adaptable genre, would Lee criticize its constraints on the writer?

We need to remind ourselves that the essay is a genre that developed its liberal form within a British context. The British reader was more accustomed to a conversational tone even within fields of scholarly expertise. On the Continent, especially in German historiography, which Lee was studying extensively, scholarly writing was still dominated by a fact-ridden, "pedantic" methodology that kept even the pioneer of cultural history, Jacob Burckhardt, on the margins of scholarship. Still, Lee's experience with German historiography alone cannot explain her concerns. While the variety in nineteenth-century nonfiction styles indicates a more diversified reading and writing public, we should not overlook the subtle hierarchy within the genre which was predicated by a shift in intellectual authority. It is true that the open form of the essay offered new possibilities for women and other nontraditional groups of writers, but presentations of knowledge were increasingly valorized to the extent that they complied with academic standards. Toward the end of the nineteenth century, journalism and dilettante writing were not ranked (and compiled for recirculation) in the same way as academic publications. Under

Arnold's influence, the "serious" essay, separated from the mere (literary) review essay, was elevated as a more professional genre through a firm rooting
in academic standards. The short review essay had advised the public what
books to read, but the formal, critical essay gradually replaced the book itself
in communicating new knowledge and telling audiences what to think. The
formal essay, different from the personal type, became more and more the site
of cultural authority dominated by academically trained experts and public
intellectuals who came from the ranks of the church, the professions, the
universities—all male-dominated institutions.

Vernon Lee, like other women essayists, lacked the weight of tradition,
community, or an academic institution. Although her readings were remarkably
extensive, she did not have the "cultural capital" (Bourdieu) of systematic training and the institutional (or national) power that lends public authority to the intellectual. Thus, her appeal for more genre flexibility draws attention to a double
standard in essay writing that separated academic from nonacademic styles, male
from female, as later attacked by Virginia Woolf in *A Room of One's Own*.

Twentieth-century literary history describes nonfictional prose largely as
a male domain, a view based purely on intellectual criteria developed by academic professionals. The books on Victorian prose by Holloway, Landow, and
Leavis accept these standards without questioning the grounds of their origin.
But recent studies of nonfictional genres—especially as they appeared in Victorian periodicals—have not only broadened the notions of genre but also revealed a much greater variety in the category of nonfiction. After all, as Carol
Christ points out, "to speak of nonfiction prose as a single category is something of a misnomer, in that the Victorians did not treat it as a distinct genre"
(23); nonfiction prose entered the canon in our century in the garb of "heroic
masculinity" unified by a college curriculum that had ensured the dominance
of a handful of "eminent" sage writers including Carlyle, Ruskin, and Arnold.
However, prompted by new studies of Victorian sage writing, journalism, and
other forms of nonfiction, scholars have compiled and made available a great
variety of prose writing within and without the academy that until recently
had been excluded and left unevaluated.[9]

The gendered categories which have shaped our understanding of literary
genres also feature a sociopolitical dimension. In the mid-nineteenth century,
when writing, like other commodities, had become subjected to the laws of the
expanding market, the role of the critic as mediator between artist and public

became crucial, as the critic's judgment could make or break a writer. Although we know now that Tuchman and Fortin's study, *Edging Women Out,* exaggerated the influence of men in setting literary standards, it is evident that women were met with varying degrees of skepticism depending on the discipline. Based on her extensive study of *Athenaeum* reviews from 1860 to 1900, Ellen Miller Casey has shown that gender stereotypes in novel reviews were becoming less rigid toward the end of the nineteenth century and "greatness" was no longer attached to sex (158). However, women were largely considered ignorant on subjects like the classics, law, politics, history, the army, university life, and so forth. In fact, criticism "was closely bound up with the presumption that each sex had its characteristic subjects" (156).

Women as a group were clearly absent from the executive level of the production and distribution system. In nineteenth-century Britain, the powerful machinery of publishing and editing was regulated almost exclusively by men (Sherry, 21). Successful writers had to stay in close contact with the agents of the big publishing houses, which also set the standards of writing. Most women, because of their domestic duties, generally could not afford to be away from their homes for too long, and thus often could not maintain valuable business contacts.[10] Especially when London became the center for the publishing industry, it was helpful for writers to stay close to the market and to maintain a steady network. Vernon Lee knew of these difficulties, but less for domestic than geographical reasons. Her busy social schedule—luncheons, teas, dinners, receptions, almost on a daily basis—was not simply a reflection of her upper-middle-class lifestyle but first and foremost a professional necessity. From 1881 on (the year she saw *Belcaro* through the press), she took annual trips to London to establish or rekindle important connections. We glean the tiresome toil of networking from her numerous letters to her mother that speak of financial worries, ailments, and fatigue. It was not until the end of the century that the picture changed and aspiring writers came to see *her* for advice and introductory letters at her villa Il Palmerino near Florence.[11]

Even though the nineteenth-century book market did not clearly separate male and female novelists, there are reasons to believe that essay writing remained a more masculine genre. The essay was understood to employ worldly experience, wisdom, and contemplation, none of which were usually expected from the way a woman's life was organized. Like the bildungsroman, the essay was considered the site for the expression of the writer's actual experience to be translated into observations on life in general. The "universal" voice exuded an authority which established itself as a given standard. Because of women's different status in the social and the symbolic order, identification with such a universal viewpoint was problematic. Theirs had to be an assumed position, a situation that created what feminist critique has called a "split vision." The female essayist had to write against herself, especially since the auctorial voice in this genre derived its authority from an assumed union of knowledge and discourse (Christ, 29). This, in a sense, makes the essay more "masculine" than, say, the novel, wherein experience can be rendered through a variety of voices and other narrative factors.

As Joeres and Mittman remind us in *The Politics of the Essay: Feminist Perspectives,* the essay "was not to all intents and purposes within the woman writer's domain for the first three hundred years of its existence as a genre, and those women who chose the form in the last century did so within a decidedly patriarchal context" (16). Even if the form of the essay arguably became more "feminized" in the nineteenth century, most of the subject areas reflected masculine domains: for "the whole of the century disciplines such as history, Classics, science, philosophy and theology were mainly the preserve of men" (Fraser and Brown, 20). However, the era's propensity for intellectual relativism did also exert an influence on the gender politics of the literary genres:

> If at the beginning of the century Coleridge's presuppositional that "Women . . . rarely or never thoroughly distinguish between fact and fiction" was tenable, much literature produced as the century progressed, such as that by Pater and Landor, could be described by the words in which Coleridge described the feminine form of the modern novel, as a "jumble of the two." (20–21)

Because of the assumed "feminization" of the essay, genealogies of this genre often mask its masculine lineage, which Joel Haefner's "dual father theory" addresses (258–73). The father system assimilated the personal (feminine) traits into its own self-division. From the Romantic to the late-Victorian period, male-dominated literary forms increasingly absorbed what was traditionally called the feminine element, but without actually becoming accessible to women. Until well into the nineteenth century, essay writing was somewhat elitist in terms of gender and social class, that is, it was performed by a small group of highly educated men (Joeres and Mittman, 13). Virginia Woolf's "The Modern Essay" calls attention to the thorough masculinization of the genre, although she may have stretched the point to accentuate her own feminist position.[12] If we follow Woolf's account, it seems that it was not until the end of the nineteenth century that women staked their own claim in this literary form.[13]

Female essayists were often exposed to male condescension and paternalistic pedantry. As we have seen, J. A. Symonds's letters to "Violet Paget" are full of hypercritical corrections, and similarly, Karl Hillebrand's revisions of *Ottilie* impose the pedantic standards of German scholarship. Symonds speaks to Lee from the position of an angered father whose precocious child should be less "cocksure" about herself (which in fact Symonds himself is here):

> I feel that you imagine yourself to be so clever that every thing you think is either right or else valuable. And your way of expressing yourself is so uncompromising that your belief in yourself grates upon my sense of what is just and dignified. . . . I am the very last to conceive that any one should withhold his opinion from the world, or (what is in my eyes a sin) should make concession to age, established reputation, & the like. Yet there is a certain grave and measured way of expressing difference with accepted wisdom, a certain caution and reserve in asserting our own opinions, especially when these had not stood the test of a lifetime, and I have always been sorry to see you miss [ . . . ] I cannot help thinking you would be really greater and more effective, if you were (to use a vulgar phrase) less cocksure about a heap of things. (4 April 1884, Colby)[14]

Few critics have studied the subject of women and essays from a feminist perspective. Virginia Woolf may be the first one to have done so, expressing her uneasiness as a female essayist and her ambivalence toward her metier. In her diaries, she often describes fiction writing as her real work (her art) and her essays, which she saw merely as paid work, as a distraction from it. Closely observing Bloomsbury standards, she placed the art of fiction above the essay's prose. Not unlike Lee, Woolf experimented with both of these literary forms. *The Years,* for instance, was first meant to be a mixture of essay and fiction, and *A Room of One's Own* delivers an argument as fiction.

Woolf is critical of essays displaying too much of a domineering voice, which she often associated with the male-ego.[15] Such essays, she says, allow the reader to indulge in personal egoism and speculation which would be out of

place elsewhere. Since essayists need not really know anything about their subject, they make the text a forum of "I think," "I feel" without meaning it:

> Confronted with the terrible spectre of themselves, the bravest are inclined
> to run away or shade their eyes. And thus, instead of the honest truth which
> we should all respect, we are given timid side-glances in the shape of essays,
> which, for the most part, fail in the cardinal virtue of sincerity. ("Decay of
> Essay-Writing," 7)

As a modernist, Woolf praises Pater's "pure" style, which brings before the
reader a vision of his subject as a whole through the form of his material alone
("Modern Essay," 42). Woolf, too, directs the reader toward her subject and
away from herself. She discards the authorial "I" and replaces it by the communal "we" that connects her ideal of the disinterested voice with the community of
"common readers," a term that should not delude us about its exclusiveness in
Bloomsbury usage.

Woolf's apparently self-effacing aesthetics coincides with her avoidance of
the "carping female." She feared that women's self-conscious presence would
reinstate the stereotype that women were unserious writers. To avoid this re-
direction into femininity, Woolf withdraws her voice from the subject position
and shifts the task of signification to her material. But her detachment is not
without problems. As Deborah Pope pointed out, the feminist denial of "self"
would be translated in the rhetoric of the universal subject as the nonfemale
(and therefore, male), and she would forfeit woman's chance of showing her
face ("Notes toward a Supreme Fiction," 27).[16]

I have made this excursus on Virginia Woolf as essayist because she was one
of Vernon Lee's most outspoken critics despite their obvious similarities. She resented Lee's uncontrolled language flow and untidiness, particularly her un-
veiled subjectivity. On Lee's *The Sentimental Traveller* Woolf writes in 1908:

> Her method then, so far as the portrait of the place is concerned, is purely im-
> pressionist, for if she were to concentrate her mind upon the task of seeing
> any object as exactly as it can be seen there would be no time for these egotis-
> tical diversions. (*Essays,* 1:157)

And on Lee's *Art and Life* (1909): "images and symbols, unless they spring from
a profound understanding, illustrate not the object but the writer" (279). Woolf's

criticism reflects her discomfort with women's self-consciousness. Obviously, she sees Lee's subjectivity as emulation of an egocentrism which modernist aesthetic tried to neutralize through an unmarked, "androgynous" viewpoint dissipated in different parts of speech. It is interesting that Woolf's criticism of Lee is rendered in almost the exact words that Victorian critics had chosen to describe Pater's style.[17] But Pater is not on Woolf's "blacklist." On the contrary: she considers him the precursor of pure modernist style. Does Bloomsbury aesthetics win out over her feminist zeal to establish a literary tradition for women? For the Bloomsbury writers, who tried to distance themselves from overwrought Victorian morality and exhausting elaboration in order to establish a purely aesthetic form of writing, Lee's Victorian barrage embodied the tradition from which the modernists wanted to divorce themselves. Woolf thus picked on Lee's Victorian leanings but failed to take note of her irony, with which she distanced herself from the self-centeredness of her peers, as in her sarcastic essay "Nietzsche and the Will to Power" (*Gospels of Anarchy*).

The discord between Lee and Woolf is best understood as a conflict between two generations of women writers, which means that the older generation of women still had to assert itself against a tradition which the later generation no longer had to confront. Carol Smith-Rosenberg gives a plausible explanation of the generation conflict between Victorian and modernist feminists in "The Body Politic."

> As the New Women of the 1920's and 1930's developed their new discourse, they divested themselves of older female-rooted discourses, those of Victorian matrons and of the first generation of New Women. The older discourses, by their specific attacks upon male power and by their very separateness, had affirmed women's political solidarity and the uniqueness of women's experiences. Ceasing to speak with these older female words, the New Women of the 1920's lost their ability to speak with the older women. The political solidarity of the successive generations of New Women slipped away. (120)

While Woolf positioned herself as a feminist in rebellion against her paternal history, she also distanced herself from Victorian womanhood. This implies that she saw in Lee too much of a Victorian, and too little of a woman writer struggling with that tradition herself. Thus it will be useful to take a closer look at Lee's own strikes at the "male ego" and her assertion of an alternative subjectivity.

# 4 Literary Form and Alternative Subjectivity

## THE VOICES OF THE WOMAN WRITER

Lee's theoretical texts deliver their messages in an interesting overlay of individual and general voice using the common "we" or "one," by which she could pass as a male writer.[1] The question for us is how innovative or subversive discourses can be recognized as such or if they become pointless once they can be read in the familiar terms. The complex dialectics of innovation and tradition, famously addressed by T. S. Eliot, became a central issue in modern critical theories. What we can carry away from this discussion is our awareness of the relationality between old and new, same and other: "an invention always engages closely with cultural practices and systems as it deforms or disjoins them" (Attridge, 23). Applied to the area of critique, innovation—specifically feminist innovation—cannot, as Rita Felski says,

> occur outside ideological and social structures in some privileged space, but constantly interacts with the very frameworks it challenges. The current equation of social and symbolic structures with phallocentrism and of the feminine with the marginal is unable to conceptualize adequately feminist practices, which cannot be seen as either authentically "feminine" or as passive reflection of existing patriarchal structures, but rather engaged in a much more complex appropriation, revision, and development of existing cultural frameworks. (*Beyond Feminist Aesthetics,* 59)

76

Evidently, Lee keeps a dynamic critical potential alive in her texts by neither claiming a position outside authorized discourses nor simply adopting them. Her subjectivity is not expressed but rather *performed* as just another possibility. This subjectivity is intangible at times and yet the driving force in her text. It is not stable, but moving. And it keeps suggesting, as Stephen Greenblatt has put it, "that it could all have been otherwise" (60).[2] Lee circumvents absorption in a male-defined discourse, most obviously in the way she represents gender or sexuality. Reacting to the increasingly gendered polarizations of her time, she assumes the perspective of the generally human, "Homo, der Mensch" (in "The Economic Parasitism of Women"). Her references to male or female as collective identity are seldom specific, or rather, given the pervasive gendered idiom of the time, conspicuously absent.

Late-nineteenth-century England, having been exposed to the influences of French symbolism, decadence, and the emerging psycho-medical discourses, found its literary language to be more openly sexual than in earlier years. This new sexual language was defined by the men who ran the institutions where it became fashionable. Autonomous female subjectivity began to be linked more often with sexuality claimed by New Women writers from Olive Schreiner to George Egerton to Sarah Grand, whose fiction was typically banished from "high" art as being too sexual.[3] But since the categories of sex and gender answered to the dominant heterosexual system of representation, women's use of sexual language seldom worked in their favor. For contemporary male critics, the female writers' concern with sexuality was often seen as evidence of their tendency to focus on particularities rather than on abstract or universal issues. Just how alarming the emphasis on sexuality was can be seen, for instance, in Henry James's criticism of Vernon Lee's novel *Miss Brown,* in which, he felt, she had vested the aesthetic movement with too much sexual motivation.

The structure of literary discourses produced a "no win" situation for women writers. If they chose to retain female identity, they would implicitly renounce their (male) potential of producing works of force and value. Therefore, many nineteenth-century women writers were reluctant to speak of sexuality. As Ann Ardis has shown, there also emerged besides the eroticized New Woman fiction a kind of asexual feminist discourse, which split the political from the sexual. But the female writer's escape into a language of "sexual (in)difference" (de Lauretis)[4] led, as in Woolf's genealogy of the essay, to the effacement of female difference.

Against this background, it becomes more understandable why Vernon Lee would sound almost "puritan" when speaking of sexual allusions in literature, especially in what Buchanan called the "fleshly school of poetry." She attacked writers like Baudelaire, Swinburne, Gautier, Maupassant, and Zola as unartistic, an argument which oddly echoes the contemporary criticism of New Woman fiction. Baudelaire's poetry appeared particularly "dangerous" to her (and other Victorians) because she found that he misused the freedom of art to promote selfish masculine yearnings veiled as a new aesthetic form. Aware of the manipulative power that writers have over their readers, she feared that the hidden lure in some decadent writing would corrupt the unconscious layers of the readers' psyche.

Lee's indignant attacks on the "mystico-sensual" school of writers made it difficult for her to sustain her argument of the separateness of morality and art, which is the basis of her essays in *Belcaro* and *Euphorion*. So she resorts to the *ut pictura poesis* debate by distinguishing between visual and verbal art. In "A Dialogue on Poetic Moralism" (*Belcaro*), one of her characters argues: "I have always laughed at the Ruskinian idea of morality or immorality in architecture, or painting, or music, and said that their morality and immorality were beauty and ugliness. . . . But with poetry the case is different" (249–50). Her argument seems somewhat strained here. The reader senses that she is not able to justify her dislike of decadent art in the monolithic abstractions of "art" and "morality." While she could temporarily evade this polarization in her historical argument, it remained an issue in her criticism and fiction.

Sexuality in Lee's texts, as in Victorian literature generally, is highly coded. She sometimes indulges in surprisingly sensual descriptions, as in "Lombard Colour Studies" (*Juvenilia*), when the context is "safe," that is, when sensuality can be channeled into nature or landscape.[5]

Lee's cautious use of sexual references serves to set her apart from the hedonist side of aestheticism. She was critical of those aesthetic artists who countered moral uses of art—typically associated with the Victorians—by turning art into exclusively a domain of pleasure. She had little patience with writers who had abandoned their moral servitude to God without taking moral responsibility as individuals and who, instead, had made themselves into gods.[6] What she resented most was the "arrogant perception" of self-centered artists erecting their egos as universal points of reference. To Lee, the obsession with the sexual in literature is only one reflection of the "unhealthy" distortion of the male ego elevated into universal law. She finds such distortions, for instance, in Nietzsche whom she accuses en passant of selfishly turning his contempt for humanity into his own philosophy. Pater, who for her "began as an aesthete, and ended as a moralist" (*Renaissance Fancies,* 255), is singled out as a positive example for having made the transition from "an aesthete of the very narrow sense" to "a teacher of self-discipline and self-harmony" (256).

Lee's critique implies the difference between what Reginia Gagnier has called "engaged" and "decadent" aesthetics. Whereas the "engaged" kind of aestheticism can become an aspect of liberational politics, the "decadent" kind (which Lee named hedonism) insists on the separation of art from life practice, thus denying social responsibility. Lee condemns any "school" that advertises self-interest under aestheticism. At the same time, she reclaims from aestheticism its value as a socially and politically responsible discourse.

Lee's equation of self-centered aesthetic discourse and sexual motivation is thematized especially in her fiction, where masculine desire is the motif for possession, knowledge, or other forms of control. She sees sexual attraction not as essential biological function, but rather as an interaction of uncontrollable forces aroused by gender images operating as visual and sensual stimuli. She repeatedly sketches images of womanhood as constructions of male minds, thus altering the trope of the dangerous woman into that of the "unknown" woman, who has so far been defined only through her relationship to man. As she explains in "The Economic Parasitism of Women":

> For one of the paradoxes of this most paradoxical question is precisely that, with all our literature about *La Femme* . . . we do not really know what women are. Women, so to speak, as a natural product, as distinguished from women as a creation of men; for women, hitherto, have been as much a creation of men as the grafted fruit tree, the milch cow, or the gelding who spends six hours in pulling a carriage, and the rest of the twenty-four hours standing in the stable. (294)

This characterization, of course, portrays the situation of the middle-class woman whose confinement to idleness became an issue for many nineteenth-century feminists, prominently described in Florence Nightingale's *Cassandra.* If middle-class men defined themselves through their work, their profession, why shouldn't women? Applying a utilitarian definition of the human subject as "homo economicus," Lee has to infer that no one can know what women are. Consequently, she does not need to get involved in the contemporary argument of woman's nature but rather explores the historical conditions under which women's roles are constructed.

By stressing the relationality of gender images, Lee alleges that men's fragmentary vision of women also prevents men from recognizing their own identity, for woman "is made in the image of man." But if she is only a part of man, she cannot be his mirror of recognition. Consequently, Lee's male characters cannot fully understand themselves since they cannot know the female, that is, perceive woman in other than man's terms. She wonders (in the "Introductory" to *Althea*) whether "we can know even ourselves only very slightly; for knowledge means comparison; and what is there to compare with?" Women cannot know themselves, as they can only be compared to men, and men, for lack of a true counterpart, are precluded from acquiring any knowledge of themselves through narcissistic self-mirroring. "Hence, we naturally imagine that everything is made for us, and that everything not made for us . . . must be made in our image"—she notes sarcastically (*Althea,* xiii). Her use of "we" is ambivalent here. In the second quotation, she speaks as the male subject, and her words can be read as an assumed self-assertion of "man." She implies that male subjectivity will remain incomplete and searching and will lead to such "despair of men like Byron and Baudelaire" as long as it draws only upon itself. She sees "the aridity of spiritual egoists, knowing no soul except their own, like Pascal" as the result of wearing themselves out "in the solitude of ambition" (xvi). Under these conditions, human identity must remain incomplete and can be nothing else than the worship of only one side of the male ego set up as the universal subject.

In a Lacanian sense, Lee sees the male ego as a delusion, an imaginary construction, which constitutes the ideal "I" in a unified subject she sees as the (faulty) "modus operandi" by which the world is interpreted and ruled.

> Because, so far as I can see, it is not sufficiently admitted that it is also the modus operandi of most grown-up so-called civilized folk, and has been of all established religions. There is nothing in the world but me, nothing at least of any importance, that is the beginning; nothing not for me, is the next step; nothing not like me; whence class arrangements, domestic and international morality, and the desire to reduce all persons to the same conduct and opinions. (xiv)

According to Lee, knowledge can be meaningful only if it is not self-centered or homogenous but an exchange between self and others. She illustrates this in her character Althea, who embodies the "serenity of satisfaction with one's own . . . powers and opportunities of happiness extended to others." Althea represents an alternative for the agonized modern (male) individual since, "never making any claims for herself," she will "never go through the disappointment which underlies most Weltschmerz" (xvii).

Althea can be read as Vernon Lee's ideal of her writerly self, the generally human ("genus homo") which, contrary to tradition, Lee locates in a female personage. She is not interested in yet another definition of "woman"; rather, she dismantles traditional assumptions *about* "woman." For that purpose, she dramatizes identifiable intellectual positions, playing them off against each other in a citational mode to organize a new consciousness and maybe another potential subject. In "The Economic Parasitism of Women," for example, Lee "translates" Charlotte Perkins Stetson's (Gilman's) *Women and Economics* for a European audience by expressing her thoughts in the contemporary terms of intellectual male authorities: Darwin, Durkheim, Marx, Michelet. Through her mimicry of male voices—ironically reflected in the term "parasitism"—Lee gives clout to Gilman's (female) viewpoint, which she apparently supports. But she builds her argument by exposing the foibles of the male discourses she cites. In this witty article, Lee declares her advocacy of the Woman Question, but we cannot be sure whether she really speaks as a feminist or merely uses the Woman Question as another exercise in her rhetorical repertoire. How, indeed, are we to relate the term "feminist" to Vernon Lee?

## VERNON LEE: A FEMINIST?

The term "feminist" needs some explication. Along with "female" and "feminine," or the more inclusive "gender," it has become a central category in modern criticism. Feminism requires constant redefinition or reconceptualization because of its roots in active political struggle. As we have come to realize, "feminist" marks a plethora of heterogeneous positions and coalitions. Cora Kaplan's well-known distinctions between humanist feminism, socialist feminism, and psychoanalytical and semiotical feminisms (*Sea Changes*, 149–50) have long been expanded by the voices of women of color, Chicana, Third-World, and "generation

X" feminists. Aware of its diverse subjects, modern feminist criticism distances itself from its origins in the white middle classes who promoted the Woman Question at the turn of the century and again in the 1960s. The smallest common
denominator of the different feminist approaches may be Toril Moi's definition of
feminists: "As politically motivated critics, feminists will try to make the political
context and implications of their work explicit, precisely in order to counter the
tacit acceptance of patriarchal power politics which is so often presented as intellectual 'neutrality' or 'objectivity'" ("Feminist, Female, Feminine," 117). Moi dis-
entangles a multitude of similar expressions that are not always clearly
distinguished. Thus she differentiates "between 'feminism' as a political position,
'femaleness' as a matter of biology and 'femininity' as a set of culturally defined
characteristics" (117). I will adopt her definition of feminism as a working term
that certainly needs modification, not only to do justice to Moi's complex analysis,
but also to avoid imposing a fixed methodological set on Vernon Lee.

Feminist writing implies the assumption of an anti-patriarchal and anti-
sexist position, which involves a certain consciousness of female subjectivity, an
awareness of the historical construction of sex and gender relationships, including one's own participation in them, and a desire for change. A feminist position
that sets itself against a male-based unified subject needs to present itself in terms
that may imply incoherence, inconsistency, multiplicity. But today, feminists
have moved away from any simple notions of male subjectivity because they
found themselves only corroborating the binary structures in which subject
building occurs. After all, subjectivity enters the cultural text as an imagined concept that exerts control. Acknowledging the different historical trajectories of
men and women, feminists are moving away from the postmodern denial of subjectivity toward a definition of different *kinds* of subjectivities "shaped by a historically specific set of interrelations between socio-economic conditions and
ideological and cultural processes" (Felski, *Beyond Feminist Aesthetics,* 60). As Felski
sees it, female identity is a necessary but not a sufficient condition for feminist
consciousness, which also involves an awareness of the possibility for change.
Subject transformation is a major site of political change, which cannot occur
outside individual consciousness but, in order to be politically effective, also must
involve public manifestations.

Since feminist literary criticism has paid little attention to Vernon Lee, it
might be interesting to investigate her relationship to the women's movement.
Lee's first explicit statement on the Woman Question occurs in her essay "The

Economic Dependence of Women" (1902).[7] Lee's essay is singular in her work in addressing explicitly a feminist issue unmediated through a fictional voice.[8] She confesses her former reluctance to address the "Woman Question," precisely because it *is* the Woman Question that singles out women from the "genus homo." But she admits that Gilman's book, *Women and Economics: A Study in Economic Relations Between Men and Women as a Factor of Social Evolution* (1898) has made her a "convert" because it points to the socioeconomic and, therefore, man-made construction of woman through her sex.[9] Lee expressly separates her opposition to the "Woman Question" from the general arguments by male adversaries. Her hostility to the question stems from the term "woman," which reduces the female to a nonhuman species; she argues that

> the inevitable harping on what can or cannot be done by women, because they are not men . . . produces a special feeling . . . due to the one fact sex, while the other fact of human nature, the universal, chaste fact represented by the word Homo as distinguished from mere Vir and Femina seemed for a moment lost sight of. (*Gospels,* 266)

In this essay Lee draws on her studies in aesthetics, literature, anthropology, and political economy to investigate the positioning of woman in society. Like Gilman, she argues that the Woman Question can be settled only in conjunction with the economic question, that is, by addressing the injustices inflicted upon social groups by a system that privileges personal property over the common good. Lee enters the women's rights debate from a socialist position of sorts, blaming gender inequity on the double standards created by the complicity between capitalism and its most outdated institution, marriage.[10]

Lee shares Gilman's anthropological approach which implies that the education of human offspring takes longer than that of other species. This means that woman is tied up at home for an excessive amount of time during which she cannot support herself, so that her livelihood becomes the responsibility of the male species. Economic necessity thus is constructed ideologically as a system of ownership, most notably in the concept of the "Father," meaning the supporter and owner of woman and children. In the nineteenth century, however, education was largely assigned to the government so that woman is condemned to "semi-idleness." She becomes an economic "parasite" exempt from competition and social selection.

Lee turns around Emile Durkheim's theory of the gradual degeneration of the female brain to show that woman's alleged regression has not been caused naturally but by social circumstances. Lee prides herself that she does not even have to speak from a woman's standpoint because the evidence emerges directly from the (male) theories:

> For, to such readers as have reason (perhaps owing to their superior knowledge) for giving much weight to similar statements about prehistoric civilizations; and to such readers also as feel that the fact of having possessed any particular desideratum in the past constitutes a better claim to its possession in the future, to both these classes of readers, it must be much more satisfactory to be assured of the original and primeval importance of womankind by M. Durkheim . . . than to take it on the authority of Mrs. Stetson herself, who, of course may be suspected of partiality. (274)

Her sarcastic remark that her use of a man's evidence releases her from the suspicion of partiality also reveals the bias of Durkheim's argument. Lee shrewdly plays off one male scientist against the other: she refutes Durkheim in Darwin's terms by demonstrating that women's so-called degeneration is the result of their adaptation to the limited and dependent status in the service of a single man.

From an economic standpoint, Lee explains, women's limitation is wasteful, depriving "the whole race" of a valuable work force. Women's confinement to domesticity—for which being female seems to be the only qualification—excludes them from professional competition and therefore from developing skills useful for the national economy. Thus, the progress of the whole nation is curbed because only half of its potential workers are gainfully employed. The maldistribution of human work and wealth creates within the community a double standard of "virtuous egoism and rapacity." Outside the home, man has to be greedy because, as "a good father," he has to make enough money for the family. The (middle-class) woman has to keep a certain standard of appearance to create the impression that the husband's business is flourishing, which means that she has to ask him for more and more money. In so doing she cooperates with a system that maintains her economic parasitism. Lee's argument is not altogether new. The idleness of the middle-class woman was first addressed by Mary Wollstonecraft and became a public issue in the latter half of the nineteenth century. The clash of community and individual interest which Lee emphasizes here was also an argument in Bebel's *Women in the Past, Present, and Future* (1885), which had great influence on British feminists, and among the New Women, such as Mona Caird, who did, however, distrust a radical socialist solution. What is new in Lee's argument is, first, that she brings together different arguments of the Woman Question, especially the construction of "woman" in the complex relationships between economic, social, national, and aesthetic forces. Second, she applies a rhetorical strategy which, unlike the teleological proclivity of contemporary feminist activism, does not speak of what *woman* would gain through emancipation, but how *man* would benefit from it. Lee presents the economic advantages from a male point of view and thus lends her argument the relevance that, as she claims, a woman's voice was not granted at the time.

Lee's clever argument comforts even those who fear a moral decline brought about by women's emancipation. Equality with men need not deprive women of their femaleness—including such traits as unselfishness—because this side has already been inscribed in the form of "general human virtues," for instance, in Christianity. What women will lose, though, is their exclusively sexual role, defined in relation to men. Whereas men can relate to one another in different capacities—as comrades, competitors, enemies—women's relationship to men is limited to the sexual identity. By detaching "femaleness" from sex, Lee clears the path for change. Economic independence will change woman's existence but not necessarily make her less attractive to man. Because of the relationality of gender, Lee prophetically assures her readers, "those men will change, too" (295). If it can be assumed that woman is not an invariable sexual type, man need no longer be afraid of those "men-destroying monsters [who] do everything to make themselves agreeable" (Ruskin's words, which Lee uses as epigraph for her essay). Sexuality may change its character altogether when women become economically independent and no longer have to capture a providing male through their sexual powers. Lee traces the image of woman as "oversexed" from the story of Eve to female characters in the modern French novel as expression of man's guilty desire projected onto the perpetual vision of La Femme. The very qualities of womanhood which the opponents of emancipation would like to preserve are also the ones which constitute her "evilness."

By turning again to Darwin, Lee shows that cultural adaptation, *not* natural constraints, have kept women out of the process of social selection. Thus nobody can know (yet) what women "really" are, and they remain "the last scientific survival of the pre-Darwinian belief in the invariability of types" (295). Lee compares women to organisms that develop by constantly adapting to their cultural environment. For instance, the "masculine" Englishwoman is an assimilated complement to the "out-of-door, athletic, sporting, colonising Englishman," whereas "the ultra-feminine woman belonged, quite naturally, to the effeminate (French) man" (296). As wife, daughter, sister, and companion, woman is required to be "not unlike but like himself." And so there is a "family resemblance, after all, between the men and women of the same country" (295). Lee links aesthetics with Darwinian notions of "change, of adaptation, of evolution" to show that gender is a cultural (national) construction and not an "eternal type." Again, her own experience ("living, as I do equally among Latins and Anglo-Saxons"), qualifies her to speak on this issue. Gender, Lee argues, is not an immovable category but like national identity, an aspect of human behavior shaped by the "habits and preferences" of certain civilizations. Thus Lee's rhetoric moves a cultural category like gender from a metaphysical into a historical frame of reference.

"The Economic Parasitism of Woman" shows Lee to some extent as a feminist. Like many socialist feminists, she challenges the naturalness of sex, gender, and class distinction. But she differs from them, first, by including the family as an important suture between private and public functions of gender; second, by not simply assimilating the "Woman Question" into the social question (as the Fabians did) but by revealing their mutual complicity; and third, by complicating social and gender categories by adding a national dimension that the international thrust of socialism would not acknowledge.

In general, Lee uses a detached, "universal" voice in order to convince a larger, potentially critical audience of her argument. Only once does she stray from her slightly ironic position to become the angry female. When accusing French novelists of presenting their own version of woman as "eternal" type, Lee appears overly indignant and a little too absorbed in national bias herself, claiming

> it is these selfsame Latin countries, with all their filthy talk about *La Femme,* her ailments and powers, who bore us Anglo-Saxons almost equally with their talk about the miraculous virtues of *La Mère,* who is, after all only *La Femme* . . . well, as the Latins would put it, when she is too old or too busy to be *La Femme.* (292)

The passage on French writers from Dumas fils to Michelet shows her talent for satire, but it is also the least convincing part in her otherwise clever argument. After finding important leads to connect women's aesthetic representation with their socioeconomic position, she does not follow them to conclusion. She convincingly prepares the ground with pointed questions and arguments, but then dissolves them aesthetically, in an androgynous vision of sameness:

> [L]et me remind Mrs. Stetson's readers that it is just the most aesthetic, but also the most athletic and the most intellectual people of the past which has left us those statues of gods and goddesses in the presence of whose marvellous vigour and loveliness we are often in doubt whether to give the name of Apollo, or that of Athena. (296–97)

Admittedly, Lee never claims to "solve" the Woman Question: "By what arrangements do you expect to make the wife the economic equal of her husband, the joint citizen of the community? I propose nothing, because I do not know" (292). Consistent with her surmise that we cannot *know* what women *are,* she refuses to speak of concrete feminist goals "because the practical detail depends upon other practical details which the continuance of the present state of things is hiding from us, or even forbidding" (292). And since woman can only be known "as a creation of man," that is, in images, the best solution Lee can offer us is to (dis)place the Woman Question in the realm of aesthetics where woman can at least be re-imagined.

Returning to my initial question as to whether we can regard Vernon Lee as a feminist, I am still hesitant to do so. If we understand feminism as a political form of consciousness-raising from a "discernible anti-patriarchal and anti-sexist position" (Moi), we must deny that Lee reveals such political concern. In her cultural and historical criticism, the Woman Question is not a key issue, and even in "The Economic Parasitism of Women" she turns the political issue into an aesthetic one.

Could we then say that Lee "lived" feminism more than she expounded it? Interested exclusively in a literary career, Lee rejected marriage as anachronism, not unlike many New Women novelists of the period. Since she had the support of her mother's income, marriage was not an economic necessity either. Financially, she did not even have to rely on her writing, which she yet pursued with great seriousness. In her mobility and exclusive devotion to her profession, Lee's life resembled that of many male writers of her time. Her biography challenges the gender-based division of labor and reflects the image that many Victorians had of the independent, "mannish" New Woman. But from the feminist debates, rampant in the periodicals around the turn of the century, Vernon Lee is noticeably absent. Likewise, we will look in vain for her name in the lists of New Women.[11]

Is there a connection between Vernon Lee's omission from literary history and her absence from contemporary feminist debates? Or is her reluctance to speak on the Woman Question a manifestation of a feminism on her own terms? In *The Forgotten Female Aesthetes,* Talia Schaffer has analyzed the strained relationship between feminism, New Women, and female aesthetes. I agree with her in that, "with the best of intentions," feminist critics have too narrowly applied modern terms to the complex area of late-Victorian gender politics: "In hunting for feminists, nonfeminist genres get erased so completely that readers may not even know they are missing" (11).

We know that Lee was not unsympathetic to women's causes. She instructed working-class girls and spoke in favor of women's right to vote. She shrank from the suffragettes' militant methods but still defended women's right to vote as a historical necessity:

> For the vote . . . even if used badly or not at all, is the recognition that the times are gone by when it was opportune that women, like Milton's Eve, should live for God through Man—a mode of life definable in un-Miltonian prose as parasitic and irresponsible. ("Why I Want Women to Have a Vote," 2)[12]

But Lee was critical of women who modeled themselves too closely on male styles. Her goal was to transcend gender divisions in a "generally human" position, an ideal which she saw threatened when women drew too much attention to gender, which Lee saw less as a category by itself than as a factor partaking in other cultural structures. Gender, according to Lee, had to be treated as a coincidence to keep it from becoming a fixed position. Thus she believed that the discussions about the "Woman Question" that meant to challenge the limitations of gender instead seemed to make them even more manifest. By separating "woman" from the universal subject, she found that contemporary culture allowed women only limited authority, which made it difficult for her to speak as "woman" while addressing the "generally human." Lee refused to split men and women essentially apart and rather emphasized their common interests within a larger community. As she sees it, the struggle is not between men and women but rather between "men and women of the future against men and women of the past." Still, she acknowledges that women also "have a certain number of interests special to themselves, and occasionally conflicting with those of men," but in general, she finds "men and women . . . more intimately and completely connected than serf and owner" (1).

While Lee may not have been an active participant in the women's movements, we find that her arguments reflect and interact with feminist and liberal contemporary thought. Aware of cultural gender imbalances, she was interested in exploring the entrapments of both genders, not through political activism but rather as an intellectual exercise. Feminist criticism, which for most of the twentieth century pursued questions of patriarchal oppression and feminist resistance, has not shown much interest in Lee's feminist "agnosticism."

Nevertheless, it is important to study Vernon Lee also in a feminist context, since a recognition of her place in a something other than a male genealogy is long overdue. From her first book, *Studies of the Eighteenth Century in Italy,* she was evaluated as a somewhat lesser man of letters and measured by the standards of her peers in historiography and aesthetics. For most of the twentieth century, her literary identity was framed or mediated by a male-defined canon whose validity has become the target of feminist and other criticisms in recent years.

Lee was aware of the Victorian division of intellectual labor and reacted to the situation by attaching to her books lengthy introductions that set her up as an informed but critical authority to speak of intellectual traditions and to show that there is room for a different approach—her own. Thus we should treat these "frames" as integral parts of her main texts, as they provide the readers with the lens necessary for recognizing the "virtus dormitiva" of an alternative, female or even feminist subtext, in other words, a map for less obvious implications. The critics' delay in recognizing Lee's different voice shows that our explanatory tools have not sufficiently opened her texts thus far. Lee does not assimilate her voice to the available versions of identity—neither to the unified subject of liberal humanism nor to the "special" interest of woman—but rather seeks to promote an awareness of different options. In Julia Kristeva's terms, Lee constructs "the stranger within," that is, an identity that faces its alterity, difference, and otherness (289–90). What has often been read as Lee's lack of categorial clarity may now be understood as her way of sustaining her intellectual and historical uniqueness, which meant establishing the legitimacy of difference, not leveling it. The most obvious literary form for this goal would become her dialogic essays, *Baldwin* and *Althea*.

## TOWARD ALTERNATIVE SUBJECTIVITY: FROM *BALDWIN* TO *ALTHEA*

Vernon Lee never wrote an autobiography, but her books abound with personal memories framed as historical or philosophical studies. She writes about her own history as she would about any historical topic: in terms of the people who lived it. With the acute sensibility and observation of her own psychological and intellectual experiences, she achieves a remarkable fusion of personal and general history. In the dialogue, she found a form that would match the complexity of her subject. The dialogue—favored among her contemporaries from Landor to Wilde—enabled her to explore issues inconclusively without being forced to reduce them to the textual conformity publishers demanded. In her introductions, she goes to great length to explain why the speakers should be read as different voices of her mind. These fairly abstract personages, which are yet not types but individuals, combine internal and external, intellectual and emotional aspects without settling for a fixed identity.

The introduction to *Baldwin* can be read as a scarcely veiled autobiographical account of Lee's writerly self. Baldwin, her literary double, is addressed as a friend "on the borderline between fact and fancy." His persona (and Lee's) evolves from an amalgamation of history, education, gender, and the "genius of the place," to use one of her own prominent terms. The result is a somewhat exteriorized character study, made up of loose impressions, rather than a coherent personality.

> This abstract personage, to whom life has been scarcely more than a string of abstract experiences and resultant ideas, has two further peculiarities, that complete, so to speak, his abstract personality. . . . The accident of education, carried on exclusively at home and in exceptional solitude, has placed this not very feminine man to some measure at a woman's standpoint, devoid of all discipline and tradition, full of irregularities and individualities. (*Baldwin,* 4–5)

Baldwin's education, of which Lee pretends to be "unable to give any very definite account," is the clue to his personality. Speaking about his education allegorically, "as Pueritia reading a grammar book, Adolescentia holding a hawk," Lee reminds us that the content of formal instruction was designed for boys. "A sentimental boy, a harshly philosophic youth," Baldwin is educated "exclusively at home." But home schooling was customary for middle-class girls and also constitutes Lee's own learning experience. So we should not be surprised to find Baldwin placed "at a woman's standpoint."

In Baldwin, Lee constructs an abstract subject that is still formed by his individual history, including the complex relationship between biological and social aspects. She calls him "not very feminine," to describe a gendered style, different from his biological determination "man" and still different from the social space marked by "a woman's standpoint." Baldwin's gender is irrelevant and only one of the constituents of his perception. We *know* him as "man" through name and personal pronoun, that is, his gender is determined by the symbolic conventions implemented and recognized by his culture. But since he also exists "at a woman's standpoint," signifier and signified are not congruent.

His life is spread out, like "the wool of a sheep" and hangs "flakewise" on every part of his very real "genius loci" on Italian soil, which provides more rootedness than his inconclusive nationality—an "English Briton" who was "born upon French soil" and who "vaguely remembered Germany":

> [Italy] is the only place I have possessed in absolute familiarity . . . the only place where I have been obliged to take an interest in, or rather within whose limitations I have had to find everything . . . the complete intimacy with every turn, every path; the interest in the fern growing on certain walls, in the scarlet mushroom on a particular bank skirting a beech wood; the historical mania and fancies evoked by a few scraps, a tower, an old piece of wall, a graven hand on a milestone. (3, 14)

Baldwin's gender, nationality, and local identification are woven into a costume which is corporeal to him. Gender and nationality are his connections with the world, but as they are accidental and "devoid of all discipline and tradition," their function is variable, not fixed. He is the projection of an identity that cannot be clearly defined; an identity which constantly desires but is made to renounce. Since Baldwin is in a state of continuous unfulfillment, his desires make him what he is. He cannot be described but must speak for himself, as the use of the first person indicates:

> But making me what? The usual story: many ingredients, much fussing, and a result how out of all keeping! A creature troubled with the desire to

create, yet able only to criticize; consumed (which is worse) with the desire to affirm, yet condemned to deny; a life spent in being repelled by the exaggerations of one's friends, and attracted by the seeming moderation of one's enemies, in taking exception in the midst of assent: skepticism in a nature that desires to believe and rely, intellectual isolation for a man who loves to be borne along by the current—an unsatisfactory state of affairs, yet to me the only one conceivable. (12–13)

Baldwin's subjectivity is built on aesthetic impressions that are created somewhere between desire and restraint. He is a process of collecting likenesses, as the epigraph from Emerson on the title page to *Baldwin* suggests:

A man is a method, a progressive arrangement, a selecting principle, gathering his like to him wherever he goes.

Baldwin is Lee's projection of her writerly persona, but she claims to be distinct from him. What then is the relationship between Lee and Baldwin? We can approach the answer once more through her motif of education. Toward the end of the introduction, the focus is no longer on Baldwin's learning process but on that of Vernon Lee, the writer.

My own relations towards him? . . . They are absolutely indefinable. I am the pupil of Baldwin, the thing made by him, or he is my master, yet made by me; choose and understand, for I cannot. I agree in all his ideas; yet I can place myself at the point of view of some of his opponents. . . . And yet, Baldwin and I are distinct; he does not understand me quite; he stands outside me; he is not I. No, dear friend Baldwin, better far than I and wiser, but perhaps a little less human, you are not myself; you are my mentor, my teacher, my power of being taught; and you live, dear abstract friend on the borderland between fact and fancy. (14)

Lee's hide-and-seek game with her identity here becomes a complex act of self-mirroring most noticeable in the change of point of view when she addresses Baldwin directly. The subject Baldwin/Lee has at least three different grammatical voices: a third person, an addressee, and a first-person "I." At the same time, Baldwin and Lee form a "we" ("Baldwin and I").[13] They are sameness and difference in one. Their subjectivity simulates the constant exchange between reader and text in the act of reading. If Baldwin and Lee are an inextricable double, so are the speakers in the following dialogues, and so are, eventually, text and reader, a point she makes in *The Handling of Words*. In a manner similar to what Judith Butler describes in *Gender Trouble* as discursively produced identity, the doer is constructed in and through the deed[14]—and here, the speaker through the dialogue with the listener. There is no speaker *behind* the speech, but s/he is constructed in speech or, as Lee puts it in her ambiguous use of passive voice, "he [Baldwin] is my master, yet made by me" or "my power of being taught." If we scrutinize the semantic logic of these phrases, the relationship of subject and object begins to shift, and we are no longer sure who the agent is. This playful exchange of active and passive positions summarizes Lee's alternative subjectivity and, at the same time, reflects the dynamics of its construction.

Psychologically, Baldwin embodies what Lacanian theory outlines as the subject's entering into language (the symbolic). The child learns to recognize itself through the language of the father in a series of identifications to develop a sense of self. This learning process is visualized in Baldwin, who is a likeness of Lee's writerly self, distinct from and yet part of the "I" who speaks. Baldwin personifies the consciousness which is constructed by and in language, here marked by name and gender. But this consciousness is in conflict with "woman's position," and *her* desire to create—an inconsistency that produces "an illusive, shimmering personality, seemingly full of contradictions" (13).

Lee's charade of Baldwin's indeterminable gender position and his elusive doubling of herself leave in the reader's mind the half-conscious impression of a divided identity with which s/he will read on. As Baldwin's life "hangs flakewise" on the land, the Baldwin-Lee double "hangs" in every dialogue, spread out in the speakers who interact like the voices in a musical round. If we read the introduction carefully enough, we recognize these characters as variations of her own voice: "I have felt like Vere, I often feel like Rheinhardt, I respect Agatha, I do not utterly despise Marcel, I love and am dazzled by the beautiful transcendentalist Olivia" (13). The affiliation between Lee and her speakers is expressed in verbs like "respect," "despise," "love," signifying affective relationships different from the intellectual, conscious mode of the Baldwin-Lee connection ("I agree in all his ideas"). Thus the dialogues, apart from their expression of ideas, also set up a matrix of affective or emotional responses which may well contradict or undermine the intellectual positions as predicted in the epigraph on the book's title page:

"And if I contradict myself, why, I contradict myself."—Walt Whitman

In sum, Lee's dialogues are intellectual debates as much as indices of the multiple constituents of speech. Baldwin, who is present in every dialogue without dominating it, can be read as a homology of Lee's writerly voice, an abstract but enthusiastic "denizen of the subjective world." In these early years of Lee's career as a woman of letters, Baldwin personifies a male-female consciousness, a "borderland" figure who reflects her internal division about the intellectual traditions she yet wishes to enter. The construction of Baldwin, then, allows her to draw attention to her own discourse.

In her second book of dialogues, *Althea,* Lee replaces her "dear abstract friend" Baldwin by Althea, "who is naturally the pupil of Baldwin" (xvii). Baldwin, she tells us, "has ceased to exist."—Why?—"He belonged like so many of our dead selves, of the youthful predecessors of our identity, to a genus of ephemerae which require an universe without rain, wind or frost, in fact, made on purpose for them" (xi). This phrase suggests the metaphysical subject in Western philosophy and Lee's former male-oriented self. Baldwin's "old" subjectivity is challenged by Althea, whose lack of knowledge ("I have read very few books" [113]) embodies a new kind of consciousness. Althea speaks the language of instinct, which reminds us of Lee's characterization of herself in *Belcaro* where she asserts that she *felt* art before she *learned* the "foreign" language of art criticism. Althea, too, is

> at first, inarticulate, unreasoning, ignorant of all why and wherefore, and requires to be taught many things which others know. But, once having learned the names, so to speak, of her instincts, the premises of her unconscious arguments, she becomes, as necessarily, the precursor of Baldwin's best thoughts, the perfecter of most of them. (xvii)

In *Althea,* Baldwin is only a passing stage. His teaching helps Althea express "her instincts, the premises of her unconscious arguments" and so become part of her mind. In the end, Althea (the female) transcends Baldwin (the male), thus challenging the traditional dogma in Western aesthetics which construes man as the perfecter of woman, as the beautiful soul who has no other virtue than being beautiful.[15] According to post-Enlightenment aesthetics, the female can have access to truth only through intuition and sentiment without intellect or the will to recognition, which are imagined as male qualities. In this metaphysical arrangement, the female, by her borderline existence, constantly faces the threat of falling back into "raw" nature. Therefore, the male's "sentimentalische" faculty (manifested in art and culture) has to transform the female image into his own. Otherwise she would be an empty mirror wherein he cannot recognize his image of her.[16]

This aesthetic axiom is reversed in *Althea*. Althea is not only the central character in the dialogues, but she also becomes the "perfecter" of most of Baldwin's best thoughts and finally overcomes Baldwin's superior knowledge. Althea does not need "man's" perfection since she embodies a different epistemic system. She is one of those rare natures who "recognize truth as soon as they see it" (xvii), not through knowledge, but through intuition. Yet Althea cannot serve as a model because she is already from the beginning what others have to become through a long and painful process of learning. Knowledge and intuition should not be understood as binary opposites here but rather in terms of Lee's Kantian distinction between reason and intellect to indicate the difference between two activities of the mind: "thinking" and "knowing." Baldwin's way of "knowing" is the search for truth in organized, perfectable knowledge. Althea's "thinking," however, is more immediate and therefore a basic human condition which can only be approximated but not *known* in Baldwin's terms.[17]

Although Baldwin's "death" turns the role of the organizing consciousness over to Althea, he is not replaced entirely but survives in the more "solid existence of imaginary beings." In other words, he has become one of the mind-building components in Lee's history. Since Baldwin still has a voice in the *Althea* dialogues, his presence historicizes Lee's new subject in a diachronic/synchronic conflation. Lee's own directives in the introduction to *Althea* suggest that this new concept of subjectivity implies the consciousness of one's own history.[18]

Althea represents an evolutionary subject who retains the ontogenetic characteristics of her species (Baldwin), but also adapts herself (through Baldwin's education) and moves on to another stage of development. She is not compromised by Baldwin's maleness although, admittedly, his earlier appearance (1886) was never fully rooted in it because of his multiple identifications. If neither Baldwin nor Althea is what s/he is said to be and each is a part of the other, the center of meaning is displaced and their dialogic relationship comes into the foreground. The question is not who Baldwin and Althea are, but how they are related, and how they modify each other.

In *Althea* Lee offers a dialectical subject which displays its own contradictions in dialogue. The book's central text, "On Friendship," places Baldwin and Althea in opposition to each other. Since dialectical logic dictates that opposites be synthesized on a new level, Lee introduces a third party, the sage Signora Elena, who plays the role of a female Socrates to develop and conclude Baldwin's and Althea's argument. But in the end, Lee's dialectics is not balanced. While Althea and Baldwin seem to be harmonized intellectually, a more complete alliance takes place between the older and the younger woman—through their performance outside the logic of the argument. The full implication of this conclusion becomes apparent in Signora Elena's gestures which signify her bonding with Althea. As the women approach each other, Baldwin's egocentricity—staged as fin-de-siècle worldweariness—is fading and finally perishes like Lee's former "dead selves."

Does the female displacement of Baldwin afford a lesbian reading? What other "evidence" does suggest that Lee creates a lesbian subject position within a seemingly unmarked philosophical text? To answer these questions, I will take the main dialogue, "On Friendship," through a close reading and relate its iconography to late-nineteenth-century encodings of homoerotic texts.


## THE SUBJECT AS LESBIAN: PLATONIC HOMOEROTICISM IN "ON FRIENDSHIP"

The evocation of Platonic philosophy in *Althea* is not accidental. Besides the dialogue form, the text contains explicit references to Plato, such as the likening of Althea to one of Plato's youths in the *Symposium*. "On Friendship," the central dialogue of Lee's book, contains the greatest number of references to Greek culture and philosophy. The initial allusions to Greek male friendship, whose homoerotic implication would be instantly grasped by her audience, suggest that Lee uses the Greek context to encode a lesbian message. But are the evocations of Greek homoeroticism grounds enough to assume a lesbian subtext? We need to be aware that although the antique model afforded homoerotic identification in both sexes, the available iconography had a decidedly masculine tradition that required some recasting by the female writer.

The emergence of modern lesbian identity is often associated with the cultural transitions of the fin de siècle, when the conditions for aesthetic and sexual categories coincided and the male homosexual began to be imagined as an alternative site for identity.[19] Literary and cultural studies have described the fin de siècle as the crucial period when the extant homosexual male subculture became visible even in mainstream literature. The "homosexual code" (Dowling, 1) was at once widely dispersed in the culture and "preciously cultivated by a small 'proscribed' group within that culture" (Morgan, 316).[20] Certain Hellenic or Renaissance contexts became the metaphoric field for a secret message (Dowling, 1) which was activated by references to an aestheticized male culture.[21] Platonic friendship, for instance, served as euphemism for love between men (Dellamora, 157). Through intricate rhetorical figures and connotative subcodes, Victorian male aesthetes could speak to a minority group "of varying degrees of interest in homoeroticism" within the dominant (heterosexual) code of scholarship (Morgan, 316). Pater's elaboration on male beauty and temperament, for instance, could be read as nothing more than a scholarly comment on Hellenism, while the intertext sent a message to the homosexually oriented reader. At the same time, the reworked classicism gave same-sex love respectability since it was predicated on a superior cultural standard. It has been suggested that Pater's propagation of aesthetic masculinity is the most far-reaching in spite of his subdued rhetoric (Morgan, 328). Indeed, his association of aesthetics with a homoerotic temperament as the underlying force in Western culture reminds the reader that a pederastic eros has shaped the very notion of culture.

The new aesthetics of "Anders-streben" created the conditions in which invisible minority groups could devise alternative forms of discourse to inscribe cultural difference.[22] The preciously cultivated ambiguity of the homosexual code offered writers like Lee the semiotic spaces in which they could imagine a lesbian subject outside binary gender oppositions, a subject which was yet to be defined. In other words, the aesthetes' validation of alternative masculinity offered a venue for women writers to circumvent the bind of traditional womanhood.

Inspired by Pater's poetic readings of Plato, Lee approached philosophy through the language of aesthetic criticism.[23] To avoid being collapsed in a masculinist structure, she had to displace the male subject of Paterian aesthetics by overwriting it with her own voice. The general reader did not necessarily recognize her different intent but only deplored the departure from her mentor. For instance, a reviewer of Lee's *Renaissance Fancies and Studies* regards Pater as "her master in the subject" and laments that "her style has not the polish which endeared Pater to his readers."

In the 1880s and '90s, female writers whose social and/or sexual orientation opposed them to longstanding stereotypes of the feminine began to construct woman-centered texts which devised models of female or lesbian identification in similarly ambiguous images as those they had found in the male aesthetes.[24] Indeed, lesbian writing does not "make sense" within traditional parameters but, as Yopie Prins has elegantly observed, "enter[s] a metaphorical 'field' of writing where the crossing out, over, and through of sexual identities can be performed" (*Victorian Sappho,* 16). Such performance demands reading strategies for that which is never spelled out completely, as we can see in the poems of "Michael Field." Like homosexual codes, the lesbian text evokes narrative space for woman's "primary presence" (Adrienne Rich) through images suggesting lesbian desire in a "transgressive subtext" (Farwell 93). For the initiated reader, alternative versions of common mythical figures offered new models of identification. Pan, Apollo, Athena, and other figures associated with nature, youth, and freedom in Greek mythology became particularly popular as carriers of encoded messages. In an earlier essay, "Sappho Doubled: Michael Field," Prins has shown that the female couple Bradley/Cooper writing as "Michael Field" could draw on the established associations between Hellenism and homosexuality and "therefore open Victorian Hellenism to the possibility of lesbian reading" (169). The role of the antique also set cultural boundaries because "high culture" became the site for renegotiating (masculine) subjectivity. Thus "a refashioned past, whether Greek or Renaissance, signaled both learning and an imaginative space where the lesbian imagination might flourish" (Vicinus, 102).

Although Lee was not a self-identified lesbian, she had many close relationships with women. When she was writing *Althea,* she was living with the art historian Kit Anstruther-Thomson after a painful break-up with the poet and biographer Mary Robinson. Lee collaborated in several books with Anstruther-Thomson who was very likely a model for the protagonist in *Althea,* which Lee dedicated to her.[25] Vernon Lee also had close connections with other lesbian writers or artists—from Ethel Smyth to "Michael Field" to Amy Levy—from whom she abstracted certain themes, styles, and images, especially in her fiction of the yellow decade.

Lee's commitment to philosophical issues in an environment that slighted women's intellectuality prompted her to embrace a male-identified discourse. Her highly sublimated theoretical essays in general offer little enticement for a sexual or even lesbian reading. As a "woman thinker,"[26] she avoided drawing attention to gender and personal life in her concern to be taken seriously. Contemporary critics do not make Lee's preference for women an issue, perhaps—one may suspect—because she did not make it a public affair. Understandably so, for that would have forced her to live by the categorical limitations promoted by contemporary sexology.[27] Lee's irreverent treatment of male colleagues distressed her contemporaries more than her lesbian orientation. Reading Lee as a lesbian writer does not mean to reduce her under the false unified label of sex but to value the sexual as an aspect of her difference as a writer without letting it narrow other qualities of her literary expression. Lee's broad publishing in several areas, her conspicuous presence in the cosmopolitan intellectual communities of the late nineteenth century, and her claim to speak for the "generally human" make her a model of what Terry Castle calls "lesbian worldliness." Castle describes worldliness in terms of an "expansive, outward-looking, and multifaceted humanity" as a function of difference. Rather than looking for the lesbian in "some tiny, defensively constituted corner of the world," Castle centers the lesbian subject in "the very fabric of cultural life." The lesbian writer, argues Castle, "[n]ever let a sense of sexual alienation or 'marginality' stand in the way of her curiosity, self-education, or ambition: each sought to participate to the utmost in the rich communal life of her time (and usually did)" (16–17). The notion of "lesbian worldliness" is helpful in our analysis of late-nineteenth-century texts, such as Lee's, since the homoerotic configurations in Lee's texts are large metaphorical spaces from which she addresses mainstream audiences while also inscribing a minority discourse that becomes a controlling center as soon as it is recognized.

In "On Friendship," Vernon Lee does just that: she draws up an alternative (lesbian) subjectivity in a subtext that employs and simultaneously recasts the erotic and aesthetic forms of masculinity in Plato. In this central dialogue, Lee activates homoerotic Platonic friendship but replaces Plato's exclusive male round by men and women fashioned "in the approximate likeness" of her friends. In the course of their discussion of love, the speakers—Baldwin, Althea, and Signora Elena—shift their intellectual alliances, but through the connection of the two women the reader can forge a subtext the lesbian intimations of which accentuate the general philosophical dimension. The dialogue simultaneously invokes and undermines Plato's male-defined eros while it challenges nineteenth-century representations of heterosexual desire.

"On Friendship" takes elements of Plato's *Phaedrus* and *Symposium* through a series of discursive procedures to arrive at a new notion of love which favors multiple exchanges among souls who—to borrow Judith Butler's term—have no "metaphysical substance." While the abstract rhetoric of Lee's argument is unmarked by gender, the "stage directions" foreground the rapport between Althea and Signora Elena. In the end, Baldwin withdraws, but the women's performance prevails. Lee's dialogue officially addresses the cultivated reader interested in philosophical questions, but its performative side invokes what Thaïs E. Morgan has called a "minoritizing discourse" (316) which appeals to an inner circle of lesbian readers.[28] The modalities between rhetoric and performance give us valuable clues to the way lesbian subjectivity could be presented without being named.

Lee's endowment of Althea with "unwomanly" (but not manly) difference in a Platonic subtext could draw on Pater's portrayal of Plato, which was well known in intellectual circles of the late nineteenth century.[29] According to Pater, Plato "possessed of [an] inborn genius," he learned "by habit and rule, all that can be taught and learned" from others; he supplemented what was "unique, impulsive, underivable" with what by "docility and discipline" could be acquired (*Plato and Platonism,* 146–47).[30] Similarly, Althea, "the natural pupil of Baldwin," is "inarticulate, unreasoning, ignorant" at first; but once she has "learned the names . . . of her instincts, the premises of her unconscious arguments, she becomes, as necessarily the perfecter of most of them" (*Althea,* xvii). Lee invokes the antique model without explicitly naming it. Thus, there is always room for doubt. We cannot say with absolute certainty whether she placed "On Friendship" purposely in the middle of the whole book, exactly where Plato had placed Socrates' famous speech on eros. This curious structural resemblance—even in the same amount of text framing the speech—highlights the subject matter (eros) that is indeed the most "Platonic" in Lee's anthology. The educated contemporary reader could recognize Lee's textual interplay in such formal correlation.

Lee's opening scene immediately conjures up the "Greek" setting. After a leisurely walk through an olive grove, Baldwin, Althea, and the elderly Signora Elena come to rest on a dilapidated wall by a solitary cypress tree. Similarly, Socrates and Phaedrus had left the city walls for the open country to find a resting place under a huge plane tree. In Plato's text, landscape is used only as a coulisse to reflect Socrates' enamoration with Phaedrus. The homoerotic aspect is reinforced by the allusion to statues of Pan nearby. Obviously, Phaedrus has enticed his mentor to "set foot outside the walls," for otherwise Socrates prefers the societal urban environment of the academy and usually avoids nature: "I'm a lover of learning, and trees and open country won't teach me anything, whereas men in town do" (*Phaedrus,* 230-e). Unlike Socrates, Althea's female mentor, Signora Elena, uses nature intentionally in her philosophical lecture about the interplay of "the sun, and the sea, and the wind, and the rocks" as metaphors for human interaction. The physical elements in Lee's dialogue even become active dramatis personae, which, not unlike the chorus in Greek tragedy, continually interfere: reflecting, commenting, foreshadowing. Unlike a human character, however, the natural environment conveys only abstract emotions. It is without metaphysical substance, uncentered, and forever changing. The atmospheric elements delay, displace, and concentrate meaning without ever becoming part of the human order.

The environment seems to coalesce with Althea, who is "in some odd way closely akin to the trees and grass, and clouds and sea, the real things of the world" in the first *Althea* dialogue ("The Value of the Individual," 5). She "understands the wind and the clouds"; her ungendered beauty is more at home in the natural environment than in human society, which she does not understand "from experience, from within" ("On Friendship," 126). Baldwin, on the other hand, belongs to the realm of words, somewhat artificial since his character "require[s] an universe without rain, wind or frost." He has much in common with the Kantian disembodied subject because the essential qualities of his identity are divorced from contingent circumstances.

Baldwin and Althea together represent what recent feminist theorists have called "dialectical subjectivity," a concept which emphasizes the interaction between an "inner self" and a "constituted subject" (Linda Alcoff). Although Baldwin and Althea cannot be described in terms of exactly these categories, they represent aspects of such interactive subjectivity. Lee herself had intended for the two speakers to be read concurrently. In the introductory to *Althea,* she stresses the book's significance for her own intellectual development and its superiority over *Baldwin.* Although Baldwin appears again in *Althea,* he is reduced to Lee's intellectual strawman, self-centered and fashionably pessimistic. As "focalizer" he has been replaced by Althea, who is the origin and end of her own genius and reduces Baldwin's part to that of the necessary but eventually disposable mediator. The double Baldwin/Althea offers a kind of dialectical subject which accommodates its own contradictions. Read side by side, *Baldwin* and *Althea* constitute stages in the development of the female philosopher Vernon Lee.

Moreover, it is only through the comparison of my two books together (and
this is my reason for reverting to my former volume with so much egoism),
through the comparison of what I thought and felt with what I think and feel,
that I can achieve what I greatly have at heart, namely: to point out one road,
at least, along which we modern men and women may reach serenity of mind
after the uncomfortable resting-places of our youthful thought. (*Althea,* xi)

In "On Friendship," Baldwin and Althea are guided to a conclusion through
the correcting interlocutor, the female Socrates, Signora Elena. She critiques
their idealistic notions of love and pleads for a less ambitious "partial ideal
vested in human individuals" (132). Toward the end of the dialogue Signora
Elena's humanist expression becomes increasingly vociferous, and finally, her
coupling with Althea supersedes the Baldwin-Althea double.

The lesbian overtones in their bond can to some extent be derived from
the textual allusions to Platonic homoeroticism. The same-sex topos runs on in
a stratum below the unmarked theoretical debate—almost imperceptible for
the uninitiated reader. The terms for the two women's alliance are already set
in the opening scene of the dialogue which shows Althea and Signora Elena
making flower wreaths—a typically feminine image, we should think—for a
group of village children. A seemingly insignificant detail, the wreaths yet
provide a metonymic link to the homoeroticism in Plato's text. Not only did
the participants in a Greek symposium wear wreaths on their heads—a ritual
often imitated by the aesthetic male clubs of Oxford[31]—but wreaths were also
given to boys by the pederasts as a symbol of their wooing.[32] When Baldwin
takes "one of the daisy chains" to fasten it round the trunk of the cypress tree,
"an offering, he said, to Pales or Pan" (109), he identifies with the homoerotic
context while visually separating it from the women's sphere (and Signora
Elena's ironic "your God Pan" supports this separation). Thus, while the two
women can retain the symbolic function of the pagan ritual for their female
bonding, its male-identified sexual meaning is displaced.

Lee gives the wreath-making an unusually big space early in the text, which
seems to point to its significance for the unfolding action. The cultural implications of the scene function as a reading guide to the stage directions, that is, those
parts of the text that occur outside the actual dialogue. Following these directions, we begin to recognize the relationship between the two female characters
as separate from their philosophical communications with Baldwin. Through-

out the dialogue, Althea, assisting the elderly woman on an afternoon walk, keeps close to Signora Elena, who subtly displays her affection for her young friend. At first, she looks at the girl "tenderly and admiringly," and later takes "the hand of her antagonist . . . so very loveable." In the final scene, when Althea kisses the extended hand of Signora Elena, the attraction between the two women has become a nondiscursive force breaking the power of the word. To put it differently, the bond between Althea and Signora Elena functions as a "discursive shifter" (Farwell) that feminizes—or rather lesbianizes—the dialogue's subject. But has Lee sufficiently "dismantled the master's house," as Audrey Lorde famously puts it, to make the lesbian subject visible? To answer this question, we must once more investigate the construction of Western subjectivity.

Unlike Socrates' female mentor Diotima, whose wisdom is reported in her absence, Signora Elena speaks for herself. In a way, she combines the functions of Socrates and Diotima, thus disrupting the underlying dialectics of gender that informs Plato's philosophy. Critics have argued that in the *Symposium,* Plato appropriates the female voice by denying Diotima actual presence among the male philosophers. Although Diotima does "give birth" to Socrates' ideas, her femaleness is only symbolic (Mitchell, 141). She presents woman's perspective in a form recognizable to men, which means she is appropriated by a male paradigm. The male philosopher becomes the site of metaphysical reproduction while the female, stripped of her metaphysical otherness, is only a defective male. As David Halperin has shown, Plato's "woman" is a trope for the way Plato imagines the

> (pro)creative intercourse of male philosophers. Nothing in herself, "woman" is that pseudo-Other who both makes good what men want and exempts men from wanting anything at all; she is an alternative male identity whose constant accessibility to men lends men a fullness and totality that enables them to dispense (supposedly) with otherness altogether. (150–51)

This absolute masculinity, epitomized in Platonic eros, continues to exist in Western erotic ethos which, according to de Lauretis, has also secured the heterosexual social contract "by which all sexualities, all bodies, and all 'others' are bonded to an ideal/ideological hierarchy of males" (158). Within this framework of "sexual indifference"—that is, a single practice and representation of the sexual—female desire for another female cannot be recognized. If Lee uses the

Platonic text to inscribe alternative subjectivity, she has to renegotiate the terms of hommo-/homosexuality (Irigaray) to avoid being collapsed into the male-defined metaphysics of sex and self. Irigaray's pun, based on the French and Latin implications of hom(m)o, signifies the impossibility of representing desire between females in a language devised for male subjects. This language can only express sexual indifference (= a single practice and representation of the sexual) even when speaking of sexual difference. Woman's desire for the same would be a desire "little in demand" in the male heterosexual praxis and merely mime male homosexuality, "because it lacks masculine homologues" (Irigary, *Speculum,* 103). In this system, woman has already been constructed as a male projection reabsorbed into the male world in the semblance of the feminine.

It was not until the last two decades of the nineteenth century that male and female writers experimented with new forms of subjectivity, especially in the fiction of the New Women. Outside literature, modern lesbian identity was delineated most notably in the medical field and the propagandistic language of the debates on cultural politics. But eccentric female performance could only be conceived in the male norms dominating the symbolical system and described as "unwomanly" or "deviant." Against this background, even the trendy androgyne would still represent what de Lauretis calls "singular sexual indifference," which automatically absorbs the female in a male-defined metaphysics. "Female," on the other hand, signifies not only an imperfect subject but also stands for lack itself, which creates desire. As Elizabeth Grosz puts it, "Lack only makes sense to the (male) subject insofar as some other (woman) personifies and embodies it for him" (76). Only if the subject and its desire for wholeness (Plato)—or simply desire for desire (Hegel)—are disassembled can traditional functions of desire be abandoned. Then, the ground for (masculine) philosophy begins to shift and the female can claim her existence through desire *as and for* not-women in an erotics without (male) erôs.

To be sure, lesbian writing cannot take place outside the symbolic systems in which it has occurred after all. To overcome the impasse of being caught up in the very language one is about to transcend, the lesbian can draw attention to her "cultural dilemma" by what de Lauretis calls the paradox of thinking homosexuality and hommosexuality at once separate *and* together (177). This paradox also becomes productive in Lee's "On Friendship" where Althea can only be heard when she *is not* "woman," and yet she has to speak in the language in which she can be nothing but a woman. How, then, does Lee make Althea culturally intelligible?

On the structural level (thesis, antithesis, synthesis) Lee's dialogue seems to reinforce thinking in binaries, just as the cast of characters reflects traditional gender divisions. Althea propagates selfless love and "caritas," which Victorian ideology ascribed to women, whereas Baldwin, from an egocentric male position, defines love as an endless turn of individual desire and consumption. His narcissistic yearning, echoing the wistfulness of late-nineteenth-century decadents, originates in the male subjects' idealizing faculty to woo and to possess. "But," as Baldwin knows, "the ideal escapes, the desire fails" ("On Friendship," 127), and this awareness of eternal imperfection leaves him grieved and "barren," in the fashionable form of "Weltschmerz." To avoid pain, Baldwin stays away from any "real" affection, and withdraws into an inner sanctuary where he can aestheticize love and friendship from a distance:

> Am I not quite right in enjoying my fellow-creatures, when there is anything enjoyable about them, from a distance, and without any contact. . . . It struck me suddenly one day . . . that I possessed this soul [of a certain friend] more completely than it possessed itself. What should I want with its affection? (108–9)

Oddly enough, Althea's understanding of the love of duty toward humanity resembles Baldwin's love of the ideal. Both concepts are abstract and exclude what Signora Elena calls "human contact," but for different reasons. Althea prefers to love "abstractly" because she shrinks from a closeness that may inflict pain on others, whereas Baldwin eschews the pain he may feel himself.

Signora Elena leads the two antagonists through the argument, constantly adapting and saving what is "true." Although she disagrees with Baldwin's notion of love as insatiate desire for the perfect—"there is no reason that we should have all we crave for"—she accepts his "courtship of friends," which she deems necessary to bring people in contact with one another. Unlike Baldwin, she does not see the ideal as an end in itself. Nor does she share his sense of loss. Rather, she counters Baldwin's solitary "Weltschmerz" with the human need "to be consumed and assimilated," sustained by the metaphor of the sea, sun, wind, and rocks, "each struggling breaking against the other . . . making the beautiful life of the world" (129).

Signora Elena also reforms Althea's altruistic love, telling her not to squash her own nature for the benefit of others. The sage woman revises rather than rejects, which is also Vernon Lee's strategy of reassembling Plato in terms of his own "corrective intercourse." From Althea's altruism, Signora Elena salvages the orientation toward others, but she endows it with a modified version of Baldwin's love of self: "What if others require the thing you squash?" In the end, only Signora Elena's conclusion prevails: "refusing nothing legitimate to ourselves and others" in a continual "stirring, seeking, refraining, renouncing."

By likening love to the perpetual motion of sea and clouds, Signora Elena evokes the image of Heraclitean flux and undercuts the Socratic notion of stable knowledge which informs the Platonic dialogues. Heraclitean philosophy assumes knowledge to be varying experiences that cannot be contained, and in Lee's dialogue, such variability is enacted by weather, landscape, and the sea in an ever-changing atmospheric movement. The physical elements connect externally the figures moving through the landscape—a visual contrast to Plato's stationary lovers in the villa (*Symposium*) or under a tree (*Phaedrus*).

Cyclical rather than teleological ("making and unmaking"), Lee's mindscape avoids dialectical progression toward an imagined ideal, a philosophical concept which answers to Elizabeth Grosz's configuration of lesbian erotics, "an entry into an arrangement, an assemblage of other fragments . . . becoming a component in a series of flows and breaks, of varying speeds and intensities . . . being swept beyond one singular position into a multiplicity of flows" (76). Or in Lee's words:

> Sea and wind and sun, ever varying colours and ever varying sound, the music of the surf containing all manner of instruments and phrases: the swish of the wave unfurling and rushing forwards . . . feelings and impressions also, drenching us, rolling us, carrying us on their surface, drowning us in their depth, as we feel ourselves carried along, overwhelmed, by the rushing sea sound. ("On Friendship," 121)

In this sensuous philosophical fluidum, neither fixed positions nor coherent subjects have a place.

> Is not our mind the collection of things outside us. We are not definite, distinct existences . . . we are forever meeting, crossing, encroaching, living next one another, in one another, part of ourselves left behind in others, part of them become ourselves: a flux of thought, feeling, experience, aspiration. (133)

But Heraclitean philosophy itself cannot carry a lesbian subtext. Pater himself was fascinated with the allure of Heraclitean flux and made it an integral part of his aesthetics. To recapitulate Althea's special subjectivity: she can be represented only in the ever-changing atmosphere because she is not part of the cultural order. Her statement "I don't know much about human beings and their feelings" (124) obviously sets her apart from human society. Since Althea does not occupy a social or a gendered space, she does not fit familiar concepts of identity. Like the wind and the sea, she has no metaphysical core, a condition which discourages characteral coherence or essential definition. Her mystical union with the elements insubstantiates her, draws her outside. Lee keeps Althea before the reader as a view (always directed toward the sea). At the same time, she draws the reader's attention repeatedly to the resplendent physical environment in which Althea partakes. Her radiance deflects the beholder's glance, turning it in the same direction as hers. She relates to others not as opposites but in a "journey side by side."

However, by representing Althea as part of nature, Lee runs the risk of reinforcing the etiological link between woman and nature and returning her to the traditional male-female dichotomy. She can avoid the ideological snare by lending Althea the looks of a boy. With her "boy's cap" and "her face rather of a beautiful boy than of a woman," she is unfeminine—yet not masculine; she is neither male nor female. In Althea the genders are not blurred as androgyne,[33] but we recognize the boy in the woman, which points to the "cultural paradox of hommo/homosexuality" (de Lauretis) while it suggests a new kind of gender.

Althea's appearance like "one of the youths in Plato's dialogues" not only links her with the antique model of homoerotic love but also exemplifies the contemporary practice of using the boy image as a sign for lesbian difference. What made the boy image so attractive for lesbian self-representation in the Victorian age was "his chaste innocence as representative of a special, lost quality of the modern world" (Vicinus, 100).[34] Without the negative connotation of male effeminacy, the boy image could become a signifier beyond heterosexual boundaries. The general interest in boys' stories gave the lesbian writer the opportunity to address mainstream audiences and simultaneously a special group. Similar to the homoerotic code, the lesbian subtext sent the specific message to those who "knew" while concealing it from the general reader. As Martha Vicinus describes it in her intriguing essay, the boy image works like a looking glass for the lesbian text: "We repeatedly are asked to look—and then

look again—to see the hidden meaning of the beautiful boy" (92). Lee employs
the figure of the "beautiful boy" elsewhere in her work, for instance, in her
fantastic tale, "Prince Alberic and the Snake Lady," in which the protagonist
appears as the "Sapphic" disciple of a snakewoman from the mythological
past. Here, as in other texts from the 1890s, the boy image centers lesbian
imagination as it bypasses heterosexuality. Beneath the straight, argumentative surface of "On Friendship" appears a complex subtext, which translates
antique homoeroticism, a boyish protagonist, and a wordless alliance between
two women into a hidden (lesbian) and yet "worldly" message.

Althea is beckoned to Signora Elena at the very moment the older woman
propagates friendship as the "marriage of true minds"—another signifier of
homoerotics in late-nineteenth-century England. Althea's celebration of
friendship as sameness, the "journey side by side," of "creatures living off the
same interests, the same aspirations, staying together because they both were
attracted to the same things" (135) is enhanced when Signora Elena invests this
friendship with the sacred bond of marriage, though in a version superior to
conventional wedlock: "Friendship is, after all, something akin to wedlock;
only, being restrained by none of wedlock's legal and natural bonds, and not
limited to one individual, of a freer, more sensitive sort" (136). Marriage in traditional society, as she seems to suggest, is limited not only by legal, but most
notably, by "natural" relations, then understood as heterosexual. The absence
of these "legal and natural bonds" privileges (Platonic) friendship over the
(heterosexual) marriage.

Exactly at this point in the argument, the subtext foregrounds the physical
approchement between the two women which has to remain abstract for Baldwin. Signora Elena can lead her male reader merely to an intellectual understanding of women's love, whereas her looks and gestures, expressive of her
growing affection, reach the "impersonal" but "lovable" Althea beyond logos:

> Signora Elena took the hand of her antagonist, so strangely impersonal in her
> abstract passion for right, and yet with her face rather of a beautiful boy than
> of a woman, and her restrained tenderness of manner, so very lovable. (140)

"You speak like Mr. Baldwin," wonders Althea. "You seem to admit all his
notions . . . then how is it that you do not come to the same conclusion?" And
Signora Elena replies that it is "the simple, commonplace thing called love"

which makes the difference. But love has now gained a special meaning through her performance outside the dialogue. Signora Elena no longer communicates her ideas verbally but literally leads Baldwin to the place where Althea already is: "She had taken Baldwin's arm, and walked slowly to where Althea was still standing, absorbed in the sea, or in her own thoughts" (128).

The performative side of the text first coincides with and then surpasses its argumentative outline. Addressing herself to Althea, Signora Elena refutes Baldwin's notion of love based on the premise of insatiate (male) desire which originates in an isolating and soul-consuming idealism ("what philosophy and justice clamour in vain for," 135). She reveals this idealism as "a mere imaginative fancy," which is in fact "the craving for submission of other souls to our soul," and therefore an act of tyranny. To her, Baldwin (ab)uses love to disguise his self-interest as philosophy.[35] In contrast, she explains love as a function of exchange *and* consumption. But her understanding of consumption is different from Baldwin's self-centered burnout. On the premise that humans are neither whole nor separate selves, she finds that any love that excludes or prefers *one* (love or lover) is too limiting. Thus she pleads for a liberal and geneous type of love of the many.[36]

In the end, Signora Elena's bond with Althea exemplifies the experience, discipline ("restrained tenderness"), and sensuousness of love in the real, experiential sense. The older woman performs her love for Althea at the same time as she is defining it, while Althea ("philosophy in person") enacts its meaning. In the final scene, it is Althea's silence, not Baldwin's speech, which supports Signora Elena's philosophy. In a gesture that transcends all logos, Althea kisses the extended hand of the older woman, an act, as the text tells us, "more meaningful than words."

The scene is "real" and symbolic at the same time. It expresses what Vernon Lee calls Althea's "unconscious poetical vision," which through a "unio mystica" creates an understanding between two women. Althea's gesture can be completely understood only if the reader responds to her intuitively rather than intellectually. For an instant, the silent gesture seems to return Althea to the preverbal realm of her origin. And yet, she is far from it. Her education has led her through Baldwin's logos and through the Platonic text; but it does not end there. Male language is insufficient for expressing women's love for women and the text has to fall silent in the end. As Althea and Signora Elena seal their conjunction in a last gesture, the unrepresentable lesbian subject emerges as a function of wordless performance. The new meaning of erôs is not described but suggested. It requires a new reader—perhaps a lesbian reader—to grasp it.

The "lesbian" performance at the end of the dialogue seems to embody what "Michael Field" wrote to Vernon Lee a few years earlier about Katherine Bradley's and Edith Cooper's identity:

> "The woman or two" that, friends say, goes to the making of Michael Field thank you much for your valued confidence, and more valued trust. We wait for the introductions given by man—while the spirit, if we will but listen to its intimations, is providing for our most delicate + varied affinities. (20 January 1890, Colby).

Like Plato, with his "peculiar gift of verbal articulation," Lee has expressed "as if for the eyes, what except to the eye of the mind is strictly invisible" (*Plato and Platoism,* 143). She has appropriated and subverted the male eros in Plato through women's performance. Her text creates subjectivity, not as an autonomous self but as fluid exchange and subject *orientation;* in other words, the identification not *as* woman but *with* woman (Sedgwick, 62). Subjectivity, then, is invested in a new relationship between women who are "not women," and in this sense it is lesbian.

# 5 Miss Brown— An Aesthetic Bildungsroman?

**W**hen Vernon Lee's first novel, *Miss Brown,* was published in 1884, it provoked a scandal. Friends such as the Rossettis and Oscar Wilde who recognized themselves in her roman à clef avoided contact with her— some for years. A letter from her friend Mrs. Stillman, shortly after *Miss Brown* appeared, gave Lee a taste of the novel's reception: "There are several characters too easily recognizable, they will naturally object to being held up to ridicule and their friends are indignant" (27 December 1884, Colby). Cosmo Monkhouse, who critiqued the book for the January 1885 *Academy,* was quick to discover the real-life identities behind the thinly veiled characters: "the au- thor has, indeed, effectually confused their identities, but has nevertheless ridi- culed them individually as well as collectively" (6–7).[1] Since then, critics have often described *Miss Brown* as a nasty or unfair attack on "The Fleshly School of Poetry" (Robert Buchanan's famous polemics against Pre-Raphaelite art). The timing of Lee's novel was surely impeccable: *Miss Brown* appeared just as the memory of Buchanan's decade-old invective against Dante Gabriel Ros- setti's art had faded and William Michael Rossetti had set out to create the grand legend of his late brother. But this coincidence explains only partially the outrage over *Miss Brown.* Critics attacked the novel's exaggeration and im- plausibility as violations of aesthetic standards. Henry James's commentary was particularly shattering. After purposefully delaying his reaction to *Miss Brown,* he sent Lee this trenchant comment:

> The imperfection of the book seems to me to reside . . . in a certain ferocity. It will probably already have been repeated to you to satiety that you take the aesthetic business too seriously, too tragically, and above all with too great implication of sexual motives. . . . You have impregnated all those people too much with the sexual, the basely erotic preoccupation: your hand was too violent, the touch of life is lighter . . . perhaps you have been too much in a moral passion! That has put certain exaggerations, overstatements, grossise-ments, insistences wanting in tact, into your head. Cool first—write after-wards. Morality is hot—but art is icy. (10 May 1885, Colby)[2]

James questioned especially the credibility of the protagonist: "her offering to marry Hamlin strikes me as false, really unimaginable. Besides: *he* wouldn't, I think: he must at last have been immensely afraid of her." His commentary apparently left Lee contrite and remorseful, refusing to write another novel for the next two decades. So what was this "nasty" novel all about? A brief summary of the plot may help readers understand the contemporary outrage.

Anne Brown, an exotic-looking Italian nursemaid who unmistakably bears the traits of Jane Morris, is "discovered," wooed, and educated by the aes-thetic painter-poet Walter Hamlin, a pale replica of Dante Gabriel Rossetti. Hamlin adopts the young Italian as his muse and model, planning to endow her beauty with a soul that would love and inspire him. He draws up a con-tract that includes an independent income for her and a special covenant that binds him to marry her if *she* so wishes, but with no adverse effect on her finances if she does not. Anne becomes the celebrated object of desire for his aesthetic friends, but to Hamlin's chagrin, his beautiful Galatea refuses to play her part and develops her own mind. Dreaming of a career at Girton, she studies political economy with her cousin, Richard Brown, a member of Par-liament and social reformer, and takes up teaching working-class girls in an evening school. Walter Hamlin's morals and art meanwhile deteriorate under the influence of his Russian-born cousin, the attractive but sinister Sacha Elaguine. At the end, Anne decides to marry Hamlin despite her alienation from her debauched benefactor, hoping that she can retard his further decline.

Contemporary criticism was prompted by the book's alleged immorality:

that Anne—free from any economic constraints—marries a man she detests. Lee was accused of having violated good taste, literary standards, and even her own aesthetic beliefs. She was denounced for crude caricature informed by unseemly anger and the ignorance of an outsider who had not been in London long enough to have grasped the subtleties of aestheticism. In light of Lee's biography, it is telling that the first part of the novel is written from Hamlin's viewpoint and in the lighter tone of satire, which turns somber only when Anne's moral earnestness becomes the narrative center. Even then, the diatribe against "the clique-and-shop shoddy aestheticism" of the pretentious "poeticules"[3] is not altogether heavy-handed, but has burlesque and comic moments reminiscent of Du Maurier or Gilbert and Sullivan poking fun at the eccentricities of aesthetic art.

Putting aside for a moment Anne's exaggerated moralism (not uncommon in New Women novels), we find in *Miss Brown* some unusual angles on the psychological subtleties of aesthetic sensationalism. Through Lee's main character we participate in her skeptical evaluation of aesthetic lore from a woman's point of view.[4] Female participation in aestheticism, as Elaine Showalter reminds us in *Daughters of Decadence,* did not have high priority for literary history, so that "[w]hen we think of literature of the fin de siècle, the writers who come most readily to mind are men" (x). Women were ubiquitous in aesthetic and decadent art, but their images—romanticized fallen women or dark, devouring femmes fatales—were informed by antifeminism and misogyny. On the surface, women's aesthetic texts of the 1880s and '90s circulate similar images; but as studies such as Martha Vicinus's "The Adolescent Boy: Fin-de-Siècle Femme Fatale?" have revealed, the familiar images are informed by women's different policies and are now being analyzed to question the categorical premises for the entire era.[5] Similarly, Lee's female protagonist has all the qualities of beauty worshipped by the aesthetes, but, because of her independent mind, her looks have a very different meaning for herself. Behind the exotic beauty of Anne Brown we find a morally outspoken woman who has no patience with the erotic visions of her artistic friends. Anne's aesthetic views may appear shrill and outlandish, but her crass reactions also elucidate the impossibility of a female position within the aesthetic male agenda.

On the surface, *Miss Brown* is a "typical Victorian novel" with a happy ending, as Vineta Colby's summary shows:

A beautiful but poor heroine rescued from the misery of a servant-life by a well-to-do poet and artist who educates and ultimately marries her. There is a sinister villainess who lures the hero away temporarily and a stalwart rival suitor for the heroine, but the intrigue, having padded out the requisite number of volumes, is evaporated by the inevitable happy ending. (255)[6]

But Colby also tells us that the story is more complex. The heroine's inner monologue of disillusion and doubt subverts the romance plot and turns it into a mockery of itself. Parallel to Anne's personal "awakening," the novel gradually unmasks the affectation of high aestheticism, which appeals to Anne only as long as she does not understand it. Despite her aesthetic education, she reveals an old-fashioned taste for morally straight art and finally turns into a neo-Platonic idealist who equates the beautiful with the "good." From this position she attacks her weak-willed mentor, who worships the darker side of poetry, which Lee associated with the subversive erotics of Swinburne and Baudelaire. Walter Hamlin's and Anne Brown's positions complement each other as aesthetic extremes of the time: he identifies unapologetically with morbid art, which her almost ridiculously purist moral obsession has to condemn as "impure" and "filthy."

Critics who rebuked *Miss Brown* for its staunch moralism have also identified the protagonist with the author, expressing their surprise at Lee's departure from aestheticism. Some have attributed her "leap of faith" to her first encounters with aesthetic London in the early eighties.[7] "Her growing knowledge of aesthetic literature, and of the writers themselves, revealed the decadent and erotic strain latent in aestheticism, and it disgusted her" (Ormond, 151). If we accept the parallel between author and protagonist, the novel strangely deviates from Lee's theoretical writings of the same period, wherein she advocates her version of art for art's sake against her "strawman," Ruskin:

> And to this constant moralizing, hallowing, nay, purifying of art, are due, as we have seen, the great number of Ruskin's errors; his system is false, and only evil can spring from it. . . . He has made the enjoyment of mere beauty a base pleasure requiring a moral object to purify it, and in so doing, he has destroyed its [art's] own purifying power. (*Belcaro,* 226)

Lee tries to explain Ruskin's "ethical system of aesthetics" as a bridge between the natural pull he felt toward art's sensuality and his puritan education, which constrained him to castigate such natural impulses. Ruskin's split self represents to her "the strangest battles and compromises which are daily taking place between our moral and our artistic halves" (*Belcaro*, 201). At the same time, her passionate account of Ruskin's rare combination of "an artist, a critic, and a moralist" reveals how much she identified with him:

> He has possessed within himself two very perfect characters, has been fitted out for two very noble missions:—the creation of beauty and the destruction of evil; and of these two halves each has been warped; of these two missions each has been hampered by the very nobility of the man's nature: . . . by his heroic and lamentable clinging to his own belief in harmony where there is discord, in perfection where there is imperfection. There are natures which cannot be coldly or resignedly reasonable, which despite all possible demonstration, cannot accept evil as a necessity and injustice as a fact . . . . Such a nature is John Ruskin. (201)

Lee's psychological picture of Ruskin's dual character has obliquely entered her novel. The "Ruskinian dilemma," embodied in the two protagonists, Walter Hamlin and Anne Brown, also reflects Lee's own ambivalence over her role as an aesthetic critic. Being both attracted to and alienated by aestheticism, Vernon Lee creates a double perspective through her main characters, each representing a different side in her struggle with the rights and wrongs of the movement. Lee obviously conceived *Miss Brown* as a satire on aestheticism but became increasingly engrossed with the evolving character of her female protagonist. This growing identification with Anne Brown turns the novel into a moral battleground. Lee was surprised at the critics' identification of Anne Brown as her spokesperson. But is it credible that Lee—as she claimed in a letter to Mary Robinson—had ascribed to herself the role of the selfish, cold, vain, trifling, and degraded Walter Hamlin?[8]

The novel shows that Lee was troubled by a form of aestheticism that worshiped woman's sexual beauty but limited her self-determination. She resolved to make her own voice heard in the aesthetic discourse so as to arrest its subsuming of hedonist styles that attended to male desires while professing to enhance artistic beauty. In *Miss Brown,* Lee mingles two different aims: first, to create a female viewpoint within the male-defined movement and second, to explore the social effects of aestheticism. These aims explain her switch from one protagonist to the other and her abandonment of satire to finish the novel as a moral tale.

*Miss Brown* reflects Vernon Lee's own story: the making of an aesthetic critic

with a social conscience. The form of the novel allows Lee to explore her personal experience while concurrently testing aesthetic doctrine in a social environment.[9] *Miss Brown* affords us an unusual angle: as seen through the eyes of a
woman from a lower class *and* a different country, aestheticism is severally removed from the familiar view. Anne Brown, like Lee, studies "aesthetically correct" literature and art, but her staunch morality, intensified by her cultural
difference, keeps her at a distance from her mentor. The uneducated Italian servant girl and the fashionable aesthetic luminary form an "odd couple," antagonistic and complementary at the same time. Their multiple doublings (male-female,
upper class–lower class, master-servant, teacher-pupil, aesthete-moralist) set the
ideological limits for the narrative.

Doubling male and female characters was not an uncommon strategy in
nineteenth-century novels, from Emily Brontë's *Wuthering Heights* to Sara
Grand's *The Heavenly Twins* (1893) and including Lee's own brother-sister
novella, *Ottilie* (1883). In *Miss Brown,* the doubling is framed as a master-pupil
relationship which was to become a key motif in Lee's exploration of subjectivity (as in *Baldwin* and *Althea*). Anne Brown is so infused with her mentor's
ideas that she can hardly be imagined without him. Their relationship bears a
certain resemblance to Vernon Lee's perception of her own tutelage under her
male mentors John Ruskin and Henry James, but especially Walter Pater. As
Anne was borrowing her education from Hamlin, Lee was borrowing her language from her "masters." But the equation is more complex. The unstable
Walter Hamlin, in spite of his suggestive first name, is not a simulacrum of
Walter Pater. Lee had the highest respect for Pater's literary discipline and
valued his civil, gentlemanly kindness. She would scarcely have attributed to
the Oxford don any of the depraved or lascivious traits depicted in Walter
Hamlin. The latter's dual talent as a painter-poet, his sensuous artistic styles,
and his works' titles rather allude to Rossetti or Swinburne, of whose artistic
sincerity Lee was particularly suspicious.

But we should not overestimate the obvious biographical resemblances in
Lee's work. For her fictitious characters, she liberally borrowed traits from her
friends and acquaintances. Her methods were not different from those of other
writers, only less discreet. As a critic, Lee discouraged autobiographical readings.
Literature was the projection of life into style; highly metaphorical and much too
"widened, generalized by the universal experience" to become a "real unveiling"
of the author. To Lee a writer should be conceived as a function of "modes of life

not as a person, a man with an address and a biography, but as a Writer" (*Handling of Words*, 109–10).

Lee's texts disappoint any mimetic interpretation. Her abstracted biographical recordings are exercises in transcribing new forms of consciousness and point of view. Her pseudonym in itself invites our identification of Vernon Lee (and here we can repeat her own words) "not as a person, . . . with an address and a biography," but as an agent in the tradition of aesthetic construction of cultural identity. In the nineteenth century, one of the prominent places for this construction is the bildungsroman.

## FEMALE "BILDUNG" AND THE NOVEL

*Miss Brown* has all the ingredients of the traditional (male) bildungsroman, in which the hero engages in the double task of consolidating his identity and integrating his self into an adverse or antagonistic society. His journey or education implies rebellion, struggle, and personal growth. Under ideal conditions, he evolves into a constructive and happy member of society, but his eventual reintegration requires him to renounce some part of his original quest for perfection. The female bildungsroman follows a similar trajectory: through the struggle against an irrational or hostile environment, the heroine gains maturity and happiness—in her case, usually found in marriage.

In accordance with the narrative tradition, Anne Brown's individual striving appears to be reconciled to the laws of society through her marriage. To meet the middle-class standards of her new life, the former servant girl has to be elevated through her "Bildung." In fulfillment of her earliest aspirations (and of Hamlin's desire), she becomes "worthy" to marry her teacher and guardian. But the terms are strained. We can read *Miss Brown* as a traditional Victorian bildungsroman only by ignoring the heroine's inner contradictions, a condition that is next to impossible, as she is the "focalizer" (Genette) of most of the book. A closer look at the heroine's struggle for self-determinacy reveals the incongruity between her awakening to multiple possibilities in life and her resigned assent to marriage. What is worse, she is fully aware of the despairing note in her project: renouncing her early desire for improvement, she settles for an unsatisfactory status quo. "[S]he could not make him [Hamlin] grow better; her position would be as that of a woman who devoted herself to nurse a person sick of an incurable disease" (1:278). Anne's decision seems absurd. It is made under no material, legal, or social pressure and contradicts the inner growth she has achieved through her "Bildung." We suspect that such self-immolation points to something else. When at the end of this nine-hundred-page book the protagonist eventually subjects her life to the laws of narrative convention rather than to the logic of her reality, the novel's "meaning" is seriously undermined. Does the ending reflect an incongruence between subject matter and literary form? Is a deviation from the romance plot, as Rachel Blau DuPlessis argues in *Writing beyond the Ending,* woman's attempt "to change story," which "signals a dissent from social norms as well as narrative forms" (20)? If events, emotions, or endings are no longer recognizable, the reader becomes distanced, not only from the expected narrative but also from the learned "patterns of response." In this light, the inconsistency of *Miss Brown* points, beyond the novel proper, to the literary tradition of the bildungsroman, which Lee subverts even when using its structure.

Lee seems to anticipate what twentieth-century feminist critics find wrong with the female bildungsroman. Although female heroines populate the bild-ungsroman genre increasingly in the nineteenth century, we should not speak of a female bildungsroman in its strictest sense before "Bildung" became a reality for women.[10] The masculine origin of the genre is evident in its assumption that the protagonist is free to move about and has access to social options and experiences from which women were excluded. If, as Charlotte Brontë puts it in *Jane Eyre,* women desire the same as men and if the constraints for women are greater, then it follows that the female search for self-definition must take a different path. While women could develop a sense of identity within the familiar determinants of the patriarchal context, they could do so only as "others" or "strangers," not unlike the alienated Romantic male hero.[11]

We may not quite agree with Lorna Ellis's pessimistic reversal that for the female protagonist "growing up involves growing down" (32), but we can see why the heroine's path cannot be represented in the traditional idiom of the bild-ungsroman. A woman's development, as Mary Poovey has shown, may even involve a form of masquerade, since the code of propriety for women demanded that "self assertion had to look like something other than what it was" (29). In fact, bildungsroman heroines often gain a form of empowerment while at the same time appearing more submissive. In *Jane Eyre,* for example, the reader cannot quite decide whether Jane's consenting to marriage intimates a happy ending or an ironizing impulse on Brontë's part. This ambiguity, as Lorna Ellis suggests, depends on the double-edged portrayal of female development, both conservative and subversive: "The protagonists are reintegrated into society through traditional marriages, but their growing ability to understand and to manipulate societal expectations has subversive aspects and implications" (34). The question of whether the female bildungsroman presents a model for rebellion or for "coping" (Ellis, 40–41) has to be investigated in the tensions between the genre and its individual enactment. Often enough, the heroine's unchartered subtext implies an authorial commentary that subverts the main text but would not have been possible without the bildungsroman structure.

Similar tensions exist in *Miss Brown*. Initially, the heroine is eager to fit into aesthetic society but, with her growing knowledge, she despises and reacts against her peers. Her "Bildung" does not reconcile her to society but actually encourages her to rebel. Yet, she is not able to build an independent position against the aesthetic (male) standards which evidently collide with her (female) reserve. This discrepancy "lead[s] to a disjunction between a surface plot, which affirms social conventions, and a submerged plot, which encodes rebellion" (Abel, Hirsch, and Langland, 12).

A break in textual unity can reveal forms of patriarchal oppression, but it does not necessarily dismiss them. Instead, the female bildungsroman designs ways for women's self-assertion *within* societal limitations. Similar to the romantic forms of alienation in the (male) bildungsroman, women's patterns also include withdrawal into interiority. However, the male version of withdrawal typically results from the hero's inward belief in his superior character, which gives him the illusion of independence from society's expectations. In the nineteenth-century female bildungsroman, inwardness symbolizes women's ability to cope with their frustration over their legal or economic dependency (Ellis, 38). The heroine's struggle is a form of coping that seldom removes the cause of frustration but transforms it into emotional or spiritual fulfillment, compensating her for material or legal inequality.

Anne Brown's situation is slightly different. She suffers no material alienation and has access to (aesthetic) "Bildung," which means that she occupies almost a male position. Her frustration is caused by the constraints created by social and sexual expectations placed on women. Although Anne's exotic beauty corresponds to a new aesthetic ideal of womanhood, her androgynous saintliness contradicts her appearance and resists the masculine search for pleasure. In this last aspect, *Miss Brown* resembles other New Woman novels, where purity or asexuality is often "constructed around the collapse of heterosexual relationships" (Heilmann, 85). The reading of purity can be taken even further, as Kathy Psomiades has done, so that it "signals sexually dissident desires" (25). In this sense, Anne's statuesque sexlessness, like Pater's Winckelmann, can also point to an alternative sexual style so that "the prude is just a pervert who refuses to admit it" (27).

In *Miss Brown* the discourse of purity is directed against heterosexuality as a serious impediment for women's self-realization. Anne can only slip into ready-made roles, aptly symbolized by the dresses Hamlin designs for her. She can play only decorous or ancillary roles: model, artwork, wife, mistress, or nurse. She can choose, but she cannot create her part. Should we then read her final consent to marriage as her recognition that female existence outside heterosexual markers is impossible? Anne does not have the imaginative power to see herself beyond the reality that her London environment provides. She encounters what Lee later formulated as one of the main problems in women's self-definition: the uncertainty of what women "really" are other than "women as a creation of men" ("The Economic Parasitism of Women," 294). In Anne's resignation to marriage, the novel picks up the thematic limitations of the female bildungsroman: it cannot provide even the imaginary space for female autonomy or self-definition. Therefore, "different" women like Anne Brown cannot step out of it to explore "the thing which they expect, with which their soul seems, in some pre-natal condition to have become familiar as the one great certainty" (*Miss Brown*, 3:276).

The bildungsroman narrative cannot express Anne Brown's arcane desire and merely describes her frustration with women's present status: "But with Anne Brown it was different. Some few women seem to be born to have been men, or at least not to have been women" (2:307). Such women, the narrator explains, have no social reality (yet) and thus are defined only in negative terms: "Masculine women, mere men in disguise, they are not . . . but women without woman's instincts and wants, sexless—women made not for man but for humankind" (2:309). While I agree with Kathy Psomiades that Lee's avowal of sexlessness here conveys an alternative sexual identification that has a destabilizing effect on gender categories (24–25), I would not read the sexless code to mean invariably the presence of same-sex desire. It appears that Lee is equally interested in the question of how to represent a different, autonomous female voice, in other words, how to exit the status of "woman" without becoming "man."

It remains to be seen how Lee resolves aesthetically the conflict between traditional narrative and her representation of an alternative female subject. For this purpose, it might be helpful to return briefly to the ideological implications of the bildungsroman. With the rise of the middle class in the eighteenth and nineteenth centuries, the ideology of the individual came to imply increasingly the aspect of agency in the self-defined human subject, which is reflected in the bildungsroman. It is not sufficient for the individual merely to ingest the standards of society; the "free citizen" must consciously and affirmatively recognize the standards of the world as his own.[12] This element of the bildungsroman, as Ellis has argued, reveals its conservative aspect (40). Its fusion of external compulsion and internal impulse into a new unity arguably creates a socially agreeable subject. We find such acquiescence, for instance, in *Wilhelm Meister* where "harmonious objects" return to their creator and reduce the distance between subject and objective world. Growth is endorsed in the form of objects that can be reappropriated by the individual, in other words, culture or "Bildung" (Moretti, 116). "Bildung" supposedly creates a realm where alienating social forces intrude less severely. In this sense, education is aesthetic and functions (as does beauty) as a trope for wholeness, harmony, and perfection. "Bildung" thus can restore aesthetically the autonomous and wholesome (male) individual:[13]

> Instead of directly confronting the great powers of social life, it [aesthetic education] creates a new realm of existence in which those abstract and deforming forces penetrate less violently and can be reconstituted in syntony with the individual aspiration toward harmony. This realm is organized according to the dictates of "beauty" and "play"; it is pervaded with the "happiness" of the individual; and the Bildungsroman is its narrative explication. (Moretti, 119)

The concept of "Bildung" was defined by social (male) elites.[14] But in the late nineteenth century, when new social groups claimed access to power and public life, the character of "Bildung" began to change, and the bildungsroman increasingly featured female protagonists. Conventional aesthetics believed women to be incapable of achieving aesthetic perfection through their own agency (an important point of criticism in Elizabeth Barrett Browning's *Aurora Leigh*); because they were assumed to need a male mediator or perfecter,[15] aesthetic education was not meant to give women the same sense of autonomy. Consequently, we find women's educational ends invariably related to and mediated by men and sanctioned by marriage.

In *Miss Brown,* the heroine emulates the masculine "struggle after the ideal," while woman's traditional goal, love for a man, is "a mere secondary concern" (2:308). But when Anne Brown sacrifices her ideal for a less than ideal male character (Hamlin), she succumbs to the narrative convention of the bildungsroman. Her inability to assume female identity independent from man reflects the limitations of the genre: the female subject is "harmonized" in a marriage which, despite its hollowness, binds her in a male-centered plot.

Traditionally, the "choices" for female heroines in nineteenth-century novels are sanctioned either by marriage or by death. According to Rita Felski, these stereotypical endings could not be transcended until the twentieth century in the so-called self-discovery narrative in which women writers massively redrew the confines of heterosexual romance plots (*Beyond Feminist Aesthetics,* 124). Felski links the transformation of the novel to a wide range of changes in women's socioeconomic status, but cautions the reader not to see fiction and social reality in a direct relationship of cause and effect. At the level of the "social imaginary," where cultural meanings are produced and distributed, alternative ways of existence for women became more widely dispersed in the "New Woman" novels around the turn of the century. Their alternative plots motivated new and more differentiated variations of the female bildungsroman, which feminist critics from the 1970s began to call "Entwicklungsroman" (development novel), to show that the female bildunsgsroman articulated a different sense of subjectivity for women as they moved more visibly into the public sphere (137). Not all critics have been optimistic. Gilbert and Gubar described the female bildungsroman as "a story of enclosure and escape" with an "almost unthinkable goal" (338–39); and Bonnie Hoover Braendlin observed of the modern bildungsroman that it focuses on "the crisis occasioned by a woman's awakening . . . to the stultification and fragmentation of a personality devoted not to self-fulfillment and awareness, but to a culturally determined, self-sacrificing, and self-effacing existence" (19).

The situation in *Miss Brown* resembles the more troubling definitions of the bildungsroman as a form of entrapment. Anne's life story appears circular rather than progressive. Like Maggie Tulliver in *The Mill on The Floss,* Anne has become lost in the exploration of her inner landscapes, unable to find any exterior actualization for them, either in her work or in her love. Anne's turn to marriage is not the act of a free individual, since the social forces she has internalized do not give her true freedom of choice.

The happiness, therefore, which she was losing—the independence, the activity, the serenity . . . was only a distant and unsubstantial thing; she had never experienced it, and it could not well be realised. But she knew by experience, familiar with its every detail, the unhappiness which lay in the future as Hamlin's wife, for this future would be but a return to the past; and she felt as might a person lost in a catacomb, and who, having got to a chink, having seen the light and breathed the air, would be condemned to wander again, to rethread for ever the black and choking corridors leading nowhere. (3:277)[16]

The ironic discrepancy between the heroine's intellectual self-knowledge and the restrictions of her internalized socialization is thematized in several late-nineteenth-century novels. Unlike earlier Victorian novels, New Woman fiction in particular, from Sara Grand's *The Heavenly Twins* (1893) to Emma Frances Brooke's *A Superfluous Woman* (1894), reveals the traditional choices available to women as increasingly stifling and repressive.[17] Novels like Olive Schreiner's *The Story of an African Farm* (1883) or Mona Caird's *The Daughters of Danaus* (1894) depict traditional marriage as confinement but do not offer viable alternatives. Similarly, Anne Brown desires a path beyond marriage but finally gives up her education for Hamlin. Her inability to leave Hamlin, in spite of her material and intellectual independence, shows that her moral bonds to Hamlin keep her in place even against her better judgment. Her exaggerated sense of duty and perverse self-depreciation pull her back into "tragic passiveness." The novel here thematizes a subtle and less visible form of women's dependency rooted in the habitual memory of the body.[18]

The discrepancy between women's intellectual liberation, on the one hand, and their moral fetters, on the other, cannot be resolved in the idealistic plot of the bildungsroman nor by the bourgeois ideal of "Bildung," which harmonizes external and internal worlds. *Miss Brown* does not offer imaginary solutions for real contradictions but instead, through the plot's incongruities, forces us to look more closely at the impediments of internalized roles. Lee dis-places an Italian servant girl in aesthetic London to make visible the social contradictions in this scenario. The bohemian artists reject the very middle-class values that help Anne advance socially: high standards of work and morality and the belief in personal improvement. Ennui and self-indulgence, considered "hip" by the aesthetes, can only appear decrepit to her. Through Anne's limited, lower-class perspective,

Lee exposes the aesthetes' "false consciousness" brought on by snobbish ignorance and ideological blindness.

Anne Brown's absurd transformation from a poor, plain servant girl to a
fashionable aesthetic critic reveals the ideological side of educational ideals:
education cannot be universally desirable because it is always informed by
specific class and gender interests. Anne's "useless" aesthetic training adjusts
her to a leisurely aesthetic life-style, but alienates her from her working-class
background so that "she could not well understand how she came to be where
she was." Temporarily, she rebels against her new social status, for instance, by
refusing to take a carriage and, instead, walking "through the London streets,
in murky spring weather," to readjust herself to what she sees as the appropri-
ate life-style of a working-class woman. "Anne had made it a rule for the last
two or three months to deprive herself of all luxuries. She did not wish to enjoy
everything that she had a right to" (3:56).

In her endeavor to be socially useful ("To gain her bread, no matter how
harshly; to be of some use, to teach at school or nurse at a hospital"), her aesthetic
education proves to be utterly worthless (3:52). Her offer to teach medieval literature to working-class women is scoffed at: "political economy is what we want
the most." Anne's experience reveals that the contemporary promotion of education for the underprivileged cannot have any liberating effect unless it is embedded in a larger political context. The harmonizing value of aesthetic "Bildung"
only helps perpetuate upper-middle-class values. Anne's education turns her
into a lady which implies that she becomes an adornment for her would-be husband, Walter Hamlin, but otherwise "useless," not only for her own class but for
society at large.

Although Lee attempts to "mirror" Anne's consciousness realistically, her
flexible use of free indirect style, known from Jane Austen's novels, allows Lee to
insert into the text her own interpretation which challenges the logic of Anne's
character "of one piece."[19] Thus she can show us that Anne's struggle for self-
determinacy is caught between individual autonomy and social responsibility,
both representing conflicting positions in bourgeois liberalism. Anne's female
sense of obligation toward Hamlin adds a gendered dimension to this conflict.
Through her sense of personal debt, she feels bound to Hamlin, in spite of the freedom of choice he provides for her. Their contract, supposedly drawn up between
two independent individuals, ignores the fact that the conditions for this relationship are constituted somewhere else: in their unequal class and gender positions.

Hamlin's seemingly noble gesture, which grants her the magical sum of £500, even if she does not marry him, is gradually revealed as his calculated, adhesive possessiveness. He plans his courtship in every detail. More in love with his idea than with the woman of his choice, he knows "that either Anne Brown must bloom for him and by him, must be his most precious possession and his most precious loan to the world—or that Anne Brown must be simply and deliberately buried under a bushel" (1:120). She has to become either "the avowedly most beautiful woman in England" or remain "a sordid nursery governess." This is not sympathy for a lower-class girl, but selfish desire to invest female beauty with his own fantasies so that "Walter Hamlin's life should be crowned by gradually endowing with vitality, and then wooing, awakening the love of this beautiful Galatea whose soul he had moulded" (1:121). Anne, unsuspecting of his scheming, is generous in her praise of

> Hamlin's generosity and delicacy of the mind—of the quixotic way in which he had bound himself while leaving her free—of the chivalrous way in which he had dowered her, making her feel almost as if all this money, which placed her on his own level, was her own inheritance, and not his charity. (3:48)

From her naive viewpoint, Anne can only perceive Hamlin's generosity without any visible profit for himself as an unselfish act. Taking for granted her own inferiority, she is tortured by doubts as to whether she could be "worthy" of him. Hamlin welcomes her fixation on himself since he is "rather pleased that the creature whom he was going to teach how to think and how to feel, did not manifest any particular mode of thinking and feeling of her own" (1:201).

In the end, Hamlin has calculated right, and Anne takes the bait he has laid out for her. Through this "sacrifice," she not only pays back her personal debt, but also fulfills her social role as a woman and as a servant. Her decision is based on an ideological deception: what she sees (subjectively) as an individual obligation is (objectively) an effect of the socioeconomic condition of inequality. The generous education that Hamin provides does not liberate her but tightens her ideological bind. "Bildung" makes her conscious of choices in life, but it fails to help her transform this awareness into social or political energy.

*Miss Brown* offers a projection of what may happen when a nineteenth-century woman is educated as a man, that is, as a subject, although in the ideological context she cannot be anything but a woman and an object. The ideal of "Bildung," designed for man's autonomy, has to fail for woman because of her mediated existence. Lee's novel mocks the genre of the bildungsroman by refusing to resolve the ideological contradictions it submerges in "Bildung." And yet she had to use the very form she mocked.


## AESTHETICISM, CLASS, AND THE FEMALE VOICE

The question that remains to be addressed is why Lee would turn against aestheticism in *Miss Brown* although her theoretical writing at that time reveals her identification with the movement. Leonee Ormond suggests we look for an explanation in Lee's disenchantment with aestheticism when she personally encountered members of the aesthetic set in the early 1880s. The loosely knit intellectual circle included, among others, Ford Madox Brown, Justin McCarthy, William Sharp, Alfred O'Shaughnessy, Mrs. Humphry Ward, Theodore Watts-Dunton, and Edmund Gosse. Vernon Lee came into contact with this group through the Robinson sisters (Mary and Mabel), but soon became critical of the artists' affectation, "mutual admiration," and latent erotic strain.

In *Miss Brown,* Lee ostensibly departs from the aesthetic positions she adopted in *Belcaro* (1881), where she emphasizes that form in art has to be divorced from moral content. Similarly, in *Euphorion,* published in the same year as *Miss Brown* (1884), her historical approach clearly follows aesthetic principles. It seems almost as if Lee's moral and aesthetic attitudes are divided between her theoretical and her fictional work. Did she believe that aestheticism could preserve its idealizing virtue when encased in the more abstract language of the essay? Does the novel, because of its reliance on character and social detail, reveal a side of aestheticism that is concealed in nonfictional language? It is evident that Lee's novel offers more insight into her self-understanding as a female aesthete than do any of her theories. In *Miss Brown,* Lee's projection of a female voice is suspended in the dialogue between her two protagonists. This dual perspective reflects Lee's own dilemma, that is, her intervention into aesthetic male discourse in a split voice. Anne's moral position gives her strength as a person but not as an art critic. Her judgment is qualified by personal emotion in comparison to Hamlin's detached view. However, from the novel alone, we cannot be sure which position Lee endorsed. By reading *Miss Brown* against Lee's aesthetic theories in *Belcaro,* especially the essays "Ruskinism," "In Umbria," and "A Dialogue on Poetic Morality," we gain a better understanding of how she attaches her characters (and herself) to the aesthetic debates in the early 1880s.

In "Ruskinism," Lee positions herself as anti-Ruskinian, refusing to evaluate art by any moral or religious guidelines at all. She goes to great lengths explaining that art and morality belong to separate realms, pleading for aesthetic autonomy, an argument which placed her in the camp of the contemporary "l'art pour l'art" movement. In "In Umbria," she approaches the same issue from a slightly differ-ent angle by investigating the correlation between art and artistic personality. She extracts art once more from any auxiliary function by arguing that the artist's role is to create beauty and not to dilute his genius with other concerns. In a Kan-tian analysis Lee proposes that beauty be produced separately from life (meaning the artist's character) by defining artistic talent as a faculty which can be divorced from the artist's human existence.

> The work is produced by the man, but not by the whole of him; only by that portion which we call the artist; and how much that portion is, what relation it bears to the whole man, we can ascertain by asking ourselves what faculties are required for the production of a work of art. (*Belcaro*, 177)

Based on this assumption, she argues that an artist's "impure" personal life can-not affect his art. Her prime example is Perugino who, in spite of his cynicism and greediness, produced some of the most gentle and spiritual paintings of the Italian Renaissance. Aesthetic and moral excellence may emerge from the same sources (*Belcaro*, 208), but they cannot be linked in a causal chain, as Ruskin sug-gested. Art and culture do not deteriorate because of societies' moral decline, but they die of their own essential principles.

> Art, if it lives, must grow, and if it grows it must grow old and die. And this fact gradually, though instinctively, beginning to be felt by all thinkers on art, Ruskin, with his theory of moral aesthetics, could never recognize. (*Bel-caro*, 217)

To be sure, Lee's difference from Ruskin is not, as she claims, in applying evolu-tionary principles, but in her denial of cause and effect. If the quality of art were an effect of morality, she adds, is it not strange that those "anomalous times of social dissolution" bring forth "our greatest art"? (173).

It is interesting that Lee's homage to beauty for its own sake should apply only to visual art and that she is less permissive when it comes to writing. In "A Dialogue of Poetic Morality," she argues that beauty in poetry, which stands for literature at large, can be achieved only through the poet's lifelong struggle for purity. Lee's reasons for exempting visual art from the strictures she places on literature are not fully convincing. Reminding the reader of the *ut pictura poesis* debate, she forces, in a slight variation of Lessing, a hierarchical distinction between painter and poet. To her, language, unlike art, is informed by both sensual *and* intellectual sensations. The visual artist can be reduced to an "optic machine," whereas the poet, "whose works are made up of all that which nature perceives," puts the greatest part of his entire personality in his work (*Belcaro,* 190). Poetry, to a much larger extent than painting, is intertwined with ethics: "Now, in poetry, one half of beauty and ugliness is purely ethical, and if the poet who deals with this half, the half which comprises human emotion and action, has no sense of right and wrong, he will fail" (250). Thus the poet's work bears the highest ethical responsibility of any art form. It is interesting that in *Miss Brown,* poetry or prose (in other words, language) appears always more corrupt than painting. Obviously, since language was her medium, the writer's responsibility was of more concern to her. She realized that in an expanding literary marketplace, writing could become a powerful instrument in forming opinions and judgments.

In her last *Belcaro* essay, "A Dialogue on Poetic Morality," Lee reinforces this concern when she describes literature as a prime influence on the public's morality.[20] Convinced of her good cause—but not always convincing—she cautions writers of their manipulative potential. The imaginative power of literature, she argues, enters a reader's mind and easily settles "fluctuating opinions" beyond the control of consciousness. Particularly in an era of shifting values, literature has to be much more aware of itself than in previous centuries. People can no longer "tie their boats to rocks of religion or deistic mysticism, or of social *convenances,* which we have now discovered to be by no means granite, but some sort of sea deposit, of hardened sand, whose formation we understand and no longer rely upon" (*Belcaro,* 255). While aesthetic art was still mocking Victorian earnestness, Lee worried about the threats of mass manipulation and the triumph of vulgarity and self-indulgent pleasures that society denied ordinary individuals in real life.

Since art affects the human psyche at the level of the unconscious, to Lee, art needs to be as remote as possible from what is "most necessary in nature." She was suspicious of Swinburne, whom she accused of slipping sexual allusions into the readers' minds under the pretense of artistic freedom. Poetry to her should not be the meritless expression of what is merely our nature but a lifelong struggle for purity. She requires the poet to practice conscious ethics, not in the sense of a duty toward God, but as a responsibility toward modern society.[21]

Lee's aesthetic argument in "A Dialogue on Poetic Morality" leaves off where *Miss Brown* begins.[22] Like Cyril, the cynical artist in the dialogue, Walter Hamlin experiences a crisis in creativity. Cyril is troubled by his loss of ideals and doubts the relevance of art in a modern world. Hamlin also experiences a loss of purpose, but in the more fashionable form of ennui. He feels paralyzed by a melancholy indifference toward contemporary art, which celebrates him as an idol but offers him no inspiration. Both Cyril and Hamlin are thrown into doubt by their awareness of a "hideous reality," but each practices his own version of escapism. Cyril debates whether he should give up art, wondering "what moral right a man has to consume his life writing verses, when there is so much evil to remove" (*Belcaro*, 232). Hamlin, on the other hand, tries to secure art's exclusivity:

> The world is getting uglier and uglier outside us; we must out of the materials bequeathed to us by former generations and with the help of our own fancy, build for ourselves a little world within the world, a world of beauty, where we may live with our friends and keep alive whatever small sense of beauty and nobility still remains to us, that it may not get utterly lost, and those who come after us may not be in a wilderness of sordid sights and sordid feelings. (*Miss Brown*, 1:274)

Both Cyril and Hamlin despair because art has become too limited, but Cyril's interlocutor, Baldwin, offers another position.[23] Assuming that art has a vital function in any social context, he proclaims "the professional creators of good—they work not only for their immediate circle of like-minded friends, but for the world at large" (*Belcaro*, 242–43). According to Baldwin (and Lee), "[literature] can do both much more harm and much more good than it could do before" (271). Therefore, the "innocent" pleasure in art is its sole moral function left, which is to "fend off evil." Neither Cyril nor Hamlin sees the artist as a destroyer of evil. They echo Wilde and Pater in their creed that the artist is "made of infinitely finer stuff than other men." So it is his duty *not* to waste himself for

moral battles, but to devote himself exclusively to beauty. Cyril even argues that
the artist engaging in social issues is a hypocrite who has failed in his mission.

> We shall say that, in order to indulge in the moral luxury, the moral amuse-
> ment, of removing an imperceptible amount of pain, he has defrauded the
> world of the immense and long-lasting pleasure placed in his charge to give;
> we shall say that, in order to feel himself a little virtuous, this man has simply
> acted like a cheat and a thief. (*Belcaro*, 243)

Hamlin no longer believes in artistic calling. He finds that the modern artist no
longer has "the mission of artists in former days; it is much humbler, sadder, but
equally necessary" (*Miss Brown*, 1:274). He belongs to a later generation of artists, bored by worn-out mannerisms and craving new inspiration in "strange
beauty," personified in Anne, his "beautiful Galatea" (1:121), She is model and
artwork in one: Hamlin paints from her as well as into her, a kind of narcissistic
self-mirroring made visible in the model's image. Her soul has to remain abstract and empty so it can reflect Hamlin's own desire, fantasy, and creative
power:

> He wished to see more of her, but to see more only of her superb physical ap-
> pearance, and of that sullen, silent, almost haughty manner which accompa-
> nied it. As to anything there might be, intellectual or moral, behind this
> beautiful and dramatic creature, he did not care in the least, and would rather
> have seen nothing of it. . . . [T]he man respects the unknown woman as a god-
> dess and respects himself for having discovered her divinity. (1:50–53)

We find in this statement what Pater calls "Allgemeinheit:" "to seek the type
in the individual, to abstract and express only what is structural and perma-
nent, to purge from the individual all that belongs only to him" (*Renaissance*,
51). By concentrating on Anne's form, "purged" of her individuality, Hamlin
aesthetically distances her human side. When she is passionate, he enjoys the
intense expression; when she is sullen and somber, he savors her "tragic
beauty." Thus he can maintain the illusion of a muse who reflects more of her
creator than of herself.

Denying her socially rooted identity, he need not acknowledge her as a person, which also means that he does not have to address the moral standards by

which she critiques his art. When his spell over her begins to fade, Anne attacks Hamlin's aesthetization of vice and sin, which he stubbornly defends as the truth in aesthetic art (as a simplistic adaptation of Pater). Hamlin wants art to reflect any flicker of sensation, including those conventionally thought illicit, but sadly admits that "there is nothing to nourish art nowadays. . . . Art can't live where life is trivial" (1:273). In his defensiveness, Hamlin turns into a dogmatic stock figure repeating routinely that "such things must be judged from a purely artistic standpoint" (2:97). Artistic liberty must not be impaired by considerations outside the writer's will: "Everyone may write whatever passes through his head. . . . [A]s to responsibility, I repudiate such things" (3:33).

Put in such absolute terms, the claim for artistic freedom becomes unacceptable. Proclaiming that "everything is legitimate for the sake of an artistic effect" (2:94), Hamlin overburdens the aesthetic ideal. In the reality of the novel, this leads to serious consequences: Hamlin writes a slanderous letter to the fiancé of Anne's friend, Marjory Leigh, causing the couple's break-up. This ignoble move—inserted rather clumsily into the narrative—not only reveals Hamlin's petty nature, but also furnishes an example of Lee's theoretical argument on artistic responsibility in *Belcaro:*

> The poet is the artist, remember, who deliberately chooses as material for his art the feelings and actions of man; he is the artist who plays his melodies [on] . . . the human soul, which in its turn feels and acts; he is the artist who, if he blunders, does not merely fatigue a nerve or paralyze for a moment a physical sense, but injures the whole texture of our sympathies and deafens our conscience. (273–74)

It is obvious that Hamlin does not meet Lee's artistic ideal. Although he believes he speaks as a high aesthetic priest, he is only anxious to comply with the aesthetically correct standards of his circle, thus perverting the idea of artistic freedom. The real motive, his desire for admiration, limits not only his creativity but also his artistic honesty.

Vanity, hypocrisy, and lack of responsibility are the main points in Lee's criticism of the aesthetic movement in *Miss Brown*. Her picture abounds in crass distortions and oversimplifications, but she does not malign the aesthetes indiscriminately. One of her more likable characters is Cosmo Chough, "the poet of womanhood," whose genuine admiration for Anne and naive enthusiasm for anything decadent lends him a human touch. Chough's guileless enjoyment of beauty comes closest to what Vernon Lee calls "pure" pleasure or aesthetic disinterestedness. Chough's unselfconscious enthusiasm differs from the expressed ennui of the rest of the group. Most of all, he lacks selfishness and lecherous masculinity. To some extent, he embodies the "innocence" of Early Renaissance man who is the "child" on Vernon Lee's scale of development in human consciousness. To her, Early Renaissance art represented evil without knowing it: "The blindness to evil which constitutes the criminality of the Renaissance is so great as to give a certain innocence" (*Euphorion,* 1:102). Like Lee's Renaissance man, Chough is "passionately fond of letters and art." His innocuous enthusiasm resembles Anne's early idealization of aesthetic art. Like her, Chough is also a dilettante: a clerk who writes poetry in his spare time. To increase our empathy with Chough, Lee puts him in charge of a sick wife and several small children. We may wonder though how Chough, burdened with such responsibilities, can spend so much time discussing the sins of Lucretia Borgia.

Whereas Chough can be seen as a version of Hamlin's better self, the painter Edmund Lewis represents the morbid side of Hamlin's aestheticism. To Lewis art is a "free ticket" for all kinds of immoral or socially unacceptable acts. He chooses "sinful" subjects in order to shock his viewers and savor their reaction. He gives Anne a copy of *Mademoiselle de Maupin,* in hopes of seeing her shocked (*Miss Brown,* 2:150). For the same reason, Lewis exposes his erotic nude drawings to the vicar's "very young" and innocent daughters, slyly watching the effect on them with his "glittering eyes rising like that of a snake" (2:144). Whereas Hamlin finds pleasure in painting the two girls to preserve their beautiful impression—"so perfectly fresh, and unsullied"—Lewis tries to shock them to satisfy his morbid voyeurism. This, to Lee, is a perversion of the principle of art for its own sake, which, as she puts it in *Belcaro,* should not be abused "for the sake of an excitement, which the respectabilities of society do not permit their obtaining, except in imaginative form" (247). Anne makes the same point, but with moral pique: "these vain, weak, unreal poets and artists" abuse art as an alibi for "selfish enjoyment of beauty and selfish interest in sin" (*Miss Brown,* 2:133–34). Lee sees the movement stuck because art is no longer a "life-long struggle," but a ritual of self-satisfaction (2:89). Preoccupied with pleasure, Lee's aesthetes isolate themselves from society at large. While imagining themselves to be progressive and brazen, they simply reverse convention by worshiping immorality. Baldwin's warnings (in *Belcaro*) of the dangers in the new freedom of art become manifest here in the social milieu of Lee's novel: modern aesthetics requires disciplined and responsible writers; otherwise it will only become complacent, formulaic, and finally degenerate.

Another element of criticism enters the novel through Richard Brown, Anne's cousin, a social reformer modeled on William Morris.[24] Brown works for the improvement of society through the aesthetic and moral education of the lower classes; he sneers at aestheticism as the mannered expression of the pleasure-hunting leisure class. His campaign against social injustice makes him attractive to Anne, now disillusioned by the pretentious aesthetic life-style. Weary of her own passive role in the movement, Anne longs to render herself useful for Brown by employing her education for the benefit of the less privileged.

During her early visits to England, Lee herself had become increasingly aware of the "ugliness" at the lower end of the social scale, an awareness that spurred her criticism of the privileges her own class enjoyed. From 1884 on, she stayed fairly regularly at the home of the Fords, well-known philanthropists in the Leeds area. She became aware of the industrial landscape, saw the slums in Newcastle, and accompanied her friends Emily and Isabella Ford to socialist and labor union meetings. *Juvenilia* (1887), published three years after *Miss Brown,* shows the most obvious effect of Lee's visits to the industrial midlands. She now considers her early aesthetic ambitions class-blind and elitist and instead propagates a more equal distribution of cultural goods to all classes.

Lee's social awareness is still vague in *Miss Brown,* one of the earliest New Woman novels to address the question of gender and socialism.[25] For Lee, socialism is mainly a platform from which to attack the aesthetic movement. Consequently, Anne Brown's meditations about becoming more useful are more propagandistic than introspective:

> Without exactly knowing what she could do, or even whether she could do anything at all, she felt that she must work—work with all her might; for it seemed as if all the thoughts which the people about her refused to think, all the sympathy which they refused to feel, all the work which they refused to do, and all the sacrifices which they refused to make, must all be taken upon herself—as she alone must bear this terrible weight of rejected responsibilities. (3:219)

That Anne has now shouldered the social burden as an individual is the consequence of her disappointment with socialism as simply another form of selfishness:

[Y]our religion of science is only another form of selfish aestheticism: your
friends hanker after knowledge, as my friends hanker after beautiful pictures, and music, and poetry, and women: and as my people dignify their ap-
petites with the name of religion of beauty, so do yours sanctify theirs as the
worship of truth. (2:330)

Anne's sweeping dismissal of socialism is evidently accelerated by a crucial encounter between her and Richard Brown, which shows his alarmingly
conservative view of women's roles. Anne had hoped to find a new place in the
reform movement, working side by side with Richard for social improvement.
However, when the position of a secretary becomes available, Anne is not even
considered, although she is the obvious candidate who meets exactly the re-
quirements. Her dreams are shattered when she realizes that Richard is not interested in refashioning gender relations along more equitable lines.

"There is the son of one of our head workmen, a very intelligent lad, of whom
I am thinking; but perhaps he is not sufficiently educated yet. I must have
some one who knows German and French and so forth." Anne felt a lump in
her throat. Oh that she had been a man, instead of being this useless, base creature of mere comely looks, a woman, set apart for the contemplation of aesthetes! If she had been a man, and could have helped a man like Richard
Brown! (3:63)

Anne's former zeal turns into disgust when she discovers that Brown has been
less interested in her work than in her sexuality.

"Anne," cried Richard, seizing her hand, "I love you—I love you—I want
you—I must have you!" It was like the outburst of another nature, a strange,
unsuspected ego, bursting out from beneath the philanthropist's cool and
self-sacrificing surface. (3:73)

Richard offers to "free" her from Hamlin's guardianship, only to replace it by
his own desire, showing her that he, in spite of his outspoken respect for her,
has all along pursued her as a sexual object. The scene reveals the tensions between contemporary feminism and socialism because, as Sally Alexander puts
it, "labour men were notoriously unwilling to consider women—in the ab-

stract that is—as anything other than wives and mothers" (131). In *Miss Brown,* Richard Brown's revelation further limits Anne's choices: socialism, Anne's most obvious ally for an alternative identification that would fit her gender and class, is no longer available after it has become obvious that the masculine domination in the socialist movement makes it problematic for women.

> Richard Brown loved her, wanted her; it was the old nauseous story over again; the sympathy, the comradeship, the quiet brotherly and sisterly affection had all been a sham . . . and now the one man who had remained to her as an object of friendship and respect, her cousin Dick, had preached against selfish aestheticism, had talked her into positivistic philanthropy . . . what for? that he might satisfy his whim of possessing her. (3:76)

Both aestheticism and social reform movement have put her at a disadvantage because of her sex. The male representatives pursue her as a sexual object without allowing her to investigate other possibilities. In socialism Anne finds moral earnestness but no equality. Aestheticism offers her—at least materially— a certain independence, but its frivolous pleasure hunt remains alien to the frugality of her working-class ethics. True to her social background, Anne, "to whom happiness is a mere name, a negative thing," can conceive of pleasure only in terms of self-sacrifice and martyrdom.

> She had never hoped, scarcely even wished, for happiness; the semblance of it had passed before her eyes, had, for a brief time, made her life more acutely sensitive; but she returned to the negative: it was the law of her life. (3:193)[26]

Anne's aesthetic judgment thus cannot be understood as an absolute but rather as a function of her working-class values, which are readily mocked by her social superiors. The aesthetes' scorn for Anne's artistic taste has a greater social implication; it is directed not only against an "ignorant" individual but at the social group whose "habitus" (to use Pierre Bourdieu's term) she represents. In this sense, Walter Hamlin and Anne Brown represent not just Lee's aesthetic conflict, but her attempt to concretize abstract views in terms of class and gender. Bourdieu's classic observations on the function of taste as an expression of class distinction applies here:

As for the working classes, perhaps their sole function in the system of aesthetic positions is to serve as a foil, a negative reference point, in relation to which all aesthetics define themselves, by successive negations. (*Distinction*, 57)

The aesthetes' sneering at Anne's "Wordsworthian" taste in *Miss Brown* thus can be read as a metonymic representation of class difference. We understand now the function of the Italian servant girl: through her character, the social question is ever present and the aesthetic debates can never totally lift off from their historical reality. Through Anne Brown, the aesthetic movement's class-blindness is exposed as a function of their style, which constantly reenacts the distancing of an elitist group from the socially "inferior."

For a woman from the lower classes, life and art mean the same: servitude, hardship, and moral seriousness. To Anne, art is a manifestation of high morality that has a redeemable value and thus cannot harbor wasteful pleasure. She places Hamlin on a pedestal as she believes that his generosity puts her into contact with what she imagined to be her ideal. This forbids her to accept any of his art that does not reflect her image of him as "good." When she discovers his morbid side, she accuses him of simply imitating the fashionable trend of representing "hateful things." The attack on Hamlin's sincerity reveals the paradox of her own moral postulate: although she demands absolute truthfulness in his artistic expression, she cannot ultimately accept this quality because it implies the representation of immorality that she must reject.

According to Hamlin, Anne cannot grasp the complex relationship between art, artist, and modern reality because her thinking is structured in the simple polarities of good and bad, true and false. "But Anne Brown's nature was too completely homogenous—too completely without the innumerable strata, and abysses, and peaks, and winding ways" (2:18). Therefore, Hamlin's self-conscious negotiations between imagination and reality must remain unintelligible to her. What she considers "a pose" is to Hamlin the many-layered reality of his mind.

> The sort of shimmer, as of the two tints in a shot stuff, of reality and unreality, of genuine and affected feeling, of moods, noticed, treasured up, reproduced in himself,—which existed in Hamlin, would be perfectly unintelligible to Anne. (2:57)

Unable to see the validity of intellectual sensation, Anne demands from literature real-life strategies, which—as Lee remarks with a certain irony—may lead to "ludicrous disproportionateness."

> The poor girl, not understanding how such things [mysterious temptations] will shoot up in the poetic mind as a result of mere reading, and be nurtured there for a day for the sake of their strange colour, would screw up all her might to help him, writing to him to be patient, to be strong and bold, to remember the nobility of his nature. (1:224–25)

Anne Brown fails to see the freedom of imaginary intellectual processes that enhance the scope and variety of "human" experience. Her lack of creative vision confines her perception to the level of the "real" and isolates her from Hamlin's aesthetic art of imagined feelings and desires, which describes another kind of reality.

Again, we need to be reminded that Hamlin and Anne argue from different class and gender positions. They are almost textbook cases in Bourdieu's argument that people lacking a specific aesthetic competence apply to art the "perceptual schemes of their own ethos":[27] "The result is a systematic 'reduction' of things of art to the things of life, a bracketing of form in favour of 'human' content, which is barbarism par excellence from the standpoint of the pure aesthetic" (44). Lee's lower-class study is not always convincing. For a servant with a "simple" character to be reading Dante in her spare time strains the bounds of belief. We wonder whether Lee was really able to imagine the life of the poor. She may have doubted her ability to portray classes outside of her own societal experience and, as if to remind herself, repetitively tells her readers of Anne's servant mentality and one-dimensional mind.

Lee is more convincing in the presentation of intellectual conflict. Anne lacks sophistication (if we choose to be negative) and exhibits a pragmatic concern for concrete social problems (if we take a more positive view). Both main characters are divided by their different modes of perception, as Hamlin shows in one of his rare moments of sincerity: "He [Hamlin] was deeply touched . . . because he knew how little she guessed at the self-conscious unreality of so much of him" (2:59). Only as long as they see each other ideally do they seem to be in accord. But as each ideal is just a heightened picture of the "best" self and not of the real other, their symbiosis falls apart when their different social realities intrude. Hamlin's interest in self-fulfillment and Anne's belief in social duty represent two sides of nineteenth-century liberalism, here divided along class and gender lines. As an aesthetic upper-class male, Hamlin can claim self-fulfillment and pleasure without being held morally responsible. Anne's "female" virtues of chastity and self-denial, reinforced by the servant's sense of duty, make her carry double responsibility.

Vernon Lee does not clearly privilege Anne Brown over Walter Hamlin. The first 150 pages of the novel are written from his point of view, witty and somewhat detached. When Anne leaves her "safe" Italian environment, Lee's concentration on her heroine becomes disproportionate. Although Lee seems to identify with large portions of Anne's criticism, the latter's rigid moralism must have felt alien to Lee's artistic temperament. It soon becomes obvious that the heroine's "one-dimensional" mind misses the complexity of the scene. True, Anne's pure character brings out hypocritical poses among the aesthetes, but her sense of propriety is too easily offended. Her puritanism makes Anne an opponent of, but not an authority on, aestheticism.

At the melodramatic end of the novel, Anne Brown undergoes a strange metamorphosis. When Hamlin's art and personality are weakened because of his overindulgence in vice (sexual affairs, opium, and alcohol), she tells herself that she no longer feels obliged to him and begins to consider her own possibilities. Despite her consistently moral posture, she secretly develops an almost vicious pleasure in watching Hamlin fall prey to his cousin, Sacha Elaguine. Anne hopes that Hamlin will marry Sacha, thus freeing Anne. She begins to think of a teaching career—a real choice because of her financial contract with Hamlin. Why, then, does she decide to marry him even though she detests him? Her resigned explanation that she at least she might "prevent his growing worse, [though] she could not make him grow better" (3:274) almost duplicates Hamlin's own melancholy view of his "much humbler, sadder, but equally necessary" role as a modern artist. Unlike Hamlin, Anne cannot "choose" to be melancholy. Her resignation is the result of an oppression from which not even her "Bildung" could liberate her. Anne Brown's story has followed a circular path so that at the end, she is little more than a servant. Although she has the financial means and a career plan, she is unable to use her "capital" (Bourdieu) because her perverse gratitude toward Hamlin forces her into choosing marital dependency.

Few critics have seen the full impact of Anne's indebtedness as a form of female self-crippling through the internalization of moral and social rules. This less obvious form of oppression presents little material evidence but nevertheless has a powerful, because unconscious, existence in female subjectivity. Anne is not aware of this moral bind, nor is it reflected in the contemporary feminist discourses. But Lee has shown that moral habit, anchored in the unconscious, informal memory of the body, proves to be the most sturdy keeper of cultural and social values.

*Miss Brown* reacts to one of the most powerful media in women's education, the bildungsroman, whose romance plot rewards the compliant heroine with marriage, not "Bildung." As pointed out earlier, the reading of *Miss Brown* as a novel with a "happy ending" is possible only in terms of its outward structure. The futility of the heroine's intellectual awareness points to Vernon Lee's critique of women's internalization of social norms and of a whole literary genre that continues to endorse women's bondage. In this sense, the ending of Lee's novel mocks even the reader's expectation shaped by the novelistic tradition.

# 6 Vernon Lee and the Fantastic

Although Vernon Lee's fantastic stories are less central to her work, they are better known today than her more serious critical essays. Typical of the sexual and psychological interest of the period, Lee's tales of the 1880s and '90s are laden with erotic overtones. Comparable to some of the most prominent specimens of the decadent gothic, such as Arthur Machen's *The Great God Pan,* John Meade Falkner's *The Lost Stradivarius,* or Henry James's *The Turn of the Screw,* Lee's fantastic stories range between the "uncanny" and the "marvelous" on Todorov's scale (44). She uses the transgressive possibilities of the fantastic to visualize sensations and feelings normally hidden from the external world and even from our own consciousness. Fantastic moments occur, when the reader, or narrator, hesitates between a natural and a supernatural explanation. Such "moments of hesitation" (Todorov) are often produced by the neurotic or overwrought minds of her narrators, obsessive writers and scholars as Lee herself surely was.

Lee's most prominent stories, "Amour Dure," "Dionea," and "Prince Alberic and the Snake Lady,"[1] feature mysterious women from the past whose dangerous magnetism reveals their kinship with the period's infamous femme fatale. In a slightly mocking tone, Lee exposes her narrators' possessive yearnings for the women who promise pagan pleasures—but at a price. We are never quite sure if the protagonists desire a more glamorous past or an exquisite sexual experience, since both become interchangeable in their self-conscious rhetoric. At times, Lee's fantastic stories strike us as extensions of her historical project, a visual display of the way she perceived history: subjective, incidental, and full of surprises. The stories become fictional endorsements of a historical model bent on rupture and coincidence, which means that for her narrators—invariably male—the past returns as a pathological text somewhere between supernatural occurrence and realist narrative, haunting both individual and collective cultural memory.

## The Genre of the Fantastic

Vernon Lee's major supernatural tales appeared in a climate that produced some of the most potent literary myths, such as Robert Louis Stevenson's *Dr. Jekyll & Mr. Hyde* (1886), Oscar Wilde's *The Picture of Dorian Gray* (1891), and Bram Stoker's *Dracula* (1897).[2] These classic models of the fantastic reflect the age's preoccupation with the "other," the unenlightened, or the irrational of the human psyche, most often comprised in the "doppelgänger" motif. In the uncanny double, writers expressed their skepticism of a fully describable reality and their doubts whether the prevailing explanatory models of an objective world manageable by rational thinking could accommodate all ways of knowing. Spencer's social philosophy and Darwin's theories of evolution suggested that all forces in nature were not yet known and that science was an open process of cognition.[3] Scientists and philosophers explored the possibility of human growth and degeneration in an environment that was neither fully understood nor completely under human control, conditions which led them to assume that human perception is limited and all knowledge relative.

Theorists of the human mind from William James to James Ward investigated psychological processes as scientific matter and recognized them to be as real as anything physical. Vernon Lee, having studied William James's *Principles of Psychology,* proclaimed, "The things in our mind, due to the mind's constitution and its relation with the universe, are, after all, realities; and realities to count with, as much as the tables and chairs and hats and coats" (*Renaissance Fancies,* 239). The new psychological theories borrowed their language from the scientific realism of biology, anthropology, and geology; they presupposed a secular mode of thought and postulated a clear distinction between narrative as historical (and scientific) fact and narrative as fiction. Through clearly separated modes of representation, writer and reader could feel in control of the text and of their sense of reality. Contemporary fantastic stories destabilized this sense of control by meshing the real and the imaginative, creating gaps and ambiguities that the reader could not resolve. As Rosemary Jackson claims, the unsettling potential of the fantastic lies in its transgressive energies that intrude into the limiting frame of the real and subvert or dissolve the rational order (179–80).

In the course of the nineteenth century, fantastic literature produced more refined and complexly layered narrative voices which indicated that "otherness" was more intimately related to the self and its divided identities. Unlike the external horror of the early gothic, the subject matter of the decadent gothic was no longer some unknown outside force but the reaction of the human psyche to something fearful. Henry James's *The Turn of the Screw* (1898) is a paramount example of the psychological ghost story in which the horrible itself remains vague while the text unfolds a representation of the human psyche in a dialogue between self and self *as* other. The writers of the psychological fantastic, such as James, Wharton, and Lee, were no longer interested in unambiguous resolutions; instead, they fabricated intricate identities under the imminent threat of disintegration, which was to become a major issue in modernism (Block, xiv).[4]

The new perception of the human psyche figures most prominently in the "uncanny" ("das Unheimliche"), which became a recurring notion, even before Freud, in fantastic literature from Edward Bulwer Lytton's *Zanoni* to Bram Stoker's *Dracula*.[5] The writers' awareness of the unstable human psyche entered their texts in the form of an unreliable narrator. Likewise, Lee's narrators become the actual source of the uncanny. Their frantic self-reflections and obsessiveness create pathological patterns that have much in common with Browning's dramatic monologues.

Another major influence for Lee is unmistakably E.T.A. Hoffmann's *Der Sandmann,* the mastertext for Freud's notion of the uncanny.[6] In Freud's theory, the uncanny is the sentiment produced by the divergence of familiarity and strangeness in which repressed and supposedly surmounted infantile or primitive fears return to haunt us. What is experienced as uncanny is a projection of the subject's anxieties onto external shapes,[7] which means that Freud assumes a different, unconscious discourse outside our conscious thinking. But we should be mindful of the limitations of this model because it occurs, after all, within a rational descriptive discourse. Moreover, by drawing on fiction to describe the uncanny, he turns literature into "a paradigmatic illustration of a truth exterior and anterior to it [the uncanny]" (Kofman, 159). Freudian theory imposed a positivist closure on the fantastic spaces that Hoffmann had deliberately kept indeterminate and not necessarily resulting from repression. Lee championed Hoffmann's approach in "Faustus and Helena: Notes on the Supernatural in Art" (*Belcaro*), her "manifesto for the writing of supernatural fiction," as Brian Stableford calls it (3). In the indeterminacy of a fantastic moment, its obscurity and ambiguity, Lee sees the most powerful instigator of our imagination. Particularly in the unshaped oral narratives of traditional folklore and legends—not in the more finite forms of art—she finds the most powerful archetypes of the uncanny.

More recent theories of the fantastic have relied less on Freud than on Todorov's classic study, *The Fantastic: A Structural Approach* (1975), which is based strictly on formal criteria. Todorov's concept resembles Lee's insofar as he puts more emphasis on the textual process. Like Lee, he stresses the "duration of this uncertainty" (33), but from his structural viewpoint, he is more interested in the way the fantastic operates on the textual level, while Lee pays more attention to the reader. Todorov is not unmindful of the reading process. He assumes a rational reader who is bewildered by the ambiguity caused by an event which cannot be explained by the logic of the narrative and thus causes a "moment of hesitation" (33–34). The implicit reader "must opt for one of two possible solutions: either he is the victim of an allusion of the senses, of a product of the imagination . . . or else the event has indeed taken place." In the first instance (the uncanny), the laws of the world remain what they are, and in the second (the marvelous), the inexplicable event is part of reality, "but then this reality is controlled by laws unknown to us" (25).

Todorov's taxonomy of fantastic texts as "pure fantastic," "marvelous," and "uncanny" (4) may strike us as a little too rigid, but it seems to respond to the formal variations of Lee's supernatural tales. In his terms, her story "Prince Alberic and the Snake Lady," for instance, is "marvelous" because it builds on improbable or unbelievable affairs that violate the laws of nature. The "uncanny," on the other hand, which contains events we can explain by these laws but find incredible, shocking, disturbing, or unexpected, typifies the fantastic moments in "Amour Dure" and "Dionea."[8] But since Todorov's terms exclude psychological and ideological explanations and presuppose an ultimate way of knowing, his limitations for reading Lee are obvious. Late-nineteenth-century authors from James to Lee defer emphatically any certainties by deliberately leaving gaps in the narrators' accounts, thus "foregrounding their fear of seeing the rational world destroyed" (Callois, 44–50).

Such fear typically reflects the sense of loss in the rapidly changing cultural climate of the late nineteenth century, and neither Freud's nor Todorov's approach captures the historical momentum. Lee's own manifesto, "Faustus and Helena" in *Belcaro,* describes the fantastic as a shifting literary mode, which, in different historical contexts, has undergone material semantic changes as an effect of its transformation from medieval to modern ways of thinking. Lee illustrates the historicity of the fantastic by contrasting and comparing different representations of the Faust topos. She devises a genealogy of Faustian ghosts based on the perceived (historical) reality of their appearance. Marlowe's stock representation of evil, for instance, did not have to be evocative since the audience's sense of the real included the belief in the supernatural ("when devils still dwelt in people"), whereas the "demonic" of our modern, secular times must be a strained, sophisticated construction to have the same kind of effect.

> We moderns, disbelieving in deviltries, would require the most elaborately romantic and poetic accessories—The Mephistophilis of Marlow, in those days when devils still dwelt in people, required none of Goethe's wit or poetry; the mere fact of his being a devil, with the very real association of flame and brimstone in the world and the next, was sufficient to inspire interest in him; whereas in 1800, with Voltaire's novels and Hume's treatises on the table, a dull devil was no more endurable than any other sort of bore. (*Belcaro,* 98)

Lee here anticipates Rosemary Jackson's theory of the fantastic as a historical category that appeared as a way of knowing in an age when readings of otherness as real and subjective began to replace readings of otherness as supernatural and external. Still, Lee wants to know how one can explain the modern attraction to the fantastic. She suggests that

> we moderns seek in the world of the supernatural a renewal of the delightful semi-obscurity of vision and keenness of fancy of our childhood; when a glimpse into fairyland was still possible.... In certain words, in certain sights, in certain snatches of melody ... they were spells which opened doors into realms of wonder. (96)

By locating the desire for the supernatural in the unconscious experiences of childhood—individual and collective—Lee links historical and psychological dimensions:

but no picture, no symphony, no poem can give us that delight, that delusory, imaginative pleasure which we received as children from a tawdry engraving or a hideous doll. . . . We now appreciate and despise; we see, we no longer imagine. And it is to replace this uncertainty of vision, this liberty of seeing in things much more than there is, which belongs to man and to mankind in this childhood, which compensated the Middle Ages for starvation and pestilence, and compensates the child for blows and lessons, it is to replace this that we crave after the supernatural, the ghostly—no longer believed, but still felt. (97)

Lee's concern here is less with psychological truth than with the rendering of the fantastic in an art form which, while appealing to the secular mind, would also reveal to that mind its own unconscious, vaguely felt past.

Lee sees in the fantastic the possibility of reassessing and extending the laws of the natural to include the scientifically unproven even within realist discourse. To her, the fantastic operates as a literary complement to mainstream realism. Edwin Block and more recently Nicholas Daly argue that the fantastic extends beyond the realist period; its overt exposure of psychological incongruities and tensions rather makes it a significant link to modernity. Because of its reflexivity, self-consciousness, and emphasis on exclusion, the "psychomythic tale," as Block claims, prepared the road to modernism with its characteristic traits of irony, disintegration, and inner conflicts (xiv–xv). Vernon Lee's stories, written at the end of the realist era, display these characteristics of the incipient modernist styles. Although she makes ample use of realist detail, the organizing center of her text lies in her narrators' inner thoughts. Their obsession, hysteria, and self-delusion render their narrative unstable and create ironic distance between voice and content. By obstructing the readers' desire for authentic truth, Lee forces us to pay more attention to the psychology of narrative and character. Unlike modernist stream of consciousness techniques, Lee's narrative does not integrate inner and outer reality. Her characters' language of desire enables uncanny occurrences, the nineteenth-century answer to the culturally unintelligible—"that which cannot be said, that which evades articulation"—in the culturally acceptable discourses (Jackson, 37).

As the fantastic resists closure, it draws attention to the relative nature of such categories as the "real" with its nominal unities of time, space, and "most particularly the concept of 'character,' mocking and parodying a blind faith in psychological coherence and in the value of sublimation as a 'civilizing' activity" (Jackson, 176).

Lee's narrative exposes such futile attempts at coherence and sublimation. It is no coincidence that her stories often involve self-conscious scholars (like herself) who typically refuse to regard "the past as a closed book" (Pykett, 198) and seek in it more seductive sexual possibilities than the present seems to offer them.

With its staging of hesitation, fear, and subversion, the fantastic can give expression to the marginal, the invisible, and the unacceptable—notions that characterize Lee's complicated attachments to her writerly identity. In her stories "Amour Dure" and "Dionea," the fantastic occurrences unsettle her male narrators' inflated sense of themselves shaped by their confidence in professional scholarship, which yet cannot satisfy their emotional need for the past. "To raise a real specter of the antique," Lee writes in "Faustus and Helena," "is a craving of our own century" (*Belcaro,* 104). Such craving often resembles sexual desire which, when repressed, turns into neurotic obsession transformed into fantastic visions. Her seemingly rational narrators become unreliable mainly because they are driven by masculine desires they may hide from themselves, but not from the reader. An interesting reversal takes place: by destabilizing the male voice, Lee can give more weight to the fantastic females who appear no longer as ghosts, but as enigmas from another time, ready to be explored along "the mind's path into the unknown" (Traill, 18).

Unlike the abstract forms of horror in Henry James's stories, Vernon Lee's fantastic tales more directly point to a gendered, and therefore historical, reality. Through skillful arrangement of various subtexts, Lee encourages us to read into her historical women the complexity of modern female subjectivity, "with more freedom and more ideal" (*Belcaro,* 103), a mode which opens an alternative perspective on past and present female identity without offering any concrete answers. Since neither "Amour Dure" nor "Dionea" reinstates the reality principle, both can validate possibilities suggested by the mythical women whose seductive powers destroy the male characters' moral order. But instead of vilifying the female allure in familiar decadent fashion, Lee gradually exposes and ridicules the masculine desire that creates the women's effect by reproducing the narrators' "male gaze." In "Dionea," for instance, the narrator's voyeurism is almost overlooked at first because it operates within the socially accepted mode of aesthetic contemplation. As long as we share the narrator's cultural standards, we do not suspect his unreliability. But the rationality he professes is increasingly undermined by unseemly outbreaks of sensual intimations. Through multiple allusions, dramatic monologue, and mise-en-abyme, Lee points to her narrators' unconscious obsessions which, summoned by certain images, respond to and become themselves powerful cultural forces.

Ultimately, the shifting terrain between Lee's scholarly men and enigmatic women, like the relationship between past and present, remains unknowable. In this respect, Lee follows her own concept of the fantastic that must be allusive and suggestive enough to let her readers develop their own fantasies, because "we have all of us the charm wherewith to evoke for ourselves a real Helena, on condition that . . . we . . . remain satisfied if the weird and glorious figure haunt only our own imagination" ("Faustus and Helena," *Belcaro,* 104–5). As indicated by Todorov, the implied reader is decisive for the success of a ghost story. Lee's anticipated reader is a device through which she avoids closure and evokes (rather than describes) whole networks of cultural allusions,

> things of the imagination, born there, bred there, sprung from the strange confused heaps, half-rubbish, half-treasure, which lie in our fancy, heaps of half-faded recollections, of fragmentary vivid impressions, litter of multi-coloured tatters, and faded herbs and flowers, whence arises that odour (we all know it), musty and damp, but penetratingly sweet and intoxicatingly heady, which hangs in the air when the ghost has swept through the unopened door. (*Hauntings,* ix)[9]

Lee's fantastic stories surpass their own design. Read side by side with her nonfictional texts analyzed in this study, they not only offer insight into her role and intent as a female writer, but also stage performances of her unique historical approach. Entering the field as an art critic, she believed that objective and detached historiography has to remain silent on matters outside its assumed scientific discourse. The less systematic and less explicit sides of history for her could only be embodied by the intuitive language of art. It is no coincidence that in each of her supernatural tales music ("A Wicked Voice"), artworks ("Amour Dure," "Prince Alberic"), or artists ("Oke of Okehurst") evoke fantastic moments that push the past into the present. In other words, art can create a more immediate contact with the past than can historical scholarship. Lee's supernatural, which stages our intuitive and subjective connections with the past, thus can be seen as a metaphor for an unrealized historical method.

"Dionea" and "Prince Alberic and the Snake Lady" serve as examples of Lee's fictional resolution of the intellectual issues in her prose essays of the 1880s and 1890s. In "Dionea," Lee tackles once more the construction of cultural memory, here as Christianity and paganism in conflict. "Prince Alberic and the Snake Lady," in its lush aesthetic atmosphere and erotic overtones, typical of the yellow decade, plays with the period's interest in sexually ambiguous images interacting with power structures and, on the textual level, nonrealist narrative techniques. Both stories dramatize extreme psychological situations, as does "Amour Dure," a clever investigation of the borderlines between imagination and madness. This story, which was first conceived as a Renaissance novel Paterian style, combines most completely Lee's psychological, aesthetic, historical, and cultural interests. "Amour Dure," unlike the other two stories, tackles, in a complex intertextual dialogue with Pater, her own role as a female writer in late-Victorian aesthetics and historiography.

## "Dionea": Male Desire and Pagan Myth

In "Dionea" Lee explores once again the impingement of the past upon the present, this time in a series of inexplicable events presumably caused by an antique goddess of love. As in several other stories by Lee, the theme of female sexuality turned into vengeance is staged as a theater of the (male) mind. We observe a learned man who is as obsessed with the pagan past as he is with the female body. Lee's slightly ironic tone in "Dionea" echoes Heinrich Heine's witty critique of political and philosophical dogmatism in The Gods in Exile, one of Lee's favorite books.[10] Similar to Heine's gods, Lee's pagan deities appear in an austere (Mediterranean) community that has banned any form of sensuality. Removed from their classical context, the pagan gods—in Lee as in Heine—arouse ambivalent attraction even among the most noble characters, including the scholarly narrator.

"Dionea" is the tale of a shipwrecked waif, picked up on the shore of an Italian port after a violent storm and placed in the Franciscan Convent for a Christian education. Because of her unruly behavior she is soon expelled and left to fend for herself.[11] Dionea's story is told in a series of letters to a wealthy benefactress, Lady Evelyn Savelli, written by the official physician of the convent, Doctor Allessandro de Rosis, who is also working on a thesis on the return of the pagan

gods. The doctor finds Dionea beautiful but strange in the way she arouses un-
suitable desire among the men. His letters hint of her mysterious connection with
Dione, mother of Aphrodite.[12] When a German sculptor (Waldemar) comes to
Porto Venere, his wife (Gertrude) selects Dionea as his model, a choice that has
tragic effects: a fire destroys the studio and the sculptor is found dead, fallen off a
cliff. His pregnant wife (also dead) is stretched out on an ancient Roman Venus
altar, apparently slaughtered during a bloody ritual.

From the beginning, the text is built on a Christian-pagan dualism that
creates epistemic tensions and points to alternative meanings, typical of symbolist literature and art. But the narrator's heavy-handed allusions to paganism are too obviously parodistic to be taken at face value and instead draw
attention to his own obsession with the return of the goddess Venus and what
she embodies.[13] For instance, when the doctor is summoned to discipline Dionea for the desecration of the altar, he feigns indignation at her behavior but
can barely conceal his attraction to this "amazing little beauty," immediately
comparing the scenario to a mythological episode, "when Dame Venus
scratched her hand on the thorn-bush, [and] red roses should sprout up between the fissures of dirty old bricks" (*Hauntings,* 134).

The common people fear Dionea's magic, blaming her for any unexplained occurrence, and, in an outbreak of collective hysteria, let the children
throw stones at the "witch" with an "evil eye." Generally, the narrator distances himself from such superstition by assuming a scholarly mien, but he secretly delights in the people's reaction, since it seems to support his own thesis
on the return of the pagan gods. However, we may note that it is solely his narrative which connects the uncanny events with Dionea's mysterious powers.

De Rosis's documentary tone conveniently conceals his sexual attraction
behind his scholarly interest in the past. The reader soon catches on that ancient mythology offers him the sensual stimulus that is missing in the austere
moral environment of this community, and from there, it is only a small step
to our discovery of his secret desires. He himself is unable to admit the reality
of his sexual attraction. But for the reader, the discrepancy between de Rosis's
rhetoric and his unacknowledged carnal desire for Dionea undermines his
credibility and allows the reader a "private view" of the historian's mind. We
catch a glimpse of his suppressed desires in his all too frequent references to
her sculptural physique and erotic appeal to the male (and even female) world.

The fact that neither religious nor scholarly practices are immune to

Dionea's seductive force reveals their exclusionary politics, which we may call an overdose of Hebraism, scientism, or asceticism. Lee believed that a secularized, rational modern world increased the craving for the repressed and unexplained, for the "days of disbelief when the more logical we become in our ideas, the more we view nature as prosaic machine, . . . do we feel the delight of the transient belief in the vague and the impossible" (*Belcaro,* 96).[14] Likewise, the narrator in "Dionea" is disappointed with the possibilities of theoretical, second-hand study: "My poor little manuscript can only tell you what St. Augustine, Tertullian, and sundry morose old Bishops thought about the loves of Father Zeus" (*Hauntings,* 151–52). Unable to accept that scholarship can be dry and prosaic, he immediately evokes the poetic side of life: "The world, at times, seems to be playing at being poetic, mysterious, full of wonder and romance" (152). He repeatedly becomes so enchanted by his own aesthetic excursions that his language is no longer consistent with his official role and, fixating his glance on Dionea's form, loses himself in sensuous indulgence which arrests the flow of narration:[15]

> Dionea lies stretched out full length in the sun . . . 'tis a lovely sight, a thing fit for one of your painters, Burne Jones or Tadema, with the myrtle-bushes all round, the bright, whitewashed convent walls behind, the white marble chapel steps . . . and the enamel blue sea through the ilex-branches beyond. (131)

It seems odd that a respectable village doctor should pay so much attention to his ward's beauty: "dark, lithe, with an odd, ferocious gleam in her eyes, and a still odder smile, tortuous, serpentine, like that of Leonardo da Vinci's women" (134). Dionea's attraction is "tortuous" for him, so he displaces his "unspeakable" desire into Leonardo's art and thus into a more acceptable context.

As the story proceeds, de Rosis can scarcely conceal his arousal, even in the most inappropriate situations. When Father Domenico, a model of pure asceticism and spirituality, pines away, apparently a victim of Dionea's uncanny powers, the doctor pretends to be outraged with her conduct, but he can hardly keep his eyes off her "magnificent, radiant" beauty. As if to wipe out the unseemly sensation, he immediately shifts his glance to the dead monk's "poor thin face," and triumphantly throws a branch of myrtle (Aphrodite's sign) into "that smile like the twist of a young snake" (138). His concluding remark that he "felt glad for Father Domenico; his battle was over" (138), indicates that the monk's battle against temptation was the narrator's own.

By now, the reader is aware of the unreliability of the narrator, whose scholarly interest in ancient mythology is driven by a yearning for sensual experience. By aestheticizing the pagan past, he tries to liberate it from its "exile" commanded by contemporary religious discourse, but the subtext subtly mocks his worthy cause by revealing a sexually repressed narrator for whom the disturbing reincarnation of the pagan goddess has the same uncanny power as the female body.

Dionea's appearance in a St. Franciscan convent suggests that disparate belief systems might actually be nothing other than cultural practices separated by the effects of time. By visualizing historical time synchronically (rather than diachronically) in one and the same place, Lee develops a psychology of the "genius loci" dominated by movements of repetition and disruption. Places for Lee, like memories, submerge the collectively forgotten past, which yet comes to haunt individuals unconsciously. Such informal personal (or collective) memory, according to Paul Connerton, can only be bodily enacted. And since identities are not only abstractions but also physical realities, individuals need to make sense of their experience, which, as Connerton points out, is traditionally organized by social rituals and performances (79–102). Lee's fantastic moments seem to make visible the functions of our unconscious memory controls which are multiply embedded in various socio-symbolic categories, among them gender and sexuality. I emphasize these two, since Lee's narratives often create fantastic moments as conflation of sexual and historical dimensions. Evidently, with its momentary suspension of reality, the fantastic can become an ideal site for the exploration of the unconscious side of cultural memory as it is stored and activated in the body.

In "Dionea," Lee inserts a woman's body as connecting point between pagan and Christian symbolic systems to unsettle, but also to obscure historical memory. In the imagined space of Dionea's reincarnation, Christian and pagan traditions merge: her natural sympathy with nature, symbolized by her entourage of white doves, suggests synecdochical identification with both Aphrodite and St. Francis. The two belief systems share symbolic meanings but they become incompatible when organized around the female body. Does Dionea's sexuality obstruct our recognition of her St. Franciscan (male) spirit? Generally speaking, is historical knowledge constructed and decoded in gendered terms? We are tempted to ask if Dionea would have been associated with St. Francis if she had been a man. After all, it is odd that the narrator and the country folk seem to know everything about witches and ancient goddesses but very little about the St. Franciscan tradition in which they live.

The loss of collective historical memory, cultural amnesia, is one of the reasons why the different pasts (pagan and Christian) exclude each other and why Dionea has to remain enigmatic. She grows up in a community of St. Francis but her Franciscan attributes remain unrecognized. Ironically, Dionea's love of all creatures makes her a better ally of St. Francis than the Convent's punitive regime. Translated into gender categories, the concept of "woman" in the story's setting is socially and symbolically so far removed from "man" that she cannot be imagined in the same terms and, therefore, has to be relegated to witchcraft or paganism. Similarly, the symbolic pigeons in the legend of St. Francis and the real pigeons in the Umbrian village no longer inhabit the same historical space, even though they may occur in the same location. The past is no longer part of the present and so the once saintly pigeons have degenerated into "dirty animals."

When the reader has eventually figured out how this culture makes sense to itself, the story ends abruptly. Before capturing Dionea's figure in a work of art, the German sculptor and his wife perish in a bloody Dionysian tragedy. Dionea is gone, but rumor has it that she was seen on a strange Greek boat, "singing words in an unknown tongue, the white pigeons circling around her" (154). How are we supposed to read the final scene? The narrator suggests ritualistic murder, allegedly instigated by Dionea. But without any evidence in this murder mystery, all the traces lead back to the narrator who set us up to believe in the reality of the pagan goddess. His overwrought symbolism leaves an impression of mockery, mockery of a craving for that delicious fear of the unknown with which the decadent gothic seemed to titillate Victorian minds.

It is obvious that Lee meant to keep Dionea's ultimate identity in the dark, and it is this unresolved question which directs our attention to those who wish to control her representation. Her body becomes the constant reminder of individual and collective repression. In the end, all that is left at the place of crime is the Venus altar. And again, submerged in historical oblivion, the past may find this place, ready to repeat itself—and haunt us.


## "Prince Alberic and the Snake Lady"

The aesthetic symbolism in "Prince Alberic and the Snake Lady" makes it very much a story of the *Yellow Book* days in the same vein as Oscar Wilde's precious fairy tales. Lee's story never leaves the fairy-tale mode (in Todorov's terms). Its third-person narrator stays in the confines of the Prince's naive, childlike voice, which, combined with the stylized historical references, creates a curiously archaic point of view. Prince Alberic's consciousness suggests the developmental stage of a mythical culture different from that of the narrators in "Amour Dure" and "Dionea," who clearly speak from a secular point of view. Lee believed that the fantastic produced a mythical mode of thinking with the *possibility* of harmonizing rational and irrational elements, reality and dream, self and other. When staged in a secularized culture, the fantastic expresses a longing for such unity, no longer presumed possible and therefore purely imaginary. On the axis of binary opposites, the mythical can be ascribed to the intuitive or instinctive, qualities often associated with the feminine. The secular, on the other hand, revolves around rational principles, traditionally seen as masculine (Jackson, 179). In "Dionea," the male narrator's text represents a secular order, disturbed by a female figure who enters reality from an allusive mythical past. This arrangement is almost reversed in "Prince Alberic and the Snake Lady," where the text foregrounds the young prince's feminine bond with his mythical godmother, negating the absolutist patriarchal rule of his grandfather, Duke Balthasar Maria of Luna.

The friendship between the prince and the snake lady is foreshadowed in Alberic's lonely childhood. He grows up socially isolated in the duke's Red Palace with its unnatural and stiffly baroque decor from which all live animals have been banned. What the prince learns about nature he finds in a faded tapestry representing his ancestor Prince Alberic the Blond with the Snake Lady Oriana. She becomes young Alberic's worshiped ideal and compensates for the real companions he longs to have. Alberic is fascinated by the woman's beauty and richly ornamented dress. Strangely enough, he has seen only her upper body, since the lower part is hidden behind a chest and an iron crucifix too heavy for him to move. One day, when Alberic is about eleven, the furniture in his room is rearranged and her full picture is exposed. He discovers that the lady's lower half is not dressed in a skirt as he expected but ends in a snake's tail. But instead of being disappointed, he loves her "only the more because she ended off in the long twisting body of a snake" (31).[16]

When the duke has the tapestry replaced with one representing Susannah and the Elders—a prime example of male voyeurism—the prince slashes the replacement to pieces. He is subsequently expelled from the Red Palace and sent to the remote Castle of the Sparkling Waters, a dilapidated palace with a lush wild garden inhabited only by a poor peasant family. In the garden, near a strangely ornamented sepulchre, the guileless prince befriends a glittering green grass snake of whom he is "not afraid, for he knew nothing about snakes" (39). He is only startled by the creature's coldness, which so arouses his pity that he puts it in his pocket to keep it warm. The thinly veiled eroticism of this scene intimates pleasure without anxiety, which can be attributed to the benign nature of this snake. Uninformed by the cultural bias against snakes, the prince touches the creature without any fear or suspicion. Its body becomes a source of sensual pleasure for him, pure joy without any sense of guilt. Shortly afterward, a beautiful lady appears at the Castle of the Sparkling Waters and introduces herself as his godmother. She visits him an hour every "evening at sunset" (46), playing with him and teaching him a variety of skills, "and, above all, to love" (46).

From a peddler, the prince learns the full story of the Snake Lady, which goes back to the time of the crusades. Alberic the Blond, then the knight of Luna, had discovered and sworn to dispel the spell from the Fairy Oriana, who appeared to him as a snake in the same sepulchre where young Alberic first saw the green snake. The Snake Lady must remain bewitched, as two of Alberic's ancestors failed to fulfill the condition for her release: to remain faithful to her for ten years.[17] The Prince recognizes his "fate" and decides to rescue the lady. This also requires that he kiss the snake. Following the historical legend, Alberic puts his lips on the ice-cold creature's head, "but a coldness seized his heart, the moon seemed suddenly extinguished, and he slipped away in unconsciousness" (59). When he awakes, his head is resting on the knees of his beautiful godmother; this leads us to believe in her identity with the snake, a belief reinforced by Alberic's remark that they never turn up at the same time.

Lee's readers are led to accept the snake as a lovable creature whose nurturing quality belies its abundantly exploited image as sly and seductive. Here, the snake receives new symbolic relevance through the godmother's warmth and affection. When the Prince "put out his hand and she twisted round his arm, extending slowly her chilly coil to his wrist and fingers," snake and arm are synecdochically intertwined in an "unio mystica," the imaginary space in which the medieval legend reconciled disparate beings. The sensual image suspends the difference between Prince and snake, foregrounding once more the oneness of culturally separated images in a sensual tableau of pleasure, love, and beauty. In Lee's story, the good nature of both snake and woman suggests a doubling of positive values rather than a dichotomy of good and evil. In a departure from Lee's other ghost stories, where "otherness" turns out to be the repressed part of the same, the doubling in "Prince Alberic and the Snake Lady" conceals no Mr. Hyde but only complements itself positively. The prince's boyish innocence allows for a merging of childhood and myth as a possible site for alternative cultural knowledge.

Yet we should not read the Snake Lady's world as a secluded, noncompetitive feminine biotope. Her pedagogical program for the prince affords a comprehensive development of his mental, emotional, and physical sides in accordance with the traditional education for a gentleman. She endows him with the necessary paraphernalia for his social position (a horse, a sword, and a library) to make him "every inch a Prince," but, as we may add, without the duke's phallic power and the ideological system that attends to it. Self-aggrandizement, rivalry, bribery, and corruption—all attributes of the Duke's patriarchal system—are absent from the Edenic garden by the Castle of the Sparkling Waters. In this Paradise, the prince receives a refined chivalric education whose main ingredient is love. The Snake Lady provides young Alberic with nurture and sensual appeal, in short, everything the duke's Machiavellian rule lacks. Symbolically, the two different worlds are separated by the two gardens: the duke's rococo garden of the lifeless Red Palace, surveyed by twelve granite busts of Caesar and boasting a sublime grotto; and the prince's lush natural garden of the Castle of the Sparkling Waters, inspired by the Snake Lady's nurture and beauty.

The duke's ambassadors try to hoax the prince into an arranged marriage to resolve the estate's financial difficulties. But Alberic is immune to their bribes because his godmother has supplied everything he needs, thus making him independent from his grandfather's rule. As expected, the friendly union between the snake and the prince inspires fear and hate at the duke's court. Suspecting the snake's "evil" influence behind the prince's disobedience, the duke gives orders to kill her. Rumor has it that instead of a dead snake, a naked lady is found, disfigured and mutilated by saber cuts. When the symbiosis of prince and snake is disturbed, Alberic dies within a few days. The duke, haunted by "terrible thoughts and images," plunges into excesses of debauchery that precipitate his death and thus the end of the House of Luna.

Like many of Lee's fantastic stories, "Prince Alberic and the Snake Lady" reminds us of the intermingling of past and present personified in an enigmatic woman whose appearance brings back lost memory. Lee's doubling of female values in "Prince Alberic and the Snake Lady" favors a woman-centered and perhaps even a lesbian perspective, as suggested by the boy's image, which has been established as an icon of same-sex love in fin-de-siècle literature. Martha Vicinus famously has linked the figure of the boyish prince to similar images in contemporary lesbian literature from Renée Vivian to Michael Field. For a tacitly lesbian writer like Lee, the adolescent boy "was the defining, free agent" (Vicinus, 84) to express the other identity. As shown earlier, the boy image also plays a central role in Lee's Platonic dialogues, *Althea,* in which Greek (homoerotic) love is configured in lesbian terms. In her dialogues, Lee evokes lesbian subjectivity through the atmosphere, the scenery, and the gestures that are not actually part of the argument. Similarly, in "Prince Alberic and the Snake Lady," Lee directs our attention to the nonverbal, sensual evocations in language that point to another meaning or text. Although the original legend of Prince Alberic the Blond has been transmitted in heterosexual terms, Lee's literary enactment occurs in a symbolic natural order which could be called "lesbian" since the masculine element has been displaced.

The cut-up body of the snake woman evokes the ancient Egyptian myth of Isis and Osiris, in which Osiris's body is pieced back together through Isis's loving care. The mythical connection can also be made with Aphrodite, who sprang from the foam of the sea that gathered the severed parts of Uranus. Monique Wittig's *The Lesbian Body* makes use of such mythical "dissection" to define alternative (lesbian) subjectivity. In her poem, she dismantles mythical female figures to reconstruct their body as the same and yet as something new to enact an alternative symbolic system. Wittig reassembles bodies as open entities, marked neither by difference nor by boundaries but from a newly arranged point of view that yet needs to be defined. Is the reader of "Prince Alberic and the Snake Lady" encouraged to do likewise? Should we read the story backward, through the cut-up body of the enigmatic Snake Lady, and arrive at a different view of history?

The symbolism in Lee's story changes meaning on the preverbal level of mythological images, that is, a knowledge that escapes cognitive awareness. The secret relationship of the Snake Lady and the Prince does not produce a new dualism. Without the boundaries of gender, norms like heterosexuality are undercut and direct us to other possible relationships. From a new reference point we can construct an alternative (maybe lesbian) text. Such a conversion is exemplified in the bonding of the prince and the Snake Lady, which establishes a life principle beyond patriarchal authority. Alberic and the Snake Lady form an integral entity that supplies its own needs out of itself and whose parts are vitally important to each other. The prince cannot survive when his symbiotic other is killed, while his death prevents the snake's release from the spell. Although Lee's story is less optimistic than Wittig's assertive poem, it does not reinstate patriarchal rule since the duke survives the prince by only a few months, and "the House of Luna" becomes extinct.

In "Prince Alberic and the Snake Lady," a positive "primary presence" of womanhood (to use Adrienne Rich's term) is forged through the Snake Lady's mythical reconstruction in the boy. Her snake body, like that of the coreless Melusienne of the French saga, does not have a compact body, nor does she have a soul. Her spirit is not produced by Adam and therefore not defined in relation to him.[18] This aspect makes the snake woman an apt site for the "not-woman" (in Wittig's sense), which could be a lesbian, whose identity is not defined within a system attending to man. Thus "Prince Alberic and the Snake Lady" opens an imaginary space for the construction of "woman" beyond the definitions traditional history has offered to us.

## THE SUPERNATURAL AS INTERTEXTUAL CRITIQUE: LEE'S VERSION OF PATER'S "LA GIOCONDA"

In Vernon Lee's story "Amour Dure," an uncanny presence rises from the text.[19] It is the presence of Medea da Carpi, a woman "dead these three hundred years." Born in 1556—exactly three hundred years before Vernon Lee—Medea has come to represent a line of deathly women, the "race of Faustinas, Marzias, Bianca Capellos."[20] In "Amour Dure," the ghost of this Renaissance woman haunts an obsessive nineteenth-century historian, Spiridion Trepka, who is studying for a German university the history of the Italian city of Urbania.[21] But his growing desire for Medea da Carpi confuses his sense of reality and drives him to madness. A short newspaper clipping abruptly ends the narrative: "Professor Spiridion Trepka of Posen, in the German Empire, had been discovered dead of a stab in the region of the heart given by an unknown hand" (126).

"Amour Dure" is another clever sample of its genre. The story's multiple literary allusions—a favorite Victorian device—not only create the mystery and ambiguity of a gripping ghost story, but also reveal the overdetermined character of the cultural text. The curious effect of this story lies in its evocation and simultaneous deconstruction of another subtext: an animated version of Pater's portrayal of "la Gioconda." At the same time, "Amour Dure" can be read as a trope of the entire nineteenth-century craze for the Italian Renaissance. Evidently, Lee's phantom woman Medea da Carpi also owes a lot to Bronzino's *Lucrezia Panciatichi*[22] described as Pater's famous "presence that rose thus so strangely beside the waters" (*Renaissance,* 96).[23]

Pater's Mona Lisa figures both as origin and as culminating point of a temporality, a summation of history in which the "ten thousand experiences" of the past are swept together in one mythical image enfolding all narrative of history in the aesthetic form. Historical and mythical time are conflated in one point and one figure. But Lisa's enigma demands interpretation, Pater's interpretation, which collapses all the disparate moments of the past into each other to embody the myth of the modern spirit. In Pater's aesthetic and epiphanic rendering of history, to quote Carolyn Williams, "a temporal series of successive stages is recast as an image or spatial figure" (119).

Whereas Pater conjures up the vision of an enigmatic woman who resolves the antinomies of history, Lee reverses the mythmaking process and lets us see the mind behind it. Her female figure (Medea da Carpi) is just as "strange" as Pater's Mona Lisa. The difference lies in Lee's interpretation of the enigma, for she tells Medea's story mediated through the mind of a modern historian. Lee investigates how seemingly timeless images not only reflect but also reproduce—concretely and subjectively—collective history in individual minds. She undoes Pater's fusion of aesthetic object (the image) and subject (the critic) by placing both in their specific historical reality. By sexualizing her narrator's perspective,[24] she shows the limitations of the "modern" mind whose time-transcending consciousness simply reproduces cultural relationships between subject and object, past and present, male and female. Whereas Pater's immortal Mona Lisa melds "Leonardo's artistic development, the processes of history, and the movements of his own essay" (Williams, 111) in synchronic unity, Lee's Medea escapes from her mythical deathbed, disrupting her maker's historical text while creating her own. Although Lee employs Pater's configuration of historical transmission as aestheticized female form, she breaks it down into historical (and sexualized) components, which she then reassembles to construct woman's historical visibility—on her own terms.

In "Amour Dure," Pater's famous reverie of the modern spirit ("what in the ways of a thousand years men had come to desire") becomes literal (sexualized) history in the Renaissance femme fatale; Medea da Carpi devours her lovers as Mona Lisa devours centuries.

> Her magic faculty is to enslave all the men who come across her path; all those
> who see her, love her, become her slaves; and it is the destiny of all her slaves to
> perish. Her lovers . . . all come to an untimely end; and in this there is nothing
> unjust. The possession of a woman like Medea is a happiness too great for a
> mortal man . . . [H]e must be willing to love and suffer and die. This is the
> meaning of her device—"Amour Dure—Dure Amour." The love of Medea
> da Carpi cannot fade, but the lover can die; it is a constant and a cruel love.
> (102)

Medea's sinister and seductive smile means death, not in a mythical or symbolic sense, but frightfully real. She takes revenge and kills her lovers as her
namesake from Colchis, the mythical Medea, killed her children.

The Renaissance woman's story is "mastered" (temporarily) by Spiridion
Trepka as he retrieves her history from documents in the archives of Urbania.
But phantom-like, she soon emerges from the pages of his diary and, once out of
control, begins to haunt the hysteric historian's mind. Trepka has found in
Medea the embodiment of all of his unfulfilled desires, which are motivated by
sexual repression and loss of national identity. An exiled Pole in Germany, he
feels oppressed by pedantic German scholarship, which leaves no room for fantasy and romance. For years, Trepka had longed to "come face to face with the
Past," and he had "sighed like Goethe in Rome," full of desire for a grand passion, for a woman "for whose pleasures to die" (100). When he finally comes to
Italy, his quixotic yearning is frustrated by the profane reality of Urbania's pro-
vincialism and the barrenness of the wintry landscape. In his dismay, he flees into
the imagined reality of Medea da Carpi. His obsession for her becomes most intense around Christmas, when his yearning for Medea merges with the wistful
recollection of his eager expectation of Christmas Eve in his childhood in Poland.
Convinced that he is "reserved for something wonderful in this world," Trepka
wishes and works for the reappearance of the woman from the past who promises to be even more exquisite than Goethe's "Fraus," for he is "after all a Pole,
accustomed to something very different from 'Fraus'" (99).

Trepka's national pride, which excites his secret revolt against both German
authorities and pedantic historiography, emulates Medea's rebellion against the
relentlessness of sixteenth-century Italian patriarchy. The underlying parallel of
his own oppression as "a Pole grown into the semblance of a German pedant"
with this "imperious woman . . . treated like a chattel" makes him her elect

protector (101). Ostracized and maligned through a biased historiography, Medea becomes a model for Trepka's own disempowerment. At the same time, her untamed, uncanny sexual attraction offers him an escape from dull historical scholarship into the fantastic past of the Duchess Medea. Through her image, he endows history with romance and excitement and himself with an identity, however outside the confines of society.[25]

Trepka's narrative also mimics the wistfulness of Pater's imaginary portraits: sensitive, isolated, and somewhat esoteric characters whose search for beauty and innovation is thwarted by adverse social forces. Loyal only to their impressions, Pater's hypersensitive artists appear as the true bearers of the "modern spirit" that can be recovered only by a kindred (aesthetic) temperament, namely Pater himself. "La Gioconda," the myth of myths,[26] the "strange presence" that rises from the waters, is a symbol of the timeless moment against the flux of history. Lee takes Pater's image of the "modern idea"—"the fancy of a perpetual life, sweeping together ten thousand experiences"—and translates it into concrete historical experience. In "Amour Dure," she tracks a myth back to its making by examining a Renaissance woman through the historian's mind to find out how his imagination interacts with cultural assumptions in past and present. Trepka's quest for Medea at first merely reproduces her traditional image as a femme fatale whose history reminds one of that "of Bianca Capellos, and at the same time of Lucrecia Borgia" (90). But Medea's portrait is increasingly permeated by his intrusive self-conscious monologue, which not only disassembles the myth of the Renaissance woman but also exposes the historical conditions of its production thereby subverting the notion of myth itself.

Medea's portrait strikes us as another version of "La Gioconda":

> The face is a perfect oval. . . . Tight eyelids and tight lips give a strange refinement, and, at the same time, an air of mystery, a somewhat sinister seductiveness. . . . The mouth . . . looks as if it could bite or suck like a leech. . . . A curious, at first rather conventional looking beauty, voluptuous yet cold, which, the more it is contemplated, the more it troubles and haunts the mind, . . . I often examine these tragic portraits, wondering what this face, which led so many men to their death, may have been like when it spoke or smiled. (96–97)[27]

Like Lisa with "the unfathomable smile always in touch of something sinister in it" (*Renaissance,* 97), Medea epitomizes what men desire, but her history has come to represent rather what they fear. Between these two sensations, fear and desire (in Trepka's words, "the feeling terrifies me, but it is delicious"), the narrator pieces together what is remembered of Medea da Carpi in historical archives and folk legends. Her image gradually emerges from official documents, personal letters, and, most formidably, pictorial representations. On another level, she is evoked as an evil woman in the legends and superstitions of oral history, which is the site of people's informal cultural memory. The nineteenth-century people of Urbania still tremble at the spook of "Madonna Medea, who rode in the sky on a black he-goat" (104).

Through her name, Medea is associated with the ancient sorceress. This mythological connotation brings a pagan otherness into the Christian setting of Urbania, where "all the bells are ringing for the approach of Christmas" (116). Like a foreboding of Trepka's fate, she appears to him while he hallucinates a Christmas service in the long-deserted church of "San Giovanni Decollato" (John the Baptist) which has a picture of "the daughter of Herodias dancing upon the altar" (117).[28] In an almost surrealistic break through time, Trepka retains from his fantastic encounters two tangible tokens: a rose and a letter. These symbols are to impart Medea's historical transcendence and a larger dimension for Trepka's spiritual-erotic fantasies.

The dissolution of boundaries between imagination and reality, past and present, which brings together cultural incommensurabilities, occurs repeatedly during Trepka's plunges into heightened spiritual sensation. Through the wintry landscape, the smell of incense, and the ceremonious atmosphere created by the bright illuminations of the ongoing Christmas festivities, Trepka relives the sensations he felt on Christmas Eve in his childhood "long ago at Posen and Breslau." In these moments of recollection, "all seems a dream; everything vague and unsubstantial . . . as if time had ceased" (124). Spiridion's awaiting of the Christ Child as a little boy parallels his eager anticipation of Medea's revelation to him; and the Christian myth, which speaks of annunciation and the birth of Christ, unfolds for the reader in the substratum of the text. Medea, however, plots her own rebirth, vampire-like, because her return requires Trepka's death. In the end, his wish to be selected for something wonderful is fulfilled in a macabre sense. He believes himself to be Medea's executor in the destruction of the effigy of Duke Robert, Medea's brother-in-law and greatest rival, to enable her fantastic return into history. But the Pole's final triumph is a Pyrrhic victory, for he does not survive this task. His "mission" ends at the very moment he is about to receive

Medea's "reward." When his excitement becomes overpowering ("At last,
Medea, Medea! Ah! AMOUR DURE—DURE AMOUR!"), his narrative is
abruptly stopped (126).

Medea's fatal stroke on Christmas Eve and the fulfillment of Spiridion's
desire in the moment of death ironically reverse the traditional conception of
Christmas as a feast of birth. The "immaculate" Mother-and-Child myth, re-
vived in popular religious discourses of the nineteenth century,[29] is evoked and
mocked by the conniving Renaissance Medea who kills her lovers and her
mythological "double" who kills her children. Medea da Carpi's appearance
obviously commands traditional Christian iconography: though she appears in
the red and black garb of the Compassionate Madonna,[30] she undermines the
religious symbolism by the fear she spreads through a pattern of love as revenge. Like the mythological figure, Medea da Carpi is the "unfeminine"
woman and the "unmotherly" mother (a female Cronos), who is a latent threat
to established order. The Medea myth, especially in Euripides' version, has
been read as a trope for the historical circumstances, in which she represents
women's oppression and desperate revolt.[31] Both the antique and the Renaissance Medea are culturally unintelligible; in either case, female rage threatens
the social order and signifies an end to history as men have known it.

In "Amour Dure," Spiridion Trepka's version of Medea da Carpi's story
shows that historical circumstances, rather than her innate evilness, have created
her image as femme fatale. Throughout history—as Trepka's research brings to
light—Medea has only been visible through her fatal connections with men. The
eager Polish historian, however, shows us Medea's "hidden" text, her alternative
identity as an autonomous, intelligent, and learned woman who can "read Pe-
trach and Plato," but who is forced to play a merely sexual role in men's power
games. Although her quest for wealth and power is not different from the goals
of her male contemporaries, she appears uncanny and threatening to them because of her sex. Thus, she has gone into history as the evil seductress, while her
archenemy and executioner, Duke Robert, is praised for his rule of clemency.
Trepka reveals that either image is false and can only be attributed to the limitations of conventional (male) historiography, which renders invisible the fear and
insecurity behind the glory of "great" men. The myth of Duke Robert's clemency, for instance, hides the cowardliness of "a cunning, cold, but craven priest,"
who feared Medea as something "almost supernatural" (103). Trepka's investigation suggests that the ruler's cruelty—he had her incarcerated and then strangled

by two women—can only be justified by historiography if Medea is invested with evil powers so that the stroke against her appears as an act of self-defense. When Trepka's historical text deprives the Duke of his "goodness," Medea's alleged wickedness becomes relative. At the same time, the text shows that Medea's image is overdetermined in so many ways that it points to its own cultural construction rather than to historical "truth."

Ironically, Trepka's narrative perpetuates the maligned image of this "femme fatale" while he pretends to undo her historical distortion. His obsessive narrative shows that his desire for Medea is not different from that of other men (lovers and historians alike), in short, the desire to possess a woman through possessing her text. In this respect, Spiridion Trepka repeats precisely the patriarchal tradition. As he does not put into perspective his own role, he becomes another "victim" of Medea's revenge. Although Trepka redeems the maligned woman from her historical exile, he imprisons her again in his frenzied mind, blinded by sexual obsession and the desire for self-aggrandizement. Through what Paul Connerton would call "mythical identification,"[32] Trepka adopts the Renaissance woman's past as his own possibility. His ritualistic reenactment (signified by the Christmas celebrations) of the collective cultural memory stored in the conception of "Medea" not only reincarnates the past, but also strengthens his self-importance. In his manic desire to become Medea's elected lover, he can envision himself as having been "reserved for something wonderful" in this world: "Why should she not return to earth, if she knows that it contains a man who thinks of, desires, only her?" (118). Although he knows that all her other lovers acted in the same manner, the Pole feels exceptional because his love makes her immortal: "But she shall love me best—me by whom she has been loved after she has been three hundred years in the grave" (122). The reader recognizes the dramatic irony of Trepka's arrogance, although he is willing to pay the price for her love: "all had to die, and I shall die also. . . . The love of such a woman is enough" (122). As the hyperbolic cliché (death for a woman's love) is made literal, symbolic and realist discourse become confused.[33] Spiridion Trepka assumes a "real" position as another rival among figures who exist only on paper. This "ungrammaticality" exposes his ludicrous obsession with the masculine role. He claims to assign to Medea a new historical importance, but unable to think outside conventional gender images, he gives her, first and foremost, a sexual identity. The narrator leaves intact the traditional male-female relations, and so they will continue repeating themselves,[34] just like the run-on inscription of Medea's golden necklace with "lozenges at intervals, on which is engraved the posy or pun . . . 'Amour Dure—Dure Amour'" (97).

The round of the necklace, which illustrates the Renaissance paradox "in my beginning is my end," reinforces the cyclical movement characteristic of mythological time. Medea also speaks to Trepka in the language of myth by appealing to his unconscious. His "grandiose" insight into the nature of Medea's love— "The love of Medea da Carpi cannot fade, but the lover can die" (102)—ironically paraphrases the self-perpetuating potency of the unreflected content in mythical images. In this respect, the dramatic irony in the text is produced not by Trepka's ignorance of the repetitiveness of "fate" but by his blindness to the cultural conditions which engender the fiction of such repetition. In Trepka's quest, one of the most powerful factors to obstruct critical awareness is his unrestrained desire. Medea signifies Trepka's longing for all that is lacking in his frustrating reality as a Polish subject of the German Empire: the "at-home" feeling of his Polish boyhood, his national (and masculine) identity, and emotional fulfillment. The text does not connect these aspects explicitly, but the reader can actualize them in Medea's dramatic entrances. Paradoxically, it takes Trepka's desire to reclaim her from the mythological bind of centuries, but the same desire arrests her image subsequently in the hothouse of his imagination which re-establishes the myth of "the eternal duration of 'La Femme.'"

Still, the narrator's dramatic monologue (almost "My Last Duchess" in reverse)[35] reveals to us the text of a learned, powerful woman, obviously no more ruthless than her male peers, and their equal in craft and cunning. This particular aspect of gender "equality" becomes visible as Trepka leaves behind the traditional history of "great men" and individualizes universal identification built into historical discourse. By shifting Medea da Carpi from the margins of history to the center, he gives the Renaissance woman a new identity, which alters the historical myth and shakes the belief in its eternal duration. By presenting Medea's story through the historian's mind, Vernon Lee shows that the myths of time-transcending images are primarily constructions of a certain cultural and political reality, here the product of a craven Renaissance duke or of an overwrought Polish professor. When Trepka claims to "understand" Medea, he fails to recognize the cultural condition of his desire as well as the Renaissance woman's historical otherness. As he is not aware of the connection of his alienation and repression with his sexual attraction to the powerful woman, his fate must follow that of her former "lovers." Trepka's sense of reality dissolves to the degree that he desires Medea's presence, and he writes the Renaissance woman into history by the same movements as he is written out of it. In "Amour Dure," masculine desire becomes disturbed when the image itself (Medea) begins to desire—not erotic fulfillment, but recognition and power. The text endows Medea da Carpi with the "strange presence" of Pater's Mona Lisa, but it also shows what happens when woman desires to create her own presence. Vernon Lee's male narrator evokes a female subject, which was supposed to be an object, and manages to create a voice for a woman to overcome her traditional historical silence. Thus, Lee's story designs a possible female position in history while revealing the (male) discourses that have kept her outside.

"Amour Dure" can be read as an inversion of Pater's modern myth. Whereas he projects a picture of the romantic and enigmatic woman who resolves the antinomies of history, Lee breaks down the picture into its components. She reverses the mythmaking process and lets us see the mind behind it. Her female figure is every bit as enigmatic as Pater's Mona Lisa—but only from the male point of view. Pater, as Ian Fletcher has argued, "was trying to create an image or model, a design, into which he could pour all the female fluid matter of his understanding of the world so as to locate it there and make it legible" (13). The phrase "men in the ways of a thousand years" can then be translated into Pater himself for whom the Mona Lisa expresses what he himself desires. In this sense, Pater's "fancy of a perpetual life, sweeping together ten thousand experiences," becomes an attempt to give universality and authority to the image by arresting in its aesthetics a synoptic history of the development of civilization.

> All the thoughts and experience of the world have etched and moulded here
> ... the animalism of Greece, the lust of Rome, the mysticism of the middle age
> with its spiritual ambition and imaginative loves, the return of the Pagan
> world, the sins of the Borgias. (*Renaissance,* 98–99)

"The return of the Pagan world, the sins of the Borgias,"—is not Medea da Carpi all that, too? Are these not the metaphors of her story? And yet her image differs from that of the Mona Lisa, as it includes the viewer's perspective. "Amour Dure" not only represents the mythical female object but reveals the relationship between the object and the maker.

Whereas Pater's reverie gathers history through the heightened sensitivity of the artist whose temperament is mystically linked to the aesthetic critic of the modern age, Lee looks into history from the woman turned into myth. Similar to the way her heroine Medea da Carpi haunts her narrator's life, Lee enters historiography from the unknown female subject position. Through complex arrangements of various cultural images, Lee constructs the visibility of woman in history. She borrows her male narrator's voice and point of view so that she can speak as a "subject-I." But she keeps her narrator at an ironical distance, which is evident, for instance, when Trepka's inflated male ego deludes him into a manic competition with Medea da Carpi's previous lovers. As Trepka's madness unfolds, the historical construction of his (male) subjectivity and thereby that of his object become evident. Trepka's madness creates a potential reality for Medea's voice and allows her, if only temporarily, to become a subject in history.

Vernon Lee employs the impressionistic historical style of Walter Pater as she reenacts his subjective revisions of "objective" historical discourses, but she writes into her text a different, female subjectivity. Lee questions the validity of historiography altogether by denying that it can yield any "truth" or knowledge unless we inquire *who* is asking the questions. In other words, an understanding of history has to remain incomplete and distorted as long as it excludes woman's point of view.

Lee's fantastic stories put her in the vanguard of the English Aesthetic Movement. But she could not totally bask in the modern aesthetic spirit because it evolved from a tradition of male subjectivity. Therefore, she is writing with *and* against Pater's model. She still shares his own ambivalence about historicism's demand for authenticity and about the claim to represent "the thing in itself." In "Amour Dure," for instance, she ridicules the pedantic methods of the German historians ("dryasdusts"), whose imperious belief in the fact-producing potency of "objective" scholarship turns history into a dead object for microscopic dissection. In the climate of the arrogance that came with the newly established German Empire, historical science was becoming a powerful instrument of oppression that silenced diverging positions. Lee shows how such oppressive systems displace their own deficiencies in "otherness," while forcing noncompliant minds to withdraw into another, imaginary reality. Trepka's madness in "Amour Dure" points to the dangerous effects of such pressure. But Lee also blames the victim (Trepka) who mistakes his escapism as empowerment. To her, the early Pater (as opposed to the "mature" Pater in *Marius the Epicurean*), practiced a form of escapism in what she called his "hedonistic aestheticism," which she criticizes in *Renaissance Fancies and Studies*:

For Walter Pater started by being above all a writer, and an aesthete in the very narrow sense of twenty years ago: an aesthete of the school of Mr. Swinburne's *Essays*. . . . The cultivation of sensations, vivid sensations, no matter whether healthful of unhealthful, was, after all, but a theoretic and probably unconscious disguise for the cultivation of something to be said in a new way, which is the danger of all persons who regard literature as an end, and not a means. . . . And of this Mr. Pater's first and famous book was a very clear proof. (251)

Pater's (male) glance into history indulges a yearning for "lost contents" (Ellen Friedman), without naming *what* was lost. Historical consciousness on the verge of modernism therefore appears as nostalgic desire—so evidently captured in Pater's account of Winckelmann's longing for home[36]—for an experience which came to fill in for all kinds of "unpresentable" contents in old master narratives. Ellen Friedman argues that women's texts of the modernist period also express a yearning for the unpresentable but that their texts often evoke it as the "not yet presented" (244). Women do not look into history in the same way as men do. Being denied subjectivity and with it, agency, they have to think back through different identities. Thus they show "little regret for the no longer presentable," in other words, the old paternal order. The female paradigm for missing contents should therefore be read as a look forward, beyond patriarchy, into the unknown, the not yet presentable.

I have shown that Lee repeatedly identifies the unknowability of history with the unknowability of woman. She refers repeatedly to the possibilities of future methods to find in history what her contemporaries for lack of knowledge cannot yet see, so that they "sometimes throw away noble ore, for lack of skill to separate it from base alloy" (*Renaissance Fancies,* 251). Vernon Lee's "female aesthetic historicism," as I may call her approach for now, can be considered an attempt at a new way of reading the past. She uses the language of her mentors, but she slips into their texts a modified point of view. Lee exposes the cultural construction of historical myths by wearing the transparent disguise of a male historian whose imagination she saw conditioned by the suppressed fears of individual and collective male history. The ghost of the past, personified in the dangerously sexual woman, appears as a production of male hysteria, thus suggesting a connection between male anxieties and cultural images.

The late nineteenth century produced a number of lasting mythical images of women, of which Pater's "la Gioconda" is one famous example. Between painting and text arises the aesthetic critic's "masterpiece," meant to give universality and authority to the image and at the same time to inscribe in it moments of freedom, "exquisite pauses in time" ( *Renaissance,* 118). And so, Pater's Mona Lisa represents the male desire to "re-master" the Renaissance picture.[37] Lee's story "Amour Dure" undermines Pater's controlling symbolism: The portrait of Medea da Carpi is a (Bronzino) painting come alive—with all the forces that man has put into it. In this respect, Vernon Lee's story "Amour Dure" is a key text for her re-thinking of Paterian aesthetic historicism, as well as her exploration of the relationship between history and historian, writer and text. By focusing on the absent or suppressed female text, Lee changes history as it has been known. The end of the story leaves her narrator dead and the historical text unwritten. Medea's story is history suspended: What she was, is, or will be cannot be known—at least not in man's terms.

# Notes

1. The label "non-canonical" has become widely used in reference to neglected writers to avoid assimilating them to an established male canon. But the term is problematic in itself, as Talia Schaffer warns us in *The Forgotten Female Aesthetes,* since it may leave marginalized women writers in perpetual opposition to the mainstream list. She offers an intelligent way to rethink both groups: "When the women's presence within literary schools forces us to reshape our views of those schools . . . we have used canonization against itself" (17).

2. Two recent studies of Ruskin explore his work in terms of modernist content, thus redressing his reputation as a staunch Victorian, which had clung to him since the later part of his life. The essays edited by Giovanni Cianci and Peter Nicholls under the title *Ruskin and Modernism* (2001) attest to the multiple resonances of Ruskinism in modernist art, although the latter persistently denied his legacy. Diane Birch's anthology *Ruskin and the Dawning of the Modern* (2000) offers new ways of reading Ruskin as both opponent and contributor to cultural change, asking how his patterns of writing opened possibilities for modernist discourses.

3. The marginalization of late-nineteenth-century New Women writers by literary periodizations (especially realism and modernism) has been analyzed by Ann L. Ardis in *New Women, New Novels* (1990). Other feminist critiques of literary periods, such as Ellen G. Friedman's "Where Are the Missing Contents? (Post) Modernism, Gender and the Canon" or Rita Felski's *The Gender of Modernism,* suggest that female writers look back differently from male writers into literary history and that the discovery of neglected women writers alters the boundaries of such periods significantly.

4. Even Perry Meisel's critical study, *The Myth of the Modern,* leaves untouched the most persistent myth, which is that the "principal modern English classics" are understood to be male; and so he names "Hardy, Arnold, Pater, [T. S.] Eliot, Joyce," and has for Woolf only the group category of "Bloomsbury" (5).

5. This is especially true of Woolf's article "The Modern Essay."

6. Instead of disavowing their debt to the nineteenth century, writers like Vernon Lee and later Rebecca West tried to link themselves to their immediate predecessors. But the modernist concept of the present moment as a phenomenon isolated in time instead intensified the disjunction from the past (see Margaret D. Stetz, "Rebecca West's Criticism," in *Rereading Modernism,* ed. Lisa Rado, 41–55).

7. "Modernism," comprising a broad range of style, has often been identified with its foremost attribute, "disinterestedness." In "Modernism and Modernity," Rita Felski offers a list of features most often associated with modernist style, such as decentered subjectivity, aesthetic self-consciousness, subversion of narrative continuity, and an emphasis on paradox, contradiction, and ambiguity. Feminist critics have recently reassessed these attributes from the women writers' perspective, which gives a different evaluation of this literary period: "The impersonal and abstract formalism of a writer such as Pound, for example, is of little relevance to understanding those female modernists such as H.D. whose writing sought to evoke the intimate and fragmentary fluctuations of the psyche" (in Rado, 193–94).

8. Walter Pater's letters to Vernon Lee, 4 June 1884, Colby College Special Collections (henceforth cited parenthetically as Colby).

9. Max Dessoir, the editor of *Zeitschrift für Ästhetik,* wrote to Lee that he found it impossible to understand her essay on aesthetic psychology because she referred to her own experience instead of keeping an objective scientific focus: "Mir scheint ferner, dass die ständige Beziehung auf Ihre persönliche Entwicklung das Wesentliche, nämlich das sachliche Problem, in den Hintergrund treten lässt. Kurz, mir gelingt es nicht, einen deutlichen Fortschritt der Gedanken, einen wirklichen Beweisgang zu erkennen." [It seems to me that the constant reference to your personal development pushes the subject matter itself into the background. In short, I am unable to discern any clear progression of thought nor any real presentation of evidence.] My translation; letter of 7 October 1909, Vernon Lee Papers, Somerville College, Oxford; henceforth cited parenthetically as Somerville.

10. On this change in the role of the intellectual see T. W. Heyck's important study *The Transformation of Intellectual Life in Victorian England,* especially 221–39.

11. Later in life, Lee attempted a similarly empirical study of music enjoyment on the basis of a questionnaire she had sent out to listeners (*Music and Its Lovers,* 1932).

12. Lee's citations include Michelet, Burckhardt, and Symonds; she also includes a great number of French, Italian, and German medievalists, British scholars of the Elizabethan stage, and recent art theorists (*Euphorion,* 2:237–39).

13. For instance, in Charlotte Yonge's novel *The Clever Woman of the Family* (1865), the heroine finally has to admit that "such cleverness as that is a far more perilous gift than your plodding intellectuality has even been."

14. Karl Groos's letters to Vernon Lee (February 1901–January 1929, Somerville) show his genuine interest in Lee's work. Unlike Symonds, he does not address her as a neophyte but, respectfully, as a colleague.

15. Any accounts of gender and power, Small asserts, must be preceded by a discussion of the relationship between knowledge and authority, since power and gender have little or no meaning beyond the institutions that sanction them. Small's argument is based on an epistemology of cause and effect which assumes a one-directional (not an interactive) model of power. Thus, he can discuss the mechanisms of competition between different epistemological models in abstract, timeless terms.

16. Small discusses Lee's role in the debates about Associationism merely on a theoretical level without acknowledging her different, that is, nonacademic background, common among women writers in her time. While acknowledging her intellectual boldness, he pays more attention to her limitations. He uses only one of her minor essays from *Juvenilia* ("Lake of Charlemagne: An Apology of Association"), while quoting extensively from Arnold, Pater, and Wilde. In fairness, this imbalance may very well be the effect of the relative inaccessibility of Lee's texts in comparison to the greater circulation of the other authors. After all, Small included Lee as the only woman writer in his anthology, *The Aesthetes,* published in 1979.

17. "Gospels of Anarchy" first appeared in Lee's essay collection of the same title in 1908 and was reprinted in Broomfield and Mitchell's *Prose by Victorian Women.* The page numbers refer to the original version.

## CHAPTER 1

1. Peter Gunn, *Vernon Lee: Violet Paget, 1856–1935,* ix. The restrictions on the documents that Lee's executrix, Irene Cooper Willis, placed in the Miller Library at Colby College, Waterville, Maine, in 1951 were in effect until 1980; and the papers given as a gift to Somerville College, Oxford, were not to be used until fifty years after Lee's death as a contribution to a study of the period. According to Pauline Adams, director of the Somerville Library, the Vernon Lee papers were deposited in 1935 with a fifty-year restriction, so they have been available for consultation since 1985. Both collections comprise large parts of Lee's extensive correspondence (several thousand letters) with her family, friends, and literary acquaintances; her literary journals and personal notebooks; drafts and manuscripts of her unpublished work; proofs sheets; part of her personal library; photographs and other memorabilia. Phyllis F. Mannocchi's comprehensive list of Vernon Lee's works is invaluable for every scholar; Carl Markgraf's "'Vernon Lee': A Commentary and an Annotated Bibliography of Writings about Her" compiles and summarizes the many scattered criticisms on Lee in English and other European languages.

The archives are cited parenthetically as Colby and Somerville. Parenthetical citations of letters use the abbreviations VL for Vernon Lee and MP for Matilda Paget.

2. Lee recalls the formative years of her aesthetic outlook in *The Handling of Words* (1923) and in the unpublished manuscript "Aesthetics—My Confession," a 107-page holograph, possibly written in the last years of her life and now in the Vernon Lee collection at Colby College.

3. "Her appearance at this time was somewhat unconventional, even a little odd, by contemporary Victorian standards. . . . Among the English society in which she moved the difference in her upbringing and attitude was marked not only by the slightly foreign precision of her vocabulary and intonation but also by the frequent use of gesture, particularly Italian in its graceful appropriateness or in its vehemence, when reinforcing a point" (Gunn, 90).

4. A list of Vernon Lee's books from her personal library in "Il Palmerino" (now at the British Institute in Florence) reflects the wide range of her interests from psychology to economics and social sciences—at least half of them in French, German, or Italian. Many of them bear the dates of her reading and rereading, and are copiously annotated in different languages. Similarly, her correspondence in the archives of Colby College and Somerville College is carried on in four languages.

5. The question of the national origin of Violet Paget's father, Henry Paget, cannot be fully resolved. While it is certain that he was in Poland during the revolutionary uprisings in the 1840s, the question of whether he was of Polish or French extraction has been complicated in part by Matilda Paget's rewriting of his family history. Gardner, who has studied Eugene's narrative of Henry Paget's participation in the Polish uprising of 1846–48, has no doubt "that Henry was a Pole" (90).

6. "She was very strong on grammar; acquired an exhaustive (and to my childish mind exhausting) knowledge of the fourteen cases (including avec le peu) of the French past participle. Also she had great faith in Euclid, of whom she had mastered up to and inclusive of the fifth proposition of the first book, besides the definitions and postulates, all of which she endeavoured to convey to me during our walks, always by word of mouth, and without allowing me to glance at a diagram or even to draw one furtively in the road's dust" (Vernon Lee on her mother in *The Handling of Words*, 298).

7. From the mid-eighties on, diverging interests and viewpoints led Lee and Sargent in different directions, but Lee always remained close to John's sister Emily. John Sargent painted Lee's portrait (1881), which is now in the Tate Gallery, London, and made several pencil sketches of her, one of them archived in the Ashmolean Museum, Oxford.

8. This letter to my knowledge is the only one by Vernon Lee in the Karl Pearson papers now kept at the Library of University College London.

9. In his article "Der ästhetische Mensch," the art historian Gerd Mattenklott names as one of the origins of the Aesthetic movement the intelligentsia's reaction to the failure of the national-democratic rebellions in the mid-nineteenth century. Intellectuals in Western Europe formed an "aesthetic opposition" against the national restoration that took place in the second half of the nineteenth century (60–61).

10. Although literary history paid more critical attention to Vernon Lee than to Eugene Lee-Hamilton, the irony of fate would have it that she was buried anonymously in Eugene's grave in Florence with only his name written on the tombstone. But due to the tireless agitation of Carola Costa-Angeli (who bought the villa "Il Palmerino" after Lee's death), the Florentine and British authorities arranged a ceremonial inscription of Vernon Lee's name in March 1996.

11. To Kit Anstruther-Thomson, Lee vented her anger at Eugene more openly: "While Eugene admits his illness is caused by autosuggestion, he is doing nothing to bring himself out of it; . . . [Eugene] seems to fill the whole horizon with the thought of himself" (9/10 November 1894, Colby).

12. Roger Fry (18 June 1933, Colby) praises Lee's innovative approach to music, which, he hopes, will open new possibilities for the visual arts as well.

13. I am referring to Denisoff's article "The Forest beyond the Frame" in *Women and British Aestheticism,* ed. Talia Schaffer and Kathy Alexis Psomiades.

14. See for example "Our Library Table," *Athenaeum,* 28 November 1908, 68 (on *Studies of the Eighteenth Century in Italy*); "*Euphorion,*" *Pall Mall Gazette,* 7 July 1884, 4–5; "*The Countess of Albany,*" *Athenaeum,* 23 August 1884, 229–30.

15. Ruth Robbins makes this point, however, with regard to Lee's fiction, in her discussion of Lee's "decadent" story, "Prince Alberic and the Snake Lady" (157).

16. Hillebrand's corrections of *Ottilie* in a letter to Violet Paget (16 July 1883, Colby) illustrate his intent: "Your hero was born in 1759 (the same year as Schiller) and was between 14 and 15 (p. 86) when he made the acquaintance of councillor Moritz. Yet (p. 102) you speak of the summer 1782 as the time of this intimacy, which would make your hero a youth of 23. By changing 1782 in 1773, all comes right, and the reading of *Laocoon* as a new book becomes more natural. . . . p. 81, I would say W. was about to write a refutation of the *Dramaturgie* (not Drammaturgie), not 'had written,' as the Dramaturgie was just written in this very year. I think it would be advisable to correct with a pen the two dates (p. 102 and 120) and the word *Dramaturgie.*"

17. The first commentary is from "Books. *Euphorion,*" *Spectator* (London), 12 July 1884, 916–18, and the second from "Recent Books on Italy," *Atlantic* 97 (April 1906): 559–60.

18. Jarves here refers to Lee's "The Artistic Dualism of the Renaissance" (1879).

19. "Are Myths Necessary? Vernon Lee's Exposure of the Syndicalist Myth," *Current Opinion* 54 (April 1913): 313–14, on *Vital Lies* (1913).

20. J. A. Symonds, for instance, admired Vernon Lee's book on the eighteenth century and considered her knowledge in this field unrivaled by anybody else. For further details see Phyllis Grosskurth, *The Woeful Victorian: A Biography of J. A. Symonds,* 222–56.

21. Some of the republished essay collections are: *Baldwin: Being Dialogues on Views and Aspirations* (1886; New York: Books for Libraries Press, 1972); *The Poet's Eye: Notes on Some Differences between Verse and Prose* (1926; Folcroft: Folcroft Library Editions, 1974); *Renaissance Fancies and Studies* (1895; New York: Garland, 1977); *The Beautiful: An Introduction to Psychological Aesthetics* (1913; Folcroft: Folcroft Library Editions, 1970,1974; Norwood: Norwood Library Editions, 1977; Philadelphia: R. West, 1978); *Studies in the Eighteenth Century in Italy* (1878; New York: Da Capo Press, 1978).

22. *The Handling of Words and Other Studies in Literary Psychology* (1923), ed. Stuart Sillars (Oxford: Oxford University Press, 1996); ed. David Seed (Lewistown: Edward

Mellen Press, 1992); previous editions include one by University of Nebraska Press (1968) and another by Peter Smith in 1968.

23. The following survey of the retrievable re-editions of her stories written in the 1880s and '90s offers only a selection: "Dionea" is republished in *Nineteenth-Century Stories by Women,* ed. Glennis Stephenson (Peterborough: Broadview Literary Texts, 1997), 349–84; "Winthrop's Adventure" reappeared in *Victorian Ghost Stories by Eminent Women Writers,* ed. Richard Dalby (New York: Carroll & Graf Publishers, 1988). Other collections contain these late-nineteenth-century or early-twentieth-century stories: *Hauntings: Fantastic Stories* (Freeport: Books of the Library Press, 1971; London: Heinemann, 1978); *A Vernon Lee Anthology with Explanatory Notice by Vernon Lee,* ed. Irene Cooper Willis (Folcroft: Folcroft Library Editions, 1977); *For Maurice: Five Unlikely Stories* (New York: Arno Press, 1976); *Five Victorian Ghost Stories,* ed. E. F. Bleiler (New York: Dover, 1971), 299–340; *Pope Jacynth and Other Fantastic Tales* (London: Peter Owen, 1956); *The Snake Lady and Other Stories* (New York: Grove Press, 1954). The most recent re-editions of her original *Supernatural Tales* date from 1987 and 1990: Vernon Lee, *Supernatural Tales: Excursions into Fantasy,* with an introduction by Irene Cooper Willis (London: P. Owen, 1987); Vernon Lee, *Amour Dure: Unheimliche Erzählungen,* ed. Frank Rainer Scheck (Cologne: Du Mont, 1990).

24. "Sie ist aber nicht fähig gewesen, ein Anschauungsbild von der italienischen Renaissance zu geben, das neben den Darstellungen ihrer größeren Zeitgenossen zu bestehen vermöchte." Max Bräm, *Die italienische Renaissance in dem englischen Geistesleben des 19. Jahrhunderts, im besonderen bei John Ruskin, John Addington Symonds und Vernon Lee,* 98.

25. See Lillian Faderman's 1990 review of *The Lesbian Imagination* by Burdett Gardner. After listing the merits of Gardner's compilatory scholarship, Faderman (rightly) dismisses its usefulness: "Unfortunately, he put all that material to the primary use of rehashing antipathetic lesbian stereotypes."

26. Gardner locates Lee's lesbianism in her nature, whereas he describes the "symptoms" of her behavior in terms of the cultural decorum. Reminiscent of the early sexologists is his problematic citation of physical "evidence" to show that her "Lesbian neurosis . . . was . . . to change her physique and her secondary sex characteristics" (144). His description parallels the characterizations of female "inversion" by Lee's contemporaries Richard von Krafft-Ebing and Havelock Ellis. Krafft-Ebing, in particular, linked women's rejection of traditional gender roles and their demands for social and economic equality to cross-dressing, sexual perversion, and hermaphroditism: "Uranism may nearly always be suspected in females wearing their hair short, or who dress in the fashion of men, or pursue the sports and pastimes of their male acquaintances" (quoted in Carol Smith-Rosenberg, *Disorderly Conduct: Visions of Gender in Victorian America,* 271).

27. Similarly, Adeline R. Tintner's "Vernon Lee's 'Oke of Okehurst' or 'The Phantom Lover' and James' 'The Way It Came'" is a comparison between Lee and James, which presupposes James as the greater genius.

28. The essay was recently republished in Richard Dellamora's *Victorian Sexual Dissidence* (1999).

29. In his review of Lee's "Satan the Waster," *Nation* 27 (18 September 1920): 758–60, G. B. Shaw probably overdrew Vernon Lee's role slightly to appeal to British Liberalism, which he saw losing its influence in Britain's increasingly materialist and nationalist policy.

30. See, for instance, David Lodge, *The Language of Fiction* (1966); Kenneth Graham, *English Criticism of the Novel, 1865–1900* (1965); John Halperin, ed., *The Theory of the Novel* (1977); Eric Warner and Graham Hough, eds., *Strangeness and Beauty: An Anthology of Aesthetic Criticism, 1840–1910* (1983); Ian Small, *Conditions for Criticism: Authority, Knowledge, and Literature in the Late Nineteenth Century* (1991).

31. Vernon Lee's correspondence in the Somerville Library testifies to her being perceived as a voice of reason and understanding. As one example among many, I quote from a letter the German psychologist Richard Baerwald wrote to her after Germany's defeat in World War I: "Sehr geehrtes Fräulein Paget! Haben Sie vielen herzlichen Dank für Ihren Brief, der mich auf mannigfachen Umwegen erreicht hat. Wenn ich Ihre Persönlichkeit nicht schon aus Ihren Schriften zu erraten glaubte, durch diese echte 'document humain' würde sie mir klar werden. Sie glauben kaum, wie tröstend und wohltuend solche Briefe in dieser Zeit furchtbarster Seelennot wirken; es scheint sich ein beginnender Heilungsprozeß in Ihnen anzukündigen, der die zerrissenen Glieder der Menschheit wieder zusammenwachsen lassen will" (12 April 1919, Somerville). (Baerwald thanks her for her letter, which he calls a "document of humanity." Her writing gives him hope that "humanity, now split asunder, will grow back together again.")

## CHAPTER 2

1. In the introduction to *Studies of the Eighteenth Century in Italy* (1880), Lee snubs historians who look only for antiquarian detail as "laborious bookworms, who find broken and minute fragments of the eighteenth century as they do of every other century" (2).

2. In his own time, this Swiss scholar was criticized as "unhistorical," a judgment that leveled Pater, Symonds, and Lee, none of whom ever achieved the status of professional historians by traditional European standards. To what extent Burckhardt's *Civilization of the Renaissance in Italy* (1860) was known in England cannot be decided in all certainty. Although the book was translated into English in 1878, it had only a small run. Symonds and Pater knew it, but it did not gain its enormous influence until its second translation in 1929. Through her fluency in German, Vernon Lee had access to Burckhardt's work, which she cites in *Euphorion* (1864). She became one of the first propagators of his relativism and shared his defiance against grim Hegelian determinism.

3. In her article "'This Feminine Preserve': Historical Biographies by Victorian Women," Maitzen analyzes how female historians enabled their work by different

strategies to meet the critical hostility they anticipated when entering the male domain of history. Through their rhetoric of distinction and subordination they at least superficially adapted their work to cultural pressures.

4. Mary Beard—born in the same year as Vernon Lee—called a past described only from a male perspective "fragmentation" and advocated an expansion of historical narrative. In *On Understanding Women* (1931) and *America through Women's Eyes* (1933), she showed rather self-consciously how different history would look when seen through women's eyes (Bonnie G. Smith, 26).

5. "Art is not Art's end, and Beauty is not its end," Symonds wrote to her in March 1882; and on 18 July 1883, he lectures her that "morality is the distinctive attribute of the highest organicism known to us in Nature." He displays astonishment "at the superficial way in which it has been treated by the thinkers of your school—Clifford for instance."

6. In reference to Lee's review of Villari (see chapter 1), when he wrote to his friend T. S. Perry, Symonds was more direct: "I look forward to hearing what you think of Euphorion. It is a most remarkable & able, but very irritating book. The crudity of self-assertion & of self-assumption in it disgusts me as much as its candour attracts. . . . I don't think there is any conscious plagiarism; & Miss Paget's originality is indubitable. But there is a certain carelessness & arrogance about her, wh[ich] makes her think that she has thought out a great deal wh[ich] she has really absorbed from other writers & remembered" (30 July 1884, letter 1408).

7. Jacob Burckhardt had been one of the first trying to understand the composition of cultural and social systems anew from source material rather than from what German professors had written about Greek or Renaissance civilization.

8. Lee felt entitled through her aesthetic sensibilities to oppose her predecessors, such as Goethe and Winckelmann, and to speak as an advocate for the "other" Renaissance, which she literally does in "The Sacrifice" (*Euphorion,* 1:27–54).

9. Jacob Burckhardt also found that universal and abstract notions could not grasp the diversity of the Renaissance. To stress its special function in historiography, he asserted—like Vernon Lee—that it was a condition, not an epoch. Burckhardt uses "Renaissance" somewhat polemically against traditional periodization that had developed with the exploration of Antiquity. Compared to the "static" concept of the classicist age, the Renaissance had to appear as a quirky living thing which could not be subsumed by the cool and breezy terms of historical universality. See Burckhardt, *Die Kultur der Renaissance in Italien,* ed. Horst Günther, 1010–24.

10. Similarly, in *Althea,* her protagonist is "at first, inarticulate, unreasoning, ignorant of all why and wherefore, and requires to be taught many things which others know. But, once having learned the names, so to speak, of her instincts, the premises of her unconscious arguments, she becomes, as necessarily, the precursor of many of Baldwin's best thoughts, the perfecter of most of them" (xvii).

11. Lee generally was critical of Hegel, but followed his philosophy more closely than she would admit. In Terry Eagleton's reading of Hegel, we recognize the strik-

ing resemblance: "Theory in Hegel follows after practice, as the tardy flight of Minerva's owl; and to this extent it cannot meddle with that practice in ways harmful to its spontaneous wisdom. Spirit ripens within habitual, unconscious social activity, or 'culture'; when it forgets this location within concrete life and acts abstractly, prematurely, the result is revolutionary fanatism" (*Ideology of the Aesthetics,* 150).

12. As Lee states in her appendix to *Euphorion,* she drew much of her material from Michelet. Her emphasis on the achievements of the lower classes is probably one of her most obvious uses of the French historian. Of the many significant differences between Lee's and Michelet's concepts, I would like to point out here that Michelet associates "le peuple" with "la patrie," whereas Lee sees the nation state as adverse to the people's interests. Moreover, Lee's country people appear happy and self-reliant—altogether rather bucolic—in comparison with Michelet's bitter and dismal peasants, who have more resemblance to the urban proletariat of the industrial era. For a more detailed analysis of Michelet's "le peuple" see Stephen A. Kippur, *Jules Michelet: A Study in Mind and Sensibility* (1981), 101–5.

13. Lee often juxtaposes a talented amateur with a learned, but rather bookish, academic, as in her novel *Louis Norbert* (1914).

14. Lee often opposes "high" or academic art with the incidental, playful, or fairy-tale elements in unsophisticated folklore. For instance, her definition of the supernatural in "Faustus and Helena" (whose offspring is Euphorion) presents the medieval legend of Dr. Faustus as infinitely more powerful in its effect on our imagination than its professional version by Goethe (*Belcaro,* 71). Lee here includes as the shaping forces of culture explicitly the activities of the common people, in other words, "not only the priest and the poet, but the village boor" (77). The "real" supernatural effect can be achieved only by the less polished legends which remain alive even under Goethe's artistic but "bloodless" transformation (102).

15. Within a milieu of rising British nationalism and rivalry with France, interest in the French Renaissance was rather subdued. Walter Pater and Emilia Dilke—although pursuing significantly different approaches—were "the earliest, and most enthusiastic, British scholars of French Renaissance culture" (Mansfield, 170). It is interesting to see how both Dilke and Lee tried to distinguish themselves from Pater in similar ways: while Pater defined the Renaissance ideally, Dilke declared the French Renaissance a product of quantifiable social sources and Lee found the Italian Renaissance in the production of everyday life.

16. Pater himself mentions Vernon Lee's essay most favorably in a footnote of his edition of the 1893 text of *The Renaissance:* "Recently, *Aucassin and Nicolette* has been edited and translated into English, with much graceful scholarship. . . . The reader should consult also the chapter on "The Outdoor Poetry" in Vernon Lee's most interesting *Euphorion: Being Studies of the Antique and Medieval in the Renaissance,* a work abounding in knowledge and insight on the subjects of which it treats" (12).

17. Lee must have felt that her argument was somewhat daring, for she bolsters it by quoting from Professor d'Ancona in one of her footnotes. Today, her argument

appears rather modern. As Alison Cornish has shown in a recent *PMLA* article (March 2000), "A Lady Asks: The Gender of Vulgarization in Late Medieval Italy," the vernacularization of Latin discourse in late-medieval Italian poetry gave access to restricted knowledge while it valorized the language of the ignorant. It is interesting to note that Italy precedes France in this translation of Latin texts into vernacular because of the development of the northern Italian city-states. Note that Lee gives the "Italian commonwealths" of the late thirteenth century a similarly innovative role.

18. Lee's unconventional view of Lorenzo dei Medici was, of course, not a matter of impression but of intensive research. Her approach even found Symonds's approval: "Your defence of L. de Medici's genius interests me. You rank him higher as a poet than I do. But I believe you will find that I had (in Vol 4 of R in It) done justice to the versatility & originality of his initiative" (20 June 1884).

19. The collection *Tuscan Fairy Tales,* published by W. Satchell in 1880, is preceded by a similar claim: "Taken down from the mouths of the people." Although no editor's name is given, it is generally assumed that Lee published these fairy tales anonymously.

20. Her executrix, Irene Cooper Willis, says of her: "She was just an individual, she said, and to be an individual was a weak thing, depriving her of influence" (preface to *Vernon Lee's Letters,* xii).

21. *The Handling of Words and Other Studies in Literary Psychology* (1923). In a letter to her half-brother Eugene, in 1893, Lee also complains of having no public, but she immediately turns her marginality into a position of strength—obviously trying to impress Eugene: "I don't think it is my obscurity which prevents my being popular, but my habit and determination only to please myself, irrespective of readers. . . . At thirty-seven I have no public, but on the other hand, I am singularly far from being played out" (Fall 1983, Colby).

22. Raymond Chapman, in *The Sense of the Past in Victorian Literature,* captured this sentiment: "In the last part of the Victorian age there is a growing sense that the past is simply irrelevant. It is a mood that marks the end not only of the century but also of an age in which history was important" (187).

23. From the early 1900s Vernon Lee voiced her liberal antimilitarist and pacifist views, which became rather unpopular during the nationalist polarizations in World War I, when she regularly published her views on politics in the *Nation, Westminster Gazette, New Statesman,* and *Atlantic Monthly.*

24. In his essay "Pale Imitations: Walter Pater's Decadent Historiography," Matthew Potolsky argues that "[d]ecadent texts . . . do not merely practice imitation, they explicitly thematize it" (236). Potolsky uses Pater's "Apollo in Picardy" to show that Pater's imitations constitute historical gesture, implying that the significance of the past is never fixed. Incidentally, this essay could have been applied to Lee's historical texts in which she shows that history is always open to reinterpretation in the light of subsequent events. It is interesting to note that Potolsky treats Pater's imitation not as a stigma (attached to Lee by nineteenth-century critics) but as a purposefully employed discursive strategy.

CHAPTER 3

1. Wittig (in *The Lesbian Body*, poem 11) evokes and lesbianizes a scene of heterosexuality on Cythera, an island in the Aegean Sea, with a "magnificent temple to Aphrodite." Namascar Shaktini, in "A Revolutionary Signifier: *The Lesbian Body*" (in *Lesbian Texts and Contexts*, ed. Karla Jay and Joanne Glasgow), comments: "In a politico-poetic act, a lexical metamorphosis, Wittig has reintroduced the word 'cyprine' with new usage. Just as the phallic subject, on the bodily level, produces semen, and on the symbolic level, seminaries and seminar and seminal words, the lesbian as sexual subject produces 'cyprine'" (292).

2. Lee's rewriting of "Abélard and Heloïse" in *Renaissance Fancies and Studies* points to Rousseau's version and the way Pater "sacrifices" the female in order to emphasize the innovative spirit of Abélard. Lee puts Abélard's teachings into the context of a dehumanized Christian religion that crushes genuine love and human emotion embodied by Heloïse.

3. On the difficulty of literary categorization see, for instance, *British Women Writers: A Critical Reference Guide*, ed. Janet Todd (1989), 407–10; and *The Feminist Companion to Literature in English: Women Writers from the Middle Ages to the Present*, ed. Virginia Blain, Patricia Clements, and Isobel Grundy (1990).

4. To be sure, the terms "fiction" and "nonfiction" do not neatly map into the realms of novel and essay. In the history of both genres, there are enough examples in which the exclusionary opposition of such labels breaks down.

5. For an involved discussion of the role of gender in history and historiography see Joan W. Scott, "Gender: A Useful Category of Historical Analysis," in *Coming to Terms: Feminism, Theory, Politics*, ed. Elizabeth Weed, 81–100.

6. In *English Prose of the Nineteenth Century*, Hilary Fraser and Daniel Brown show that "English literature is full of strange hybrid works." What they describe as Wilde's and Pater's modern approach can also be applied to Vernon Lee: "It is precisely this relativist treatment of the traditional categories of fiction and non-fiction that Wilde notes in another of Pater's works, the *Imaginary Portraits*. He writes that in this book fiction has become a 'fanciful guise' for the presentation of insights that are traditionally presented as non-fiction" (16).

7. Lee's misgivings about the notion of objectivity brings to mind Montaigne's skepticism about the stability of language and his distrust of "objective" judgment (foregrounded in Bakhtin's reading of Montaigne). In "A Dialogic Approach to the Essay" (*Essays on the Essay: Redefining the Genre*, ed. Alexander J. Butrym), Thomas E. Recchio sees Montaigne's doubts reapplied by poststructuralist critics such as James Clifford, who exposes the inadequacy of the notion of objective observation in the human sciences. Almost echoing Lee's words, Recchio concludes, "observation is intention, is interpretation, and as a result, the authority of the observer is limited even as the range of what can be observed is extended" (284).

8. On the development of male/female styles of essays, in *The Politics of the Essay,*

ed. Ruth-Ellen Boetcher Joeres and Elizabeth Mittman, see for instance Eileen Boyd Sivert, "Flora Tristran: The Joining of Essay, Journal, Autobiography," 57–72, and Katherine V. Snyder, "From Novel to Essay: Gender and Revision in Florence Nightingale's 'Cassandra,'" 24–40.

9. Some of the publications that have made inroads into the study of nonfictional prose include Thaïs E. Morgan, ed., *Victorian Sages & Cultural Discourse: Renegotiating Gender and Power* (1990); Andrea Broomfield and Sally Mitchell, eds., *Prose by Victorian Women: An Anthology* (1996); and Hilary Fraser with Daniel Brown, *English Prose of the Nineteenth Century* (1997).

10. For a critical discussion of women's role in the publishing process in Victorian England, see Gaye Tuchman and Nina E. Fortin's groundbreaking study *Edging Women Out: Victorian Novelists, Publishers, and Social Change* (1989). Although the study has been superseded in parts (particularly the uncritical assumption of the separate-spheres theory), it contains invaluable empirical material on the gender politics in the publishing industry.

11. In 1894, Edith Wharton had asked Paul Bourget for a letter of introduction to Vernon Lee, who later reviewed Wharton's novel *The Valley of Decision* (1902). Wharton was grateful: "No one welcomed 'The Valley of Decision' more warmly than Vernon Lee, and it was a great encouragement to be praised by a writer whom I so much admired, and who was so unquestioned an authority on the country and the period I had dealt with" (Wolff, 884).

12. With all her zeal for uncovering forgotten women and their writings, we wonder why Woolf chose not to mention George Eliot among the "great" nineteenth-century essayists. In her introduction to *Virginia Woolf: A Woman's Essays* (1992), Rachel Bowlby criticizes Woolf's omission of Eliot in an all-male genealogy as a strategical move so that Woolf could "then give all the more force to [her] own takeover of the genre for unfemininely feminist concern" (xxvii).

13. Women became important as a growing audience from the eighteenth century, when essays began to be written for the edification of women from the leisured classes. Leslie Stephen, Woolf's father and an eminent essayist himself, found that "essays were lay sermons, whose authors condescended, it was supposed, to turn from grave studies of philosophy or politics to topics at once edifying and intelligible to the weaker sex" (*Studies of a Biographer,* 27). Although Stephens's gender conjecture is ironic, we may wonder what role his own literary "fatherhood" played in his daughter's determination to wrench the essay from the masculine prerogative.

14. Lee had obviously sensed Symonds's underlying resentment and, as his letter implies, had asked him for the background of his carping (letter 1382 of *The Letters of J. A. Symonds,* ed. Herbert M. Schueller and Robert L. Peters, vol. 3).

15. In "A Voice of One's Own," Tuzyline Jita Allen quotes from Woolf's *A Writer's Diary* on this point, where she speaks of Joyce's "damned egoistical self" (143).

16. There are other feminists who criticize Woolf's self-concealing act, such as, for instance, Elaine Showalter in *A Literature of Their Own* (1977), in the chapter "Virginia

Woolf and a Flight into Androgyny," 263–97. Jane Marcus ("Art and Anger") would have preferred a little more anger in Woolf's "polite" manner (94).

17. W. J. Stillman, for instance, a harsh critic of both Lee's and Pater's impressionism, found that Pater's *Studies in the History of the Renaissance* had taught him "not so much of the theme as of Mr. Pater himself" (unsigned review of *Studies in the History of the Renaissance* by Walter Pater, *Nation* 17 [1873]: 243–44).

## CHAPTER 4

1. I'm using "pass" here in the sense that Lisa Walker proposes in "How to Recognize a Lesbian: The Cultural Politics of Looking Like What You Are," *Signs* 18 (1993). Walker sees the role of the "femme" (as opposed to the identification model of the "butch") as an example of "passing," i.e., creating the illusion of an interior gendered self as she looks like a "straight" woman, while simultaneously parodying herself, as "what you see is not what you get" (868).

2. In his *PMLA* article "Racial Memory and Literary History" (2001), Greenblatt critiques the Western narrative of gradual emergence by pleading for an awareness of the accidental and disruptive forces ("a sense of glorious fragments [rather] than a set of coherent histories"). Following Greenblatt's argument, one might say that Lee, even though adopting the contemporary evolutionary model, still built into her text an opening for the accidental and the provisional in her subjectivity.

3. On this point, see, for instance, Ann L. Ardis's important study, *New Women, New Novels: Feminism and Early Modernism* (1990), 51–52.

4. Theresa de Lauretis, in "Sexual Indifference and Lesbian Representation" (1988), develops this theme at some length: "It thus appears that 'sexual difference' is the term of a conceptual paradox corresponding to what is in effect a real contradiction in women's lives: the term, at once, of a sexual *difference* (women are, or want, something different from men) and of a sexual *indifference* (women are, or want, the same as men). And it seems to me that the racist and class-biased practices legitimated in the notion of 'separate but equal' reveal a very similar paradox in the liberal ideology of pluralism, where social difference is also, at the same time, social indifference" (155).

5. As Carol Smith-Rosenberg observes in "The Body Politic," "it seems a tribute to the power of desire that, in their letters and diaries, the New Women were able to express such highly sensual, indeed erotic, feelings for one another. The erotic did not simply lurk as the unconscious of their letters or their lives. Time and again, it burst through all restraints and boldly claimed the name desire. But, note carefully, not the name sex" (109–10). George Buelens's recent reading of eroticized spaces in Henry James could be extended to Vernon Lee. Buelens's concept of "oblique possession" (301), which disrupts dichotomies of sexual identity, also supports Lee's dissolution of gender-based identification in landscape and scenery (as I show later in this chapter).

6. This is her basic argument in "A Dialogue on Poetic Morality" (*Belcaro*). Lee returns to this point later, for instance, in the introduction to *Althea*: "[W]hile our fathers

made themselves wretched about their unworthiness in the eyes of God, we latter-day religious folk suffered sincere misery for the opposite reason: the universe and its arrangements dissatisfied man. . . . Hence, we naturally imagine that everything is made for us, and that everything not made for us (if so be that anything is) must be made in our image" (xii–xiii).

7. The essay is included, as "The Economic Parasitism of Women," in *Gospels of Anarchy* (1908), 263–97. It first appeared under the title "Economic Dependence of Women," in the *North American* (1902).

8. I find it strange that Peter Gunn calls Lee a feminist who "has continually before him [*sic*] the understanding and recognition of the existence of a distinctly feminine point of view" (9). In Lee's books and articles, there is only the essay mentioned above and a short journal essay on the question why women should have a vote, in which she explicitly takes a stand as a feminist. Some of her fictional texts focus on female characters— e.g., *Miss Brown* or *The Countess of Albany*—but these do not necessarily make her a feminist. Even among her hundreds of letters, remarks directly addressing the "Woman Question" are rare.

9. In a letter dated 15 December 1902, Gilman commended Lee's review article as "by far the most satisfactory going review or discussion I have seen. In analysis and comparison it brings out the main points at issue, and treats them admirably." In the same letter, Gilman thanks Lee warmly for the article, which "will reach and persuade many who have not read the book and will not." The letters of Charlotte Perkins Gilman to Vernon Lee (1900–1904) are in the Vernon Lee collection at Somerville College, Oxford.

10. There is an interesting parallel between Lee's argument and Monique Wittig's "On the Social Contract" (1989), in which Wittig links the establishment of the heterosexual social contract in language to capitalism by drawing on Lévi-Strauss's thesis of the exchange of women.

11. One may wonder if it is a reflection of Lee's historical reception that even in Ann L. Ardis's extensive and thorough study, *New Women, New Novels: Feminism and Early Modernism* (1990), Vernon Lee is not mentioned. Her name does not even come up in connection with Eliza Linton and Mrs. Humphry Ward (outspoken and prolific critics of the New Woman), both friends of Vernon Lee who corresponded with her about the Woman Question.

12. I am quoting from an article by Vernon Lee in the Colby College collection that lacks publication information. Judging from its style and subject matter, it seems to have been written a little later than "The Economic Parasitism of Women" but in any case before World War I.

13. There is an earlier version of her self-positioning in the preface to *Belcaro* (1881). Lee explains her use of "we" as herself (the writer) and her addressee (her reader). To make sure that the reader does not misunderstand her use of "we" as the authoritative "we" of scholarly essays, she explains that she includes a "you" in her first-person-plural pronoun to stress the communicative aspect of her text. Writing for Lee is not a monologue, but another form of conversation:

I have always felt that someone else was by my side to whom I was showing, explaining, answering; hence the use of the second person plural, of which I have vainly tried to be rid: it is not the oracular we of the printed book, it is the we of myself and those with whom, for whom I am speaking; it is the constantly felt dualism of myself and my companion. (*Belcaro*, 8)

14. Butler argues that "there need not be a 'doer behind the deed,' but that the 'doer' is variably constructed in and through the deed. This is not a return to an existential theory of self as constituted through its acts, for the existential theory maintains a pre-discursive structure for both the self and its acts. It is precisely the discursively variable construction of each in and through the other that has interested me here" (142).

15. The conventional concept of the female soul denied her the capacity for growth and creativity as, by nature, she lacked the moral virtue of the male subject who was then to become the perfecter of womanhood. The feminine is supposed to be ancillary to man's creativity.

16. For a feminist analysis of the metaphysical subject in German Romantic aesthetics, see Silvia Bovenschen's philosophically challenging study, *Die imaginierte Weiblichkeit: Exemplarische Untersuchungen zu kulturgeschichtlichen und literarischen Präsentationsformen des Weiblichen,* 52–56.

17. On patriarchal construction of meaning and the role of sexual difference see Adrianna Cavarero, "Thinking Difference."

18. Lee's construction of subjectivity in *Althea* bears a certain resemblance to modern feminist conceptions of female subjectivity. Eileen Schlee, for instance, finds that female subjectivity is not only multiple but also conscious of its own evolutionary process: "A state of naturally shifting subject-positions entails the self in a response mode of adaptation and change. The subject, in gaining competence with language, is then constantly constructing itself" (73). The historicity of the subject is also emphasized in Linda Alcoff's "Cultural Feminism versus Post-Structuralism: The Identity Crisis in Feminist Theory": "Thus, through a conception of human subjectivity as an emergent property of a historicized experience, we can say 'feminine' subjectivity is construed here and now in such and such a way without ever entailing a universable maxim about the 'feminine'" (431).

19. Historically, the pervasive exploration of identity in late-nineteenth-century British literature can be ascribed to what Rosemary Hennessy calls "a general crisis of subjectivity" (105). In materialist terms, the search for new identities affected and was affected by major alterations in the hegemonic British subject. The general recomposition of bourgeois culture and institutions during that period commanded and modeled new subjectivities, and the discursive shifts generated an array of signifiers which operated both as disruption or as recontainment of hegemonic discourses. "Old" cultural elites were challenged by "new" aesthetic programs, which refocused the language on gender and sexuality.

20. I refer to Morgan's article "Reimagining Masculinity in Victorian Criticism," in which she shows how both Pater and Swinburne built a minority audience for their

aesthetic criticism within the majority audience of middle-class Victorian readers through their special handling of Hellenic culture.

21. As Linda Dowling has shown for the terms "poikilos" and "Dorian," references to male friendship in ancient Greece could either release the connotative charge of the "hidden code" or "pass" under the eyes of the cultivated middle-class reader, depending on the context in which they occurred (5).

22. Richard Dellamora makes this argument in "Critical Impressionism as Anti-Phallogocentric Strategy" in *Pater in the 1990s,* 127–42.

23. Pater saw her as a "follower" and praised what he considered indispensable in aesthetic criticism, namely her "picturesque, romantic, wholly modern sensibility." See Pater's review of Lee's *Juvenilia.*

24. I am reluctant to apply the epithet "lesbian" at this point as it too narrows the groups in question. If any of the more recent definitions of lesbianism should apply, I suggest again Terry Castle's notion of the "worldly lesbian," which not only liberates the lesbian from her marginal or closeted existence, but also foregrounds her erotic or sensual (not necessarily sexual) orientation toward other women. Moreover, I still find the discussion of nineteenth-century identities problematic if carried on too exclusively in twentieth-century notions of sexuality.

25. Although I agree with Peter Gunn that Althea could be modeled on the unsophisticated spontaneous character of "Kit" Anstruther-Thomson, I do not share his opinion that she serves as a "mise en scène" for Lee's own sophistication and therefore as a paternalistic gesture. Although Althea does indeed bear features of Kit (e.g., her tall and erect figure), I find it problematic to assume too readily a direct representation of biography in the text.

26. This was the language of the review of Lee's *Vital Lies* (1912), in *Current Opinion* 54 (April 1913): 313–14.

27. For instance, Havelock Ellis suggested to J. A. Symonds that Vernon Lee might be a good case study for the section on lesbianism in his *Sexual Inversion* (Grosskurth, 223n)

28. Morgan's essay features the differences that both Pater and Swinburne consider as part of their "homosexual code" in which they celebrate male beauty in the guise of art historical discourses. Morgan's intriguing analysis of homoerotic intertextuality can (within limits) be implied to Vernon Lee, who, like Pater, invited a special understanding among a minority group but was far from identifying herself as a homosexual.

29. In "Greek Maenads, Victorian Spinsters," Yopie Prins has shown how Pater's "conversion of classical learning into a queer philology appealed to women interested in turning Greek eros to their own purposes" (47). While Prins investigates Jane Ellen Harrison and Michael Field as two examples of the "many women influenced by Pater in late Victorian England" (46), Lee proves to be another prominent woman who used the discourses of Hellenism to create a new configuration of sexuality and gender.

30. *Althea* appeared one year after *Plato and Platonism.* As Lee and Pater discussed their ongoing projects on a regular basis, the intertextual relationship seems plausible.

31. Lee describes this practice in her novel *Miss Brown;* the male protagonist, Walter Hamlin, remembers "when he had been the most brilliant and eccentric of that little knot of aesthetic undergraduates, at whose strange doings as Greek gods . . . Oxford had murmured in those philistine days, and which had welcomed young Hamlin, with his girlish beauty and Pre-Raphaelite verses, as a sort of mixture of Apollo and Eros, sitting at the head of the supper-table dressed in green silk, *with rose garlands on his head*" (6, emphasis added)

32. According to Harald Patzer, Greek boys would also hold wreaths in their hands during intercourse with their male lovers. He points out that erotically involved women would also be depicted with wreaths (Patzer, 118–19). Although I am aware of Patzer's limitations in his interpretation of Greek homosexuality, which is rightly criticized by Halperin (54–71), the historical evidence in his work still has validity.

33. For a critical evaluation of the androgyne as "conservative, if not misogynist ideal" see, for instance, Kari Weil, *Androgyny and the Denial of Difference,* 2.

34. Martha Vicinus has investigated the significance of the adolescent boy image in fin-de-siècle lesbian writers, such as Michael Field, Réné Vivian, and Vernon Lee, in her essay "The Adolescent Boy: Fin-de-Siècle Femme Fatale?" (republished in Richard Dellamora's *Victorian Sexual Dissidence*), which presents an important step in our understanding of the role of lesbian writers in the male-identified movement of British aestheticism.

35. Lee illustrates her distrust for philosophy's "vicarious selfishness" in the curious but plausible image of "the philosophy of the donkey-cart" in another *Althea* dialogue called "The Spiritual Life." The donkey cart in question "is being pulled by a microscopic donkey, and driven by two stout men. . . . The philosophy thereof is as follows: The furious pace is very amusing, and, in that first coolness of the evening, extremely exhilarating to the two men, but it is difficult, painful and exhausting for the donkey. In more abstract terms: our pleasure frequently coincides with the discomfort, pain, or detriment of others; but there is nothing repulsive that warns us off pleasure; on the contrary, when we view it quite simply in regard to ourselves and the moment, it has even, besides its own specific attractions, an agreeable air of naturalness" (*Althea,* 217).

36. Without overstretching the similarities between Lee's and Plato's dialogues, it is interesting to note that in his *Symposium,* Plato wanted to prescribe a new homoerotic ethos and a model of "proper paederasty" based on the reciprocity of erotic desire, an antihierarchical project that found apt expression in the dialogue form. On this point see de Lauretis (156).

## Chapter 5

1. For a more detailed identification of the characters in *Miss Brown,* see Leonee Ormond, "Vernon Lee as a Critic of Aestheticism in *Miss Brown,*" and Richard Cary, "Vernon Lee's Vignettes of Literary Acquaintances."

2. Henry James was disappointed by Lee's first novel but delayed conveying his

response because he was embarrassed that she had dedicated *Miss Brown* to him "for good luck." When he finally did comment, six months after its publication, he carefully mitigated his criticism by calling it "a very interesting experiment." In the correspondence to his friend T. S. Perry (12 December 1884), his tone was considerably harsher: "But I may whisper in your ear that as it is her first attempt at a novel, so it is to be hoped it may be her last. It is very bad, strangely inferior to her other writing, & (to me at least) painfully disagreeable in tone. . . . It is in short a rather deplorable mistake—to be repented of" (quoted from Leon Edel, "Henry James and Vernon Lee," 677–87).

3. Vernon Lee used to speak of the Rossetti clan as "poeticules." William Michael Rossetti and his wife Lucy appear in the novel as Mr. and Mrs. Spencer. Dante Gabriel Rossetti is one of the models for the aesthetic artist, Walter Hamlin. For further identifications of Lee's characters see Richard Cary, "Vernon Lee's Vignettes of Literary Acquaintances."

4. Other New Woman novels dealing with the aesthetic and socialist movements are Netta Syrett's *Strange Marriage,* which was written much later (1931), and to some extent *Rose Cottingham* (1915), which subtly critiques the upper classes' insensitivity toward the reality of the working classes in their flirtation with socialism.

5. For a critical reevaluation of the fin de siècle see, for instance, Sally Ledger, "The New Woman and the Crisis of Victorianism," in *Cultural Politics at the Fin de Siècle,* ed. Sally Ledger and Scott McCracken, 22–44, and also Talia Schaffer and Alexis Psomiades' *Women and British Aestheticism.*

6. Among the artists of the period, "discovery" and education of lower-class girls as models, lovers, and wives were not uncommon. The stories of Elizabeth Siddal and Jane Morris, who were stylized as quintessential Pre-Raphaelite beauties, fit this pattern. Anne Brown physically resembles Jane Morris, but she also reflects biographical aspects of Elizabeth Siddal, especially her strange, melancholy relationship with Dante Gabriel Rossetti. Lee seems to have blended the two women's images to study female roles within the aesthetic milieu. There is a curious incident at the beginning of *Miss Brown,* when the children under her care bury her books (Dante and an Italian grammar) under some leaves in the garden. Walter Hamlin finds the buried books and "rescues" them. It has become legend that Rossetti had his wife exhumed a few years after her death, to retrieve for publication a manuscript of poems he had buried with her in his first grief (or for dramatic effect?).

7. For example, Gunn: "Psychologically *Miss Brown* may be just possible, but the reader does not come to regard her as a possible human type so much as a lay-figure for Vernon Lee to clothe with her own emotional, moral and sociological preoccupations and prejudices" (101). Vineta Colby assumes that Vernon Lee speaks through Miss Brown (and cousin Richard), "preaching her own brand of idealistic socialism" (256).

8. Gardner quotes Lee's reflections upon the attacks on *Miss Brown* from her journals, in which she scrutinizes her own morbid obsessions. "What if I were, in some matters colour blind, what if I had myself a morbid imagination. . . . Am I not mistaking the call of the beast for the call of God; may there not at the bottom of this seemingly

scientific, philanthropic, idealizing, decidedly noble looking nature of mine, be something base, dangerous, disgraceful that is cozening me. . . . May I be indulging a mere depraved appetite for the loathsome while I fancy that I am studying diseases and probing wounds for the sake of diminishing both?" (*The Lesbian Imagination,* 366–77).

9. In her introduction to *Belcaro,* she had declared (echoing Pater), "I have done as best I could, merely to satisfy my own strong feeling that art questions should always be discussed in the presence of some definite work of art, if art and its productions are not to become mere abstractions, logical counters wherewith to reckon" (8).

10. For an extensive study of the development of the term "bildungsroman" see, for instance, Laura Sue Fuderer, *The Female Bildungsroman in English: An Annotated Bibliography of Criticism* (1990).

11. Mary Bittner Wiseman equates women with strangers in her comparison of Socrates' exile from the Athenian world with women's exile from canonical ethics ("Beautiful Exiles," 178). Among other critics who have emphasized women's representation as "strangers" in the bildungsroman, Esther Kleinbord Labovitz (*The Myth of the Heroine: The Female Bildungsroman in the Twentieth Century* [1986], 6–7), like Annis Pratt (*Archetypal Patterns in Women's Fiction* [1981]), denies the existence of any positive female development before the twentieth century. This position has been slightly modified, especially by Lorna Ellis (*Appearing to Diminish: Female Development and the British Bildungsroman 1750–1850* [1999]), who locates more positive models of the female bildgungsroman in the eighteenth century (such as Eliza Haywood's *The History of Miss Betsy Thoughtless,* published in 1751, even before Goethe's *Wilhelm Meister*).

12. The "Künstlerroman," though, allows for the protagonist's withdrawal into creativity, which then becomes exteriorized through the work of art. But the solution of art is open only to the male hero and virtually unavailable to the young woman in the nineteenth-century novel. See Marianne Hirsch, "Spiritual Bildung: The Beautiful Soul as Paradigm," 28.

13. In *Wilhelm Meister,* the structure of the outside world is invested with "meaning" only through subjective experience, which, in turn, becomes visible only as the objective. Therefore the subjective, harmonized, meaningful world becomes the "real" world. But the individual's appropriation of the world is possible only through imaginary homogenization, which is necessarily idealizing and romanticizing. The will for education, meaning the character-building struggle of the hero against an irrational environment, supplies a model of agency for bourgeois male identity (Lukács, *Die Theorie des Romans,* 120). The bildungsroman bridges the gap between the creative soul of the romantic individual and a profane and common bourgeois subject, which is conceived as male.

14. Gerd Mattenklott, one of the leading scholars of aestheticism in Germany, argues that the new aesthetic subjectivity is a successful (if artificial) merger of artistic subject and object. ("Der ästhetische Mensch," 78–79).

15. One of the most prominent European texts to manifest this idea is Friedrich Schiller's *Über naive und sentimentalische Dichtung* (1795–96): "Die schöne Seele hat kein

andres Verdienst, als das sie ist" (The beautiful soul's only virtue is that it [she] is). (Schiller, Deutscher Taschenbuch Verlag *Gesamtausgabe,* vol. 18: *Theoretische Schriften 2, 36).*

16. Anne's fate can be described in the terms of Eurydice's story, especially in Gilbert and Gubar's reading: Eurydice, "abandoned in the labyrinthine caverns of Hades . . . is really (like Virginia Woolf's Judith Shakespeare) the woman poet who never arose from the prison of her 'grave cave'" (99).

17. Felski also quotes *Madame Bovary* and *Anna Karenina* as "emblematic" not only for the problematic heroine in the nineteenth-century novel, but for the tensions by which bourgeois society is riven.

18. Paul Connerton assumes different memory types, one of them being the habitual or informal memory. This type of memory is not activated consciously but reenacted performatively through the body: "Many forms of habitual skilled remembering illustrate a keeping of the past in mind that, without ever adverting to its historical origin, nevertheless re-enacts the past in our present conduct. In habitual memory the past is, as it were, sedimented in the body" (72).

19. My thanks to Alistair Duckworth, who pointed out to me Lee's use of "style indirect libre," which here and elsewhere resembles Jane Austen's or George Eliot's treatment of character.

20. Ian Small addresses this aspect in *The Aesthetes: A Sourcebook* (1979): "However Pater had cleverly—and presumably quite deliberately—all but avoided a key issue, that of the way in which works of literature are received by the reader. . . . Contemporary critics had of course objected—and quite correctly so—that an expressive aesthetic such as Pater (and, later, Wilde and Whistler) had proposed, failed to account for the fact that art also has a public dimension: that is, that art has an audience" (xxi).

21. Lee's plea to control selfish pleasures echoes Ruskin's argument in the chapter on "Pathetic Fallacy" in *Modern Painters,* vol. 1. (1903), where he demands that the poet be accurate and true to "pure fact" (211) and not be "over-dazzled by emotion" (208). Ruskin and Lee both require the poet to control his passion; but they differ on the question of accountability: Lee's highest instance of control is the reader, whereas Ruskin's is truth (and ultimately God).

22. In the introduction to *Belcaro,* Lee explains that she closes her book at the moment when her interest takes a different turn, from "the purely aesthetical questions" to "the wider, nobler, far more intricate and dangerous field of ethics" (14).

23. Lee here for the first time uses Baldwin as the character we know from the dialogues in *Baldwin* and *Althea.*

24. In appearance and speech, Brown is clearly an embodiment of William Morris. Although she privately mocked his rustic appearance, Lee was sympathetic to Morris's version of socialism and thus largely excluded him from her caricature of the aesthetic movement. On this point see Vineta Colby, 257.

25. Sally Ledger, in "The New Woman and Socialism," discusses Margaret Harkness's *A City Girl* (1887) as one of the first New Woman novels dealing with the rela-

tionship between feminism and socialism, which became a more important issue in the late 1880s and throughout the 1890s.

26. Lee speaks of her in almost the same manner as she speaks of Ruskin in *Belcaro:* "All this Ruskin has forgotten: he has made the enjoyment of mere beauty a base pleasure, requiring a moral object to purify it, and in so doing he has destroyed its own purifying power" (227).

27. According to Bourdieu (*Distinction*), "The bourgeoisie expects from art (not to mention what it calls literature and philosophy) a reinforcement of its self-assurance, and . . . it can never really recognize the audacities of the avant-garde. . . . One has to take into account the whole logic of the field of artistic production and its relationship to the field of the dominant class to understand why avant-garde artistic production is bound to disappoint bourgeois expectations" (293–94).

## Chapter 6

1. "Amour Dure" was first published in 1887 by *Murray's Magazine* and then in Lee's famous collection *Hauntings: Fantastic Stories* in 1890 together with "Dionea," "Oke of Okehurst; or the Phantom Lover," and "A Wicked Voice." Her short story "Prince Alberic and the Snake Lady" appeared in *The Yellow Book* in 1896. Brian Stableford's recent essay "Haunted by the Pagan Past: An Introduction to Vernon Lee" gives an excellent survey of Lee's fantastic tales, including her use of gothic elements in her works.

2. The late nineteenth century witnessed a boom in fantastic literature. The "psychomythic" tale (Edwin Block's term) was flourishing and shading off into more varied forms for a brief period in the last quarter of the nineteenth century. Even mainstream writers, like James and Conrad, used the popular genre to explore the depths and ramifications of the human psyche (Block, xv–xix).

3. For a more detailed discussion of the historical development of scientific thought see Nancy Traill, 21–33, and Robin Gilmour, 11–146. Roger Caillois, a classical theorist of the fantastic, argues that it came into existence at the same time as the idea that the world is based on the laws of natural science. How exactly fantastic and scientific modes are related is still being disputed.

4. Similarly, Nicholas Daly has boldly connected late-nineteenth-century popular romance and high literary modernism. But unlike most critics who have treated the fantastic as an expression of anxiety, Daly sees it as a positive projection of the place where the "new professional male team" can be imagined (26).

5. Rosemary Jackson establishes the uncanny as a principal concept in the development of the fantastic. Her survey of its etymological evolution shows how the uncanny runs through literary texts in the nineteenth century even before Freud published his psychoanalytic definition (63–68).

6. Lee had studied Hoffmann intensely. Like him, she delighted in fairy-tale motifs, the poetic minds of children, and the visualization of other layers of consciousness.

Her "Chapelmaster Kreisler" (*Belcaro*) is loosely modeled on his "Kapell-Meister Kreisler." Other motifs she shares with Hoffmann are the figure of the half-mad young scholar, the woman-snake double, and the monk who, troubled by a double consciousness, commits a pagan crime. Lee's "Prince Alberic and the Snake Lady" strongly resembles his *Der goldene Topf* (1813) in theme and narrative technique.

7. For a detailed analysis of the uncanny in Freudian and historical materialist terms see Jose B. Monleon, *A Specter Is Haunting Europe: A Sociohistorical Approach to the Fantastic* (1990), 11ff.

8. The available surveys of fantastic literature display a structural or formalist predilection for this genre. Examples are Nancy Traill's comprehensive *Possible Worlds of the Fantastic: The Rise of the Paranormal in Fiction* (3–20) or Dieter Penning, "Die Ordnung der Unordnung. Eine Bilanz zur Theorie der Fantastik," in Christian W. Thomsen and Jens Malte Fischer, eds., *Phantastik in Literatur und Kunst*.

9. Lee here sounds strikingly similar to Robert Louis Stevenson in "A Gossip of Romance," where he defends romance in the contemporary debates against realism. It is "not character but incident that woos us out of our reserve. Something happens, as we desire to have it happen to ourselves. . . . Then we forget the characters; then we push the hero aside; then we plunge into the tale in our own person and battle in fresh experience; and then, and then only, do we say we have been reading a romance" (77).

10. Lee mimics the tone of Heinrich Heine's "Die Götter im Exil," which she had read with great enthusiasm. In "Dionea" she even has the narrator refer to "Heine's little book."

11. "Dionea" bears the traits of Pater's "Denys L'Auxerrois." Like Denys, Dionea is of uncertain origin but of beautiful physique. Both figures are marked as outsiders who arouse ambivalent feelings among village people. The crucial line between the divine and the demonic is constantly redrawn and transgressed. The major difference in Lee's story is that the final catastrophe leaves Dionea unharmed, whereas Pater's Pagan God is barbarously killed by the mob.

12. Dione, in Homer's text, is the daughter of Oceanus and Tethys and the mother of Aphrodite. According to Hesiod, Aphrodite sprang from the foam of the sea that gathered the severed parts of Uranus when he was castrated by Cronos.

13. In the text, Venus and Aphrodite appear seemingly indiscriminate. The narrator conflates Roman and Greek culture in the term "antique" or "ancient," as was typical in contemporary usage, even among scholars. However, the text slightly differentiates between Aphrodite (associated more directly with the "real," physical Dionea) and Venus (metaphorically connected with cultural practices, for instance through Waldemar's Venus altar). Through these subtle allusions, Lee manages to differentiate among her audiences—those who pick up the nuances and those who don't. The extensive annotations in Glennis Stephenson's latest edition of "Dionea" are helpful for the modern reader to understand better the allusive subtext.

14. In "The Flight to the Real," Terry Eagleton has similarly described the effects of late-Victorian positivism, which construed humans as mere instruments of "some

ulterior altogether impersonal evolution" so that spiritualized terms or disruptions without explanations become desirable (17).

15. In "Studies in Literary Psychology," Vernon Lee describes such "jumps into the present at the moment of passion and action" and compares them to "stage representations" (*Handling of Words,* 74–76).

16. All quotations from "Prince Alberic and the Snake Lady" are from Vernon Lee, *The Snake Lady and Other Stories,* ed. Horace Gregory (New York: Grove Press, 1954).

17. It should be mentioned that Lee here uses the same classical source as Gautier and Keats (i.e., Philostratus) and, as Brian Stableford has pointed out, "takes the side of the tempting serpent against those who would banish her" (5). While not disputing the fact that Lee might have used the classical source, I would like to suggest that Lee's more immediate models are based on two medieval sources. First, the story of a noble family from Burgundy (Lusignan-Partenay) who died without a male descendent: the noble hero is bewitched by a good fairy, Mélusienne, who is not human, but a noble, virtuous spirit. She bestows material good on him and becomes a benefactress for the community. She is erotically attractive but, unlike a nymph, she is well-rounded as a lover, wife, and mother. The second source for Lee might have been the Amadis de Gaule legend, which seems to have first appeared in Spain around 1508. Amadis, an illegitimate child of a mythical king, is set out to sea in an ark. At the court of the Scottish king, Longuines, he finds and falls in love with Oriana, the daughter of the new king of England. Like the French Mélusienne, Oriana becomes the victim of political circumstances and intrigues. While the plot of "Prince Alberic and the Snake Lady" is obviously based on the first legend, the prince's reference to Oriana also suggests that Lee used the second story as a source.

18. For a detailed investigation of "bloodless" female figures see Kurt Ruh, *Die 'Melusine' des Thüring von Ringoltingen* (1985), 20.

19. All quotations of "Amour Dure" in this chapter are from Vernon Lee, *Supernatural Tales: Excursions into Fantasy,* introduced by Irene Cooper Willis (London: Peter Owen, 1987).

20. Another interesting coincidence is that the Italian painter Girolamo da Carpi, Medea's namesake, died in 1556.

21. The name as well as the historical, geographical, and architectural characteristics of Urbania suggest that Vernon Lee used the city of Urbino as a model.

22. The alleged portrait of Medea da Carpi which Lee's narrator describes is in fact Agnolo Bronzino's *Lucrezia Panciatichi,* Galleria degli Uffizi (c. 1540). Bronzino is considered the creator of "Courtly Mannerism," which dominated Florentine painting in the mid-sixteenth century. Trepka's description is precise: the red bodice, the ornate hairdo, and, most notably, the necklace with the inscription "Amour Dure— Dure Amour." It is interesting that Lee chose this portrait of Lucrezia Panciatichi (wife of the French Huguenot Bartolomeo Panciatichi), which emphasizes her more abstract and intellectual qualities despite her superb attire and evident beauty.

23. The intertextual link between Lee and Pater also has biographical reality: Vernon

Lee dedicated *Euphorion* to Walter Pater and concluded its sequel, *Renaissance Fancies and Studies,* with a eulogy on him. Lee first met Pater at a dinner party in July 1881. On her subsequent visits to England, she always spent some time at his house, where they exchanged ideas on each other's work in progress. In a letter to her mother (24 July 1882, Colby), Lee mentions Pater's plan for a historical novel in connection with a similar project of her own: "By the way, I told Pater the idea (not the plot) and he thought it very good; he himself seems to be writing something very similar in the way of a novel about the time of Marcus Aurelius." Lee did not seem too impressed with Pater's draft, as she wrote home on 20 June 1884: "he has read me part of his philosophical romance about the time of the Antonines. Fine, but I think lacking vitality" (Colby). Her own Renaissance novel, first entitled *Medea da Carpi,* was not published because Blackwood objected to the mingling of fact and fiction. Thus she trimmed it down to story length, publishing it under the title "Amour Dure" in *Murray's Magazine* in 1887.

24. To be sure, Pater's metaphor for historical transmission is also sexually charged. However, as Thaïs E. Morgan has argued, his Mona Lisa is "not a womanly 'type' in the conventional Victorian sense. Rather, it is another kind of manliness, one that Pater implicitly exalts above the womanliness of women" (328).

25. Spiridion Trepka's homelessness is evident in all aspects of his troubled life. Severed from his Polish ties, he remains an alien in the German Empire, wistfully idealizing his memory of the past. He romanticizes Italian history but remains aloof from the contemporary people, whose mundanity he disdains for fear of having his illusion dispelled.

26. See Carolyn Williams (11–123) for a discussion of Pater's mythicism.

27. Interestingly, the words here recall another portrait by Leonardo—a red-chalk drawing in the Louvre—as it is described in Pater's essay on Leonardo da Vinci. But while Pater speaks of the face being "voluptuous and full in the eyelids and lips" (90–91), Medea's beauty, although called "voluptuous," is as closed psychologically ("tight eyelids and tight lips") as it is severely perfect in form.

28. The ambivalence of the imagery (Madonna, Medea, Salomé) is reminiscent of Pater's reading of a Leonardo painting in which "Saint John's strange likeness to the Bacchus" conflates Pagan and Christian imagery in an erotically daring picture.

29. See Clarissa W. Atkinson, Constance H. Buchanan, and Margaret R. Miles, eds., *Immaculate and Powerful: The Female in Sacred Image and Social Reality,* on the obsession with allegedly "truthful" accounts of the Holy Mother's apparitions in the nineteenth century.

30. Medea's image resembles Piero della Francesca's *Madonna della Misericordia* (begun in 1445). When she appears to Trepka, she loosens "her heavy black cloak, displaying a dress of deep red with gleams of silver and gold," details which echo the open black cloak over a red dress of Piero's frontal Madonna, a massive cylindrical form which towers high above the smaller-scale human beings who invoke her. The *Madonna della Misericordia* conveys a sense of power similar to Medea's overbearing magnetism during the imaginary church service.

31. In Euripides' drama, the gods approve of her revenge because her motive is Jason's betrayal of her unconditional love. On this point see Genia Schulz, "Medea: Zu einem Motiv im Werk Heiner Müllers." Schulz argues that man can recognize woman only in the function she has in *his* social order. The archaic Medea appears on the borderline between all orders. The fear she arouses is nothing else than the effect of her oppression. To assert herself, she has to annihilate all social order and thus becomes a constant provocation to the male world. In Seneca's or Klinger's representations, Medea is the terrible reminder that civilization was built on war and oppression.

32. Based on his reading of Thomas Mann's "Freud and the Future," Connerton develops his idea of the individual's conscious repetition of the past: "We are to envisage the ego, less sharply defined and less exclusive than we commonly conceive of it, as being so to speak 'open behind': open to the resources of myth which are to be understood as existing for the individual not just as a grid of categories but as a set of possibilities which can become subjective, which can be lived consciously. . . . We might refer to his pre-modern self-understanding as a kind of imitation so long as we remember that imitation here means far more than we mean by the word today. It means something like mythical identification" (62–63).

33. Rosemary Jackson has pointed out that the fantastic often takes metaphorical constructions literally. In fantastic stories, one object does not *stand* for another but literally *becomes* that other. Fantasy resists allegory and metaphor, and it is precisely in this resistance that Jackson—like Todorov—sees its subversive power (41–42).

34. In "The Economic Dependence of Women," Lee speaks of the sexual overinvestment of women. "And here we touch the full mischief. That women are *over-sexed* means that, instead of depending upon their intelligence, their strength, endurance and honesty, they depend mainly upon their sex; that they appeal to men, dominate men through the fact of their sex. . . . The old, old story is repeated with slight variations from Schopenhauer to Nietzsche, and from Michelet to Dumas *fils*" (71–90).

35. Lee here (as in her story "The Doll") thematizes female immobilization as in Browning's Duchess, a woman doomed to look perpetually "as if she were alive" (Susan Navarette, in *The Shape of Fear,* 259 n. 55). Julia Briggs also mentions Lee's reversal of the Browning poem. Lee's acquaintance with Browning, whom she greatly admired, invites a closer analysis of their intertextual relationship. On Lee's encounters with Browning, see Gunn, 122.

36. See Pater's essay on Winckelman in *The Renaissance* (141–85).

37. In Ian Fletcher's words, "She shows the action of mind and soul, shows man dealing with his experience so as to control it, thus, giving him back his sense of freedom" (?).

# Works Cited

Archives

Vernon Lee Collection, Miller Library, Colby College Special Collections, Waterville, Maine.
Vernon Lee Papers, Somerville College, Oxford.
Vernon Lee Library, British Institute, Florence.
Karl Pearson Papers, University College London Library.

Primary Sources (Selected Works by Vernon Lee)

Lee, Vernon. "Aesthetics My Confession." Unpaginated manuscript, n.d. Vernon Lee Collection, Miller Library, Colby College Special Collections, Waterville, Maine.
————. *Althea: A Second Book of Dialogues and Aspirations.* London: Osgood, McIlvaine, 1894.
————. *Amour Dure: Unheimliche Erzählungen.* Ed. Frank Rainer Scheck. Cologne: Du Mont, 1990.
————. *Ariadne in Mantua: A Romance in Five Acts.* Oxford: B. H. Blackwell, 1903.
————. "The Artistic Dualism of the Renaissance." *Contemporary Review,* September 1879, 44–65.
————. *Baldwin: Being Dialogues on Views and Aspirations.* London: T. Fisher Unwin, 1886.
————. *Belcaro: Being Essays on Sundry Aesthetical Questions.* London: W. Satchell, 1881.
————. *The Countess of Albany.* Eminent Women Series. Ed. John H. Ingram. London: W. H. Allen, 1884.
————. "Economic Dependence of Women." *North American* 175 (July 1902): 71–90.
————. *Euphorion: Being Studies of the Antique and the Mediaeval in the Renaissance.* London: T. Fisher Unwin, 1884.

————. "Faustus and Helena." In *Belcaro: Being Essays on Sundry Aesthetic Questions.* London: W. Satchell, 1881.

————. *Gospels of Anarchy and Other Contemporary Studies.* London and Leipzig: T. Fisher Unwin, 1908.

————. *The Handling of Words and Other Studies in Literary Psychology.* London: John Lane, The Bodley Head, 1923.

————. *Hauntings: Fantastic Stories.* London: W. Heinemann, 1890.

————. *Hortus Vitae: Essays on the Gardening of Life.* London: John Lane, The Bodley Head, 1903.

————. *Juvenilia: Being a Second Series of Essays on Sundry Aesthetical Questions.* London: T. Fisher Unwin, 1887.

————. *Limbo and Other Essays.* London: Grant Richards, 1897.

————. *Louis Norbert: A Two-fold Romance.* London: John Lane, The Bodley Head, 1914.

————. *Miss Brown.* London: Blackwell and Sons, 1884.

————. *Ottilie: An Eighteenth Century Idyl.* London: T. Fisher Unwin, 1883.

————. *Renaissance Fancies and Studies: A Sequel to Euphorion.* London: Smith, Elder, 1895.

————. *The Sentimental Traveller: Notes on Places.* London: John Lane, The Bodley Head, 1908.

————. *The Snake Lady and Other Stories.* Ed. Horace Gregory. New York: Grove Press, 1954.

————. *Studies of the Eighteenth Century in Italy.* 1880. New York: Da Capo Press, 1978.

————. *Supernatural Tales: Excursions into Fantasy.* Intro. by Irene Cooper Willis. London: Peter Owen, 1987.

————. *Vanitas: Polite Stories.* London: W. Heinemann, 1892.

————. *Vernon Lee's Letters.* Ed. Irene Cooper Willis. London: Privately printed, 1937.

————. *Vital Lies: Studies of Some Varieties of Recent Obscurantism.* 2 vols. London: John Lane, The Bodley Head, 1912.

————. "Why I Want Women to Have the Vote." Unpaginated manuscript, n.d. Vernon Lee Collection, Miller Library, Colby College, Waterville, Maine.

————, ed. *Art and Man: Essays and Fragments,* by Clementia Anstruther-Thomson. London: John Lane, The Bodley Head, 1924.

## SECONDARY SOURCES

Alcoff, Linda. "Cultural Feminism versus Post-Structuralism: The Identity Crisis in Feminist Theory." *Signs: Journal of Women in Culture and Society* 13, no. 3 (1988): 405–28.

Alexander, Sally. *Becoming a Woman and Other Essays in Nineteenth- and Twentieth-Century Feminist History.* London: Virago, 1994.

Allen, Tuzyline Jita. "A Voice of One's Own: Implications of Impersonality in the Essays of Virginia Woolf and Alice Walker." In *The Politics of the Essay: Feminist Per-*

*spectives,* ed. Ruth-Ellen Boetcher Joeres and Elizabeth Mittman. Bloomington: Indiana University Press, 1993.

Ardis, Ann L. *New Women, New Novels: Feminism and Early Modernism.* New Brunswick: Rutgers University Press, 1990.

Ashley, Mike. *Who's Who in Horror and Fantasy Fiction.* New York: Taplinger, 1978.

Atkinson, Clarissa W., Constance H. Buchanan, and Margaret R. Miles, eds. *Immaculate and Powerful: The Female in Sacred Image and Social Reality.* Boston: Beacon Press, 1985.

Attridge, Derek. "Innovation, Literature, Ethics: Relating to the Other." *PMLA* 114, no. 1 (1999): 20–31.

Bakhtin, Mikhail. *Speech Genres and Other Late Essays.* Trans. Vern W. McGee. Ed. Caryl Emerson and Michael Holquist. Austin: University of Texas Press, 1984.

Bann, Stephen. "The Sense of the Past: Image, Text, and Object in the Formation of Historical Consciousness in Nineteenth-Century Britain." In *The New Historicism,* ed. H. Aram Veeser. New York: Routledge, 1989.

Beard, Mary. *America through Women's Eyes.* New York: Macmillan, 1933.

―――. *On Understanding Women.* New York: Longmans, Green, 1931.

Birch, Diane. *Ruskin and the Dawning of the Modern.* Oxford: Oxford University Press, 1999.

Bjorhovde, Gerd. *Rebellious Structures: Women Writers and the Crisis of the Novel.* Oxford: Norwegian University Press, 1987.

Blain, Virginia. Rev. of *Vernon Lee: The Lesbian Imagination Victorian Style* by Burdett Gardner. *Victorian Studies* 33, no. 2 (1990): 351–52.

Blain, Virginia, Patricia Clements, and Isobel Grundy, eds. *The Feminist Companion to Literature in English: Women Writers from the Middle Ages to the Present.* London: B. T. Batesford, 1990.

Block. Edwin F. Jr. *Rituals of Disintegration: Romance and Madness in the Victorian Psychomythic Tale.* New York: Garland, 1993.

"Books of the Week: Rev. of 'Vernon Lee's Renaissance Essays.'" *Times* (London). 13 December 1895, 13.

Boumelha, Penny. "Literary Feminism." *Australian Feminist Studies* 13 (autumn 1991): 125–28.

Bourdieu, Pierre. *Distinction: A Social Critique of the Judgement of Taste.* Trans. Richard Nice. Cambridge: Harvard University Press, 1984.

Bovenschen, Silvia. *Die Imaginierte Weiblichkeit: Exemplarische Untersuchungen zu kulturgeschichtlichen und literarischen Präsentationsformen des Weiblichen.* Frankfurt: Suhrkamp, 1979.

Bowlby, Rachel. Introduction to *Virginia Woolf: A Woman's Essays,* ed. Rachel Bowlby. London: Penguin, 1992.

Bräm, Max. *Die italienische Renaissance in dem englischen Geistesleben des 19. Jahrhunderts, im besonderen bei John Ruskin, John Addington Symonds und Vernon Lee.* Zurich: Brugg, 1932.

Braendlin, Bonnie Hoover. "Alther, Atwood, Ballantyne, and Gray: Secular Salvation in the Contemporary Feminist Bildungsroman." *Frontiers: A Journal of Women Studies* 4, no. 1 (1979): 18–22.

Briggs, Julia. *Night Visitors: The Rise and Fall of the English Ghost Story.* London: Faber, 1977.

Broomfield, Andrea, and Sally Mitchell, eds. *Prose by Victorian Women: An Anthology.* New York: Garland, 1996.

Buchanan, Robert. *The Fleshly School of Poetry and Other Phenomena of the Day.* London: Strahan, 1872.

Buckler, William E. *Walter Pater: The Critic as Artist of Ideas.* New York: New York University Press, 1987.

Buelens, Gert. "Henry James's Oblique Possession: Plotting of Desire and Mastering in *The American Scene.*" *PMLA* 116 (2001): 300–313.

Bullen, J. B. "The Historiography of 'Studies in the History of the Renaissance.'" In *Pater in the 1990s,* ed. Laurel Brake and Ian Small. Greensboro, N.C.: ELT Press, 1991.

Burckhardt, Jacob. *Die Kultur der Renaissance in Italien.* Ed. Horst Günther. Frankfurt: Deutscher Klassiker Verlag, 1989.

Butler, Judith. *Gender Trouble: Feminism and the Subversion of Identity.* New York: Routledge, 1990.

Caballero, Carlos. "A Wicked Voice: On Vernon Lee, Wagner, and the Effects of Music." *Victorian Studies* 35, no. 4 (1992): 385–415.

Caillois, Roger. "Das Bild des Phantastischen: Vom Märchen bis zur Science Fiction." In *Phaicon,* ed. Rein A. Zondergeld. Frankfurt: Suhrkamp, 1974.

Carlyle, Thomas. "Boswell's Life of Johnson." In *Selected Essays,* 165–227. London: T. Nelson, n.d.

Cary, Richard. "Vernon Lee's Vignettes of Literary Acquaintances." *Colby Library Quarterly* 9 (September 1970): 179–99.

Casey, Ellen Miller. "Edging Women Out? Reviews of Women Novelists in the *Athenaeum.*" *Victorian Studies* 39, no. 2 (1996): 151–71.

Castle, Terry. *The Apparitional Lesbian: Female Homosexuality and Modern Culture.* New York: Columbia University Press, 1993.

Cavareno, Adrianna. "Thinking Difference." *Symposium* 49, no. 2 (1996): 120–29.

Chapman, Raymond. *The Sense of the Past in Victorian Literature.* New York: St. Martin's, 1986.

Christ, Carol. "'The Hero as Man of Letters': Masculinity and Victorian Nonfiction Prose." In *Victorian Sages and Cultural Discourse,* ed. Thaïs E. Morgan. New Brunswick: Rutgers University Press, 1990.

Christensen, Peter. "The Burden of History in Vernon Lee's Ghost Story 'Amour Dure.'" *Studies in the Humanities* 16, no. 1 (1989): 33–43.

Colby, Vineta. "The Puritan Aesthete: Vernon Lee." In *The Singular Anomaly: Women Novelists of the Nineteenth Century,* ed. Vineta Colby. New York: New York University Press, 1970.

Comparetti, Alice Pattee. "'A Most Exquisite Beautiful Play' That Failed to Reach the Stage." *Colby Library Quarterly* 14 (May 1954): 220–29.

Connerton, Paul. *How Societies Remember.* New York: Cambridge University Press, 1989.

Cornish, Allison. "A Lady Asks: The Gender of Vulgarization in Late Medieval Italy." *PMLA* 115 (2000): 166–80.

Crosby, Christina. *The Ends of History: Victorians and "The Woman Question."* New York: Routledge, 1991.

Culler, Jonathan. "Literary Fantasy." *Cambridge Review* 95 (1973): 30–33.

Daly, Nicholas. *Modern Romance and the Fin de Siècle: Popular Fiction and British Culture 1880–1914.* Cambridge: Cambridge University Press, 1999.

David, Deirdre. *Intellectual Women and the Victorian Patriarchy: Harriet Martineau, Elizabeth Barrett Browning, George Eliot.* Ithaca: Cornell University Press, 1987.

de Lauretis, Theresa. "Sexual Indifference and Lesbian Representation." *Theatre Journal* 40 (May 1988): 155–77.

Dellamora, Richard. "Critical Impressionism as Anti-Phallogocentric Strategy." In *Pater in the 1990s,* ed. Laurel Brake and Ian Small. Greensboro, N.C.: ELT Press, 1991.

———, ed. *Victorian Sexual Dissidence.* Chicago: University of Chicago Press, 1999.

Denisoff, Dennis. "The Forest beyond the Frame: Picturing Women's Desires in Vernon Lee and Virginia Woolf." In *Women and British Aestheticism,* ed. Talia Schaffer and Kathy Alexis Psomiades. Charlottesville: University Press of Virginia, 1999.

Dowling, Linda. "Ruskin's Pied Beauty and the Constitution of a 'Homosexual Code.'" *Victorian Newsletter* 75 (1989): 1–8.

DuPlessis, Rachel Blau. *Writing beyond the Ending: Narrative Strategies of Twentieth-Century Women Writers.* Bloomington: Indiana University Press, 1985.

Eagleton, Terry. "The Flight to the Real." In *Cultural Politics at the Fin de Siècle,* ed. Sally Ledger and Scott McCracken. Cambridge: Cambridge University Press, 1995.

———. *The Ideology of the Aesthetics.* Cambridge, Mass.: Basil Blackwell, 1990.

Edel, Leon. "Henry James and Vernon Lee." *PMLA* 69 (June 1954): 677–78.

Ellis, Lorna. *Appearing to Diminish: Female Development and the British Bildungsroman 1750–1850.* London: Associated University Press, 1999.

Etherington, Norman, ed. *The Annotated She: A Critical Edition of H. Rider Haggard's Victorian Romance.* Bloomington: Indiana University Press, 1991.

Faderman, Lillian. Rev. of *The Lesbian Imagination (Victorian Style): A Psychological and Critical Study of "Vernon Lee"* by Burdett Gardner. *Journal of Homosexuality* 19 (November 1990): 121–24.

———. *Surpassing the Love of Men.* New York: William Morrow, 1981.

Farwell, Marilyn R. "Heterosexual Plots and Lesbian Subtexts: Towards a Theory of Lesbian Narrative Space." In *Lesbian Texts and Contexts: Radical Revisions,* ed. Karla Jay and Joanna Glasgow. New York: New York University Press, 1990.

Felski, Rita. *Beyond Feminist Aesthetics: Feminist Literature and Social Change.* Cambridge: Harvard University Press, 1989.

———. *The Gender of Modernity.* Cambridge: Harvard University Press, 1995.

———. "Modernism and Modernity." In *Rereading Modernism: New Directions in Feminist Criticism,* ed. Lisa Rado. New York: Garland, 1996.

Fletcher, Ian. "Walter Pater." In *Modern Critical Views of Walter Pater,* ed. Harold Bloom. New York: Chelsea House Publishers, 1985.

Fraser, Hilary. *The Victorians and Renaissance Italy.* Oxford: Blackwell, 1992.

Fraser, Hilary, with Daniel Brown. *English Prose of the Nineteenth Century.* London: Longman, 1996.

Friedman, Ellen G. "Where Are the Missing Contents? (Post)Modernism, Gender, and the Canon." *PMLA* 108 (1993): 240–52.

Fry, Roger. *Vision and Design.* New York: Meridian Books, 1956.

Frye, Marilyn, ed. *The Politics of Reality: Essays in Feminist Theory.* Trumansburg: The Crossing Press, 1983.

Fuderer, Laura Sue. *The Female Bildungsroman in English: An Annotated Bibliography of Criticism.* New York: The Modern Language Association of America, 1990.

Gagnier, Regina. *Subjectivities: A History of Self-representation in Britain, 1832–1920.* New York: Oxford University Press, 1991.

Gardner, Burdett. "An Apology for Henry James's 'Tiger Cat.'" *PMLA* 68 (1953): 688–95.

———. *The Lesbian Imagination (Victorian Style): A Psychological and Critical Study of Vernon Lee.* New York: Garland, 1987.

Gerhardt, Marlis. *Stimmen und Rhythmen: Weibliche Ästhetik und Avantgarde.* Darmstadt: Luchterhand, 1986.

Gilbert, Sandra M., and Susan Gubar. *The Madwoman in the Attic: The Woman Writer and the Nineteenth-Century Literary Imagination.* New Haven: Yale University Press, 1979

Gilmour, Robin. *The Victorian Period: The Intellectual and Cultural Context of English Literature, 1830–1890.* London: Longman, 1993.

Graham, Kenneth. *English Criticism of the Novel, 1865–1900.* Oxford: Clarendon, 1965.

Greenblatt, Stephen. "Racial Memory and Literary History." *PMLA* 116 (2001): 48–63.

Grosskurth, Phyllis. *The Woeful Victorian: A Biography of J. A. Symonds.* New York: Holt, Rinehart and Winston, 1964.

Grosz, Elizabeth. "Refiguring Lesbian Desire." In *The Lesbian Postmodern,* ed. Laura Doan. New York: Columbia Press, 1994.

Gunn, Peter. *Vernon Lee: Violet Paget, 1856–1935.* London: Oxford University Press, 1964.

Haefner, Joel. "Unfathering the Essay: Resistance and Intergenreality in the Essay Genre." *Prose Studies: History, Theory, Criticism* 12, no. 3 (1989): 258–73.

Halperin, David. *One Hundred Years of Homosexuality and Other Essays on Greek Love.* New York: Routledge, 1990.

Halperin, John, ed. *The Theory of the Novel.* Oxford: Oxford University Press, 1977.

Heilmann, Ann. *New Woman Fiction: Women Writing First-Wave Feminism.* London: Macmillan, 2000.

Hennessy, Rosemary. *Materialist Feminism and the Politics of Discourse.* London: Routledge, 1993.

Heyck, T. W. *The Transformation of Intellectual Life in Victorian England.* Chicago: Lyceum Books, 1989.

Hirsch, Marianne. "Spiritual Bildung: The Beautiful Soul as Paradigm." In *The Voyage In: Fictions of Female Development,* ed. Elizabeth Abel, Marianne Hirsch, and Elizabeth Langland. Hanover: University Press of New England, 1983.

Houghton, Walter, ed. *Wellesley Index to Victorian Periodicals.* 5 vols. London: Routledge and Kegan Paul, 1966–90.

Irigaray, Luce. *Speculum of the Other Woman.* Trans. Gillian C. Gill. Ithaca: Cornell University Press, 1989.

Iser, Wolfgang. *Der Akt des Lesens.* Munich: Wilhelm Fink, 1976.

Jackson, Rosemary. *Fantasy: The Literature of Subversion.* London: Methuen, 1981.

James, Henry. *Henry James' Letters.* Vol. 3. Ed. Leon Edel. Cambridge: Harvard University Press, 1974.

Jarves, James Jackson. "The Literature of Art—A New and Vigorous Writer." *New York Times,* 26 December 1879, 5.

Joeres, Ruth-Ellen Boetcher, and Elizabeth Mittman. "An Introductory Essay." In *The Politics of the Essay: Feminist Perspectives,* ed. Ruth-Ellen Boetcher Joeres and Elizabeth Mittman. Bloomington: Indiana University Press, 1993.

Kaplan, Cora. *Sea Changes: Essays on Culture and Feminism.* London: Verso, 1986.

Kippur, Stephen A. *Jules Michelet: A Study in Mind and Sensibility.* Albany: State University of New York Press, 1981.

Kofman, Sarah. *Freud and Fiction.* Trans. Sarah Wykes. Oxford: Polity Press, 1991.

Kristeva, Julia. *Strangers to Ourselves.* New York: Columbia University Press, 1989.

Labovitz, Esther Kleinbord. *The Myth of the Heroine: The Female Bildungsroman in the Twentieth Century: Dorothy Richardson, Simone de Beauvoir, Doris Lessing, Christa Wolf.* New York: Lang, 1986.

Ledger, Sally. *The New Woman: Fiction and Feminism at the Fin de Siècle.* Manchester: Manchester University Press, 1997.

Ledger, Sally, and Roger Luckhurst, eds. *The Fin de Siècle: A Reader in Cultural History, c. 1889–1900.* Oxford: Oxford University Press, 2000.

Ledger, Sally, and Scott McCracken, eds. *Cultural Politics at the Fin de Siècle.* Cambridge: Cambridge University Press, 1995.

Libbey, Elizabeth. "The Vernon Lee Papers." *Colby Library Quarterly* 8 (November 1952): 117–19.

Lodge, David. *The Language of Fiction: Essays in Criticism and Verbal Analysis of the English Novel.* New York: Columbia University Press, 1966.

Lombroso, Cesare. *L'Homme de génie.* Paris: F. Alcan, 1889.

Lukács, Georg. *Die Theorie des Romans: Ein geschichtsphilosophischer Versuch über die Formen der großen Epik*. Berlin: Sammlung Luchterhand, 1974.

Maitzen, Rohan Amanda. *Gender, Genre, and Victorian Historical Writing*. New York: Garland, 1998.

———. "This Feminine Preserve: Historical Biography by Victorian Women." *Victorian Studies* 38, no. 3 (1995): 371–93.

Mannocchi, Phyllis F. "Vernon Lee: A Reintroduction and Primary Bibliography." *English Literature in Transition* 26 (1983): 231–67.

Mansfield, Elizabeth. "Victorian Identity and the Historical Imaginary: Emilia Dilke's *The Renaissance of Art in France*." *Clio* 26, no. 2 (1997): 167–88.

Marcus, Jane. "Art and Anger." *Feminist Studies* 4 (1978): 69–98.

Markgraf, Carl. "'Vernon Lee': A Commentary and an Annotated Bibliography of Writings about Her." *English Literature in Transition* 26, no. 4(1983): 268–312.

Marks, Elaine. "Lesbian Intertextuality." In *Homosexualities and French Literature,* ed. George Stambolian and Elaine Marks. Ithaca: Cornell University Press, 1979.

Mathews, Patricia. "The Gender of Creativity in the French Symolist Period." In *Women and Reason,* ed. Elizabeth D. Harvey and Kathleen Okruhlik. Ann Arbor: University of Michigan Press, 1992.

Mattenklott, Gerd. "Der ästhetische Mensch." *Funkkolleg Kunst* 4. Weinheim and Basel: Beltz Verlag, 1985.

Meisel, Perry. *The Myths of the Modern: A Study in British Literature and Criticism after 1850*. New Haven: Yale University Press, 1987.

Michie, Elsie B. "Violet Paget." In *An Encyclopedia of British Women Writers,* ed. Paul Schlueter and June Schlueter. New York: Garland, 1988.

Mitchell, Robert Lloyd. *The Hymn to Eros: A Reading of Plato's Symposium*. Lanham, Md.: University Press of America, 1993.

Moi, Toril. "Feminist, Female, Feminine." In *The Feminist Reader: Essays in Gender and the Politics of Literary Criticism,* ed. Catherine Belsey and Jane Moore. Cambridge: Blackwell, 1989.

Monkhouse, Cosmo. "Miss Brown." *Academy* 3 (January 1885): 6–7.

Monleon, Jose B. *A Specter is Haunting Europe: A Sociohistorical Approach to the Fantastic*. Princeton: Princeton University Press, 1990.

Moore, Jane. "Promises, Promises: The Fictional Philosophy in Mary Wollstonecraft's 'Vindication of the Rights of Woman.'" In *The Feminist Reader: Essays in Gender and the Politics of Literary Criticism,* ed. Catherine Belsey and Jane Moore. Cambridge: Blackwell, 1989.

Moretti, Franco. "The Comfort of Civilization." *Representations* 12 (1985): 115–39.

Morgan, Thaïs E. "Reimagining Masculinity in Victorian Criticism." *Victorian Studies* 36 (1993): 315–32.

Navarette, Susan J. *The Shape of Fear: Horror and the Fin de Siècle Culture of Decadence*. Lexington: University Press of Kentucky, 1998.

O'Barr, Jean F., ed. *Women and a New Academy: Gender and Cultural Contexts.* Madison: University of Wisconsin Press, 1989.

Oliphant, Margaret. *The Makers of Florence: Dante, Giotto, Savonarola, and Their City.* New York: A. L. Burt, 1881.

Ormond, Leonee. "Vernon Lee as a Critic of Aestheticism in *Miss Brown.*" *Colby Library Quarterly* 9, no. 3 (1970): 131–54.

Ormond, Richard. "John S. Sargent and Vernon Lee." *Colby Library Quarterly* 9, no. 3 (1970): 154–78.

Parfitt, George. "The Renaissance." *Encyclopedia of Literature and Criticism,* ed. Martin Coyle, Peter Garside, Malcolm Kelsall, and John Peck. London: Routledge, 1990.

Pater, Walter. *Appreciations with an Essay on Style.* London: Macmillan, 1922.

———. *Imaginary Portraits.* London: Macmillan, 1922.

———. *Marius the Epicurean.* Ed. Michael Levey. New York: Penguin Books, 1985.

———. *Plato and Platonism: A Series of Lectures.* 1893. London: Macmillan, 1920.

———. *The Renaissance, Studies in Art and Poetry: The 1893 Text.* Ed. Donald L. Hill. Berkeley: University of California Press, 1980.

Patzer, Harald. *Die Griechische Knabenliebe.* Wiesbaden: Franz Steiner Verlag, 1982.

Pearson, Karl. *A Grammar of Science.* London: Walter Scott, 1892.

Penning, Dieter. "Die Ordnung der Unordnung. Eine Bilanz zur Theorie der Fantastik." In *Phantastik in Literatur und Kunst,* ed. Christian W. Thomsen and Jens Malte Fischer. Darmstadt: Wissenschaftliche Buchgesellschaft, 1980.

Poovey, Mary. "'Scenes of an Indelicate Character': The Medical 'Treatment' of Victorian Women." *Representations* 14 (1986): 137–68.

Pope, Deborah. "Notes toward a Supreme Fiction: The Work of Feminist Criticism." In *Women and a New Academy: Gender and Cultural Context,* ed. Jean F. O'Barr. Madison: University of Wisconsin Press, 1989.

Ponsonby, Mary. *Mary Ponsonby: A Memoir, Some Letters, and a Journal.* Ed. Magdalen Ponsonby. London: J. Murray, 1927.

Potolsky, Matthew. "Pale Imitations: Walter Pater's Decadent Historiography." In *Perennial Decay: On the Aesthetics and Politics of Decadence,* ed. Liz Constable, Dennis Denisoff, and Matthew Potolsky. Philadelphia: University of Pennsylvania Press, 1999.

Pratt, Annis, and Barbara White. "The Novel of Development." In *Archetypal Patterns in Women's Fiction.* ed. Annis Pratt, Barbara White, Andrea Loevenstein, and Mary Wyer. Bloomington: Indiana University Press, 1981.

Preston, Harriet Waters. "Vernon Lee." *Atlantic Monthly* 55 (February 1885): 219–27.

Prickett, Stephen. *Victorian Fantasy.* Bloomington: Indiana University Press, 1979.

Prins, Yopie. "Greek Maenads, Victorian Spinsters." In *Victorian Sexual Dissidence,* ed. Richard Dellamora. Chicago: University of Chicago Press, 1999.

———. "Sappho Doubled: Michael Field." *Yale Journal of Criticism* 8, no. 1 (1995): 165–86.

———. *Victorian Sappho.* Princeton: Princeton University Press, 1999.

Psomiades, Kathy. "'Still Burning from This Strangling Embrace': Vernon Lee on Desire and Aesthetics." In *Victorian Sexual Dissidence,* ed. Richard Dellamora. Chicago: University of Chicago Press, 1999.

Punter, David. *The Literature of Terror: A History of Gothic Fiction from 1765 to the Present Day.* London: Longman, 1980.

Purcell, E. Review of *The Beautiful. Academy,* 19 July 1884, 37–38.

Pykett, Lyn. "Sensation and the Fantastic in the Victorian Novel." In *The Cambridge Companion to the Victorian Novel,* ed. Deirdre David. Cambridge: Cambridge University Press, 2001.

Rado, Lisa, ed. *Rereading Modernism: New Directions in Feminist Criticism.* New York: Garland, 1996.

Recchio, Thomas E. "A Dialogic Approach to the Essay." In *Essays on the Essay: Redefining the Genre,* ed. Alexander J. Butrym. Athens: University Press of Georgia, 1989.

Riffaterre, Michael. *Textproduction.* Trans. Terese Lyons. New York: Columbia University Press, 1983.

Robbins, Ruth. "Vernon Lee: Decadent Woman?" In *Fin de Siècle/Fin du Globe: Fears and Fantasies of the Late Nineteenth Century,* ed. John Stokes. New York: St. Martin's, 1992.

Ruh, Kurt. *Die 'Melusine' des Thüring von Ringoltingen.* Munich: Verlag der Bayrischen Akademie der Wissenschaften, 1985.

Ruskin, John. *Modern Painters.* Vol. 1. London: George Allen, 1903.

Said, Edward. "The Politics of Knowledge." *Raritan* 11 (summer 1991): 17–31.

Schaffer, Talia. *The Forgotten Female Aesthetes: Literary Culture in Late-Victorian England.* Charlottesville: University Press of Virginia, 2000.

Schaffer, Talia, and Kathy Alexis Psomiades, eds. *Women and British Aestheticism.* Charlottesville: University Press of Virginia, 1999.

Schlee, Eileen. "The Subject Is Dead, Long Live the Female Subject!" *Feminist Issues* 13, no. 2 (1993): 71–80.

Schmidt, Gunnar. *Die Literarisierung des Unbewußten: Studien zu den phantastischen Erzählungen von Oliver Onions und Vernon Lee.* Frankfurt: Peter Lang, 1984.

Schulz, Genia. "Medea: Zu einem Motiv im Werk Heiner Müllers." In *Weiblichkeit und Tod in der Literatur,* ed. Renate Berger und Inge Stephan. Cologne: Böhlau Verlag, 1987.

Scott, Joan W. "Gender: A Useful Category of Historical Analysis." In *Coming to Terms: Feminism, Theory, Politics,* ed. Elizabeth Weed. New York: Routledge, 1989.

Sedgwick, Eve Kosofsky. "Across Gender, across Sexuality: Willa Cather and Others." In *Displacing Homophobia: Gay Male Perspectives in Literature and Culture,* ed. Ronald R. Butters, John M. Clum, and Michael Moon. Durham, N.C.: Duke University Press, 1989.

Shaktini, Namaskar. "A Revolutionary Signifier: *The Lesbian Body.*" In *Lesbian Texts and Contexts: Radical Revisions,* ed. Karla Jay and Joanna Glasgow. New York: New York University Press, 1990.

Shaw, G. B. "Satan the Waster." *Nation* 27 (18 September 1920): 758–60.

Sherry, Ruth. *Studying Women's Writing: An Introduction*. London: Edward Arnold, 1988.

Showalter, Elaine. "Hysteria, Feminism, and Gender." In *Hysteria beyond Freud*, ed. Sander Gilman, Helen King, Roy Porter, George Rousseau, and Elaine Showalter. Los Angeles: University of California Press, 1993.

———. *A Literature of Their Own: British Women Novelists from Brontë to Lessing*. Princeton: Princeton University Press, 1977.

———. *The New Feminist Criticism: Essays on Women, Literature, and Theory*. New York: Pantheon, 1985.

Sillars, Stuart. Review of *The Handling of Words* by Vernon Lee, ed. David Seed (1992). *Notes and Queries* 43 (March 1996): 116–17.

Simmel, Georg. *On Women, Sexuality, and Love*. Trans. and introduced by Guy Oakes. New Haven: Yale University Press, 1984.

Sivert, Eileen Boyd. "Flora Tristran: The Joining of Essay, Journal, Autobiography." In *The Politics of the Essay: Feminist Perspectives*, ed. Ruth-Ellen Boetcher Joeres and Elizabeth Mittman. Bloomington: Indiana University Press, 1993.

Small, Ian. *Conditions for Criticism: Authority, Knowledge and Literature in the Late Nineteenth Century*. Oxford: Clarendon Press, 1991.

———. Introduction. *The Aesthetes: A Sourcebook*. London: Routledge and Kegan Paul, 1979.

Smith, Bonnie G. "The Contribution of Women to Modern Historiography in Great Britain, France, and the United States." *American Historical Review* 89, no. 3 (1984): 709–32.

Smith-Rosenberg, Carol. "The Body Politic." In *Coming to Terms: Feminism, Theory, Politics*, ed. Elizabeth Weed. New York: Routledge, 1989.

———. *Disorderly Conduct: Visions of Gender in Victorian America*. New York: Knopf, 1985.

Snyder, Katherine V. "From Novel to Essay: Gender and Revision in Florence Nightingale's 'Cassandra.'" In *The Politics of the Essay: Feminist Perspectives*, ed. Ruth-Ellen Boetcher Joeres and Elizabeth Mittman. Bloomington: Indiana University Press, 1993.

Stableford, Brian. "Haunted by the Pagan Past: An Introduction to Vernon Lee." *Infinity plus non-fiction*. <http://www.iplus.zetnet.co.uk/introduces/lee.htm>

Stephens, Leslie. "National Biography." In *Studies of a Biographer*, ed. Leslie Stephens. London: G. P. Putnam and Sons, 1898.

Stetson [Gilman], Charlotte Perkins. *Women and Economics: A Study in Economic Relations between Men and Women as a Factor of Social Evolution*. Boston: Maynard and Company, 1898.

Stetz, Margaret D. "Rebecca West's Criticism." In *Rereading Modernism: New Directions in Feminist Criticism*, ed. Lisa Rado. New York: Garland, 1996.

Stevens, Hugh. "Queer Henry in the Cage." In *The Cambridge Companion to Henry James*, ed. Jonathan Freedman. Cambridge: Cambridge University Press, 1998.

Stevenson, Robert Louis. "A Gossip of Romance." *Longman's Magazine* (November 1882): 69–79.

Stillman, W. J. Review of *Studies in the History of the Renaissance* by Walter Pater. *Nation* 17 (1873): 243–44.

Symonds, J. A. *The Letters of J. A. Symonds.* 3 vols. Ed. Herbert M. Schueller and Robert L. Peters. Detroit: Wayne State University Press, 1967–69.

Tintner, Adeline R. "Vernon Lee's 'Oke of Oakhurst' or 'The Phantom Lover' and James' 'The Way It Came.'" *Studies in Short Fiction* 28, no. 3 (1991): 355–62.

Todd, Janet, ed. *British Women Writers: A Critical Reference Guide.* New York: Continuum, 1989.

Todorov, Tsvetan. *The Fantastic: A Structural Approach to a Literary Genre.* Trans. Richard Howard. Cleveland: The Press of Case Western Reserve University, 1973.

Traill, Nancy. *Possible Worlds of the Fantastic: The Rise of the Paranormal in Fiction.* Toronto: University of Toronto Press, 1996.

Tuchman, Gaye, with Nina E. Fortin. *Edging Women Out: Victorian Novelists, Publishers, and Social Change.* New Haven: Yale University Press, 1989.

Vicinus, Martha. "The Adolescent Boy: Fin-de-Siècle Femme Fatale?" *Journal of the History of Sexuality* 5, no. 1 (1994): 90–114. Rpt. in *Victorian Sexual Dissidence,* ed. Richard Dellamora. Chicago: University of Chicago Press, 1999.

Walker, Lisa. "How to Recognize a Lesbian: The Cultural Politics of Looking Like What You Are." *Signs* 18 (1993): 866–91.

Waterlow, Sydney. "*The Beautiful.*" *International Journal of Ethics* 24 (July 1914): 459–63.

Waters, Harriet Preston. "Vernon Lee." *Atlantic Monthly,* February 1885, 219–27.

Weed, Elizabeth. "Terms of Reference." In *Coming to Terms: Feminism, Theory, Politics,* ed. Elizabeth Weed. New York: Routledge, 1989.

Weil, Kari. *Androgyny and the Denial of Difference.* Charlottesville: University Press of Virginia, 1992.

Weir, David. *Decadence and the Making of Modernism.* Amherst: University of Massachusetts Press, 1995.

Wellek, René. "Vernon Lee, Bernard Berenson, and Aesthetics." In *Discriminations: Further Concepts of Criticism,* ed. René Wellek. New Haven: Yale University Press, 1970.

Wharton, Edith. "A Backward Glance." In *Edith Wharton: Novellas and Other Writings,* ed. Cynthia Griffin Wolff. New York: Library of America, 1990.

Williams, Carolyn. *Transfigured World: Walter Pater's Aesthetic Historicism.* Ithaca: Cornell University Press, 1989.

Williams, Raymond. *Culture and Society.* Harmondsworth: Penguin, 1963.

Wiseman, Mary Bittner. "Beautiful Exiles." In *Aesthetics in Feminist Perspectives,* ed. Hilde Hein and Carolyn Korsmeyer. Bloomington: Indiana University Press, 1993.

Wittig, Monique. "On the Social Contract." *Female Issues* 9, no. 1 (1989): 5–12.

———. *The Lesbian Body.* Trans. David Le Vay. New York: Morrow, 1975.

Woolf, Virginia. "The Decay of Essay-Writing." In *Virginia Woolf: A Woman's Essays,* ed. Rachel Bowlby. London: Penguin, 1992.

———. "The Modern Essay." *Virginia Woolf: A Woman's Essays.* Ed. Rachel Bowlby. London: Penguin, 1992.

———. Rev. of *Laurus Nobilis* by Vernon Lee. *TLS,* 5 August 1909, 284.

———. Rev. of *The Sentimental Traveller: Notes on Places* by Vernon Lee. *TLS,* 9 January 1908, 14.

# Index